Crisis Theory

CRISIS THEORY

David Z. Rich

PRAEGER

Westport, Connecticut
London

Library of Congress Cataloging-in-Publication Data

Rich, David Z.
    Crisis theory / David Z. Rich.
        p.   cm.
    Includes bibliographical references and index.
    ISBN 0–275–95722–5 (alk. paper)
        1. Business cycles.   2. Equilibrium (Economics)   I. Title.
    HB3716.R53   1997
    338.5′42—dc21   96–53945

British Library Cataloguing in Publication Data is available.

Library of Congress Catalog Card Number: 96–53945
ISBN: 0–275–95722–5

First published in 1997

Praeger Publishers, 88 Post Road West, Westport, CT 06881
An imprint of Greenwood Publishing Group, Inc.

Printed in the United States of America

The paper used in this book complies with the
Permanent Paper Standard issued by the National
Information Standards Organization (Z39.48–1984).

10 9 8 7 6 5 4 3 2 1

This work is dedicated to the memory of my beloved parents, to my mother Vanessa, and my father Joseph, and to the memory of my beloved uncle Ralph, who finally took that streetcar. This work is also dedicated to my sisters Beatrice and Shayna, to my family and friends and especially to Diana Lerner for her support and the originality with which she enhances my life.

Contents

Acknowledgments

I would like to express appreciation to my editor, Cynthia Harris, and to my production editor, David Palmer and copy editor, Betty Pessagno, for their editorial help.

My thanks to Reuben Sheffer and his staff at Ayin Nun Ayin in Tel Aviv, for their expert preparation of the camera-ready work. Special appreciation goes to Ruthie Chazanovich, Eran and Ainat Sheffer, as well as the very dedicated work of Sharona Ezer.

These ideas have been developed over years as a writer, and while I owe a great debt to the teachers and thinkers from whom I learned, the ideas expressed in this work are my own and I bear complete responsibility for their clarity.

PART I

THE PROBLEM SITUATION

CHAPTER 1

Our Contemporary Era

The simple presence of an undivided object that is identical with itself falls apart as soon as we become conscious of the net portentions and retentions in which every actual experience is embedded. The experience that is present "at the moment" is indebted to a reproducing recognition, that such differences of a temporal interval and thus also an element of otherness is inherent in the spontaneity of the living moment. The intimately fused of what is intuitively given proves in fact something compounded and produced.

Jürgen Habermas,
"Beyond a Temporalized Philosophy:
Jacques Derrida's Critique of Photocentrism"[1]

GENERAL COMMENTS

It is incorrect to maintain that the fused unity of what is intuitively given proves in fact to be something compounded and produced. Human intuition has been developed through biological and social evolution and is active in response to situations. We intuit not only as a result of our inheritance, but also as a result of our training and experiences that we acquire from our formal training and education. The role of genetics in intuition is not yet clear, because there is apparently no general intuition for populations; nor has specific intuition been demonstrated to be shared among members of the same families. Intuition, as such, is thus a property of awareness that we possess, and we use it when circumstances prevail upon us for which we require it. Still, we have no conscious control over our intuition, and therefore, we do not use our intuition for understanding the intimately formed unity of what we consider as given, for we are aware that the given is compounded and produced. Hence, intuition is of no significance here.

We do, however, often take for granted as given that which is compounded and produced, but this is only because of our familiarity with the given. For example, we take for granted our societies, our tools for working, and our products for leisure; we use our transportation systems without much consideration, and we rely on the standards of our medical care and our education systems. Although these are unique to our societies in our time, they are also to a large extent the results of social inheritance, compounded and produced in past historical eras and in the previous social times of our present historical era.

Each historical era is defined and delineated by the characteristics and properties that make it unique. For example, the Dark Ages was a historical era in which wisdom and knowledge were obtainable mostly by studying in the Church. It was an era in which religion relied on superstition to control people and in which universal education was nonexistent. Monarchs vied with religious leaders for absolute rule, and education was based on folk wisdom and the passing of skills from one generation to the next. The Renaissance that followed the Dark Ages began to a large extent with Thomas Aquinas's work, *Summa Theologica*[2] in which he incorporated Aristotelian philosophy with its concern for nature and for the teleological cause of the Supreme Being as creator of the universe. The contradictions between the Greek philosopher's theology and Roman Catholic doctrine were resolved through Aquinas's emphasis on the Aristotelian concern for nature, in contrast to the neo-Platonic emphasis on the heavenly world as interpreted by pre-Thomistic scholars.

It was Aquinas's renewed emphasis on this world as well as the next that freed the arts and philosophical inquiry into nature and the heavenly spheres, and hence led to the rebirth of knowledge—the knowledge of ancient Greece and, concerning the study of law, the knowledge of Rome. As Rome has become the center of the Catholic religion in the West—in contrast to the Church of Byzantium, which remained the Eastern Roman Empire after the fall of the Roman Empire, but which having accepted Christianity, competed with Rome as the center of the Christian faith—the great movements in the arts and sciences began in Rome and spread throughout the Western sphere of influence.

It was during the early Renaissance that artists such as Giotto made their impact on art and sculpture. Later, Leonardo da Vinci (1452-1519)—with his contributions to scientific thinking and his profound artistry—and Michelangelo (1445-1564)—with his emphasis on the human form in religious themes in his paintings and sculptures—aided in the reconsideration of nature and provided the basis for expanding philosophical inquiry into nature and the heavens. Thus, during the Renaissance, Nicholaus Copernicus (1473-1523), a canon in the Church, posed a hypothetical alternative to earth-centered astronomy, positing the sun as the center, with the earth and other planets revolving around the sun in the Ptolemaic epicycles. Copernicus had revived the ancient heliocentric system of Aristarchus of Samos, who posited a system with the sun as its center and the planets revolving around the sun in circular orbits. The circle was considered to be the most perfect form, but for the orbiting planets, their paths and motions seemed out of phase and could not be accounted for in this manner. Hence, the Ptolemaic system of epicycles maintained observational correctness but proved to be increasingly complicated. Copernicus maintained that the shift in positions placing the sun at the center and having the planets revolving around the sun in epicyclical patterns was merely an intellectual exercise in keeping with the spirit of the Renaissance.[3] It was an exercise that attracted Galileo (1564-1642) and Kepler (1571-1630) in the defense of Copernicus, and led to the development of modern science.

Galileo's defense of the Copernican system was more in keeping with the spirit of the era not because of any further work in depth in astronomy. While he was humbled before the Inquisition for his heretical support of the Copernican system as truth, and not merely as an intellectual exercise as Copernicus maintained, Galileo's greatest work was in earth physics. In the *Dialogue Concerning Two New Sciences*, he argued against the Aristotelian system of physics while placing physics within a mathematical framework, allowing for analysis and prediction.[4]

Kepler's concern with the Copernican theory was based on the notion of simplicity and, to some extent, on mysticism. The Copernican system, like the Ptolemaic system, was clumsy, cumbersome, and far too complicated. As a student and an assistant to Tycho Brahe (1546-1601), Kepler observed the same heavens but saw different things. Brahe viewed the heavens within the Copernican framework of the heliocentric system of epicycles; the alternative, that of planets traveling in circular orbits around the sun, was unacceptable because of the difficulties involved in computation. Kepler was concerned with finding the harmony of the spheres, and the Copernican system, with its cycles and epicycles, was far too cumbersome for the simple harmony Kepler sought. Relying on Brahe's observations, Kepler searched for the mathematical system that would provide the simplicity and harmony he thought existed in the heavens. The most perfect form is the circle, but in applying this to planetary motion he encountered the problem of the motion of Mars. The observations that Kepler had at his disposal were far more sophisticated than those of Aristarchus, but still, the motion of Mars provided the difficulty with the application of the circle. Kepler then posited the ellipse as the orbit of planetary motion, with the speed of the planets around their elliptic orbits varying with their relative positions to the sun.[5]

Galileo's and Kepler's theories were quite separate. Galileo, though interested in the heavens, posited a theory of physics that pertained only to the earth; he knew of Kepler's work but did not believe the astronomer was to be taken seriously. Their two systems remained separated until Isaac Newton synthesized them, and by so doing, reformulated them into a unique and unifying theory of earth and heaven physics.[6] It was the Newtonian synthesis, with its significance for mechanics as they relate to the processes of production, that brought about the demise of the Renaissance with all its artistic glory and scientific achievements, and began the next historical era, that of the Industrial

Revolution.

During this era, the economic and social processes of those countries undergoing the Industrial Revolution were not only tremendous, but also unique in the history of humankind. The village life of these countries was altered as the big cities centered around industrial developments and attracted people to work and reside near them. The emphasis on education inherited from the Renaissance not only allowed for the teaching of general subjects, but also provided courses and learning in the disciplines required by the developing industrial societies. With the establishment of large-scale industries, new auxiliary service industries were formed, resulting in the demand for greater work skills that could only be obtained by further education and training. Hence, the requirements of the Industrial Revolution made necessary more intense and sophisticated education to meet the challenges of the new era. This led to improved medical care, more efficient transportation systems for moving people to and from their workplaces, and increased ability to cope with the dynamics of the new era of industrialization.

With industrialization came the development of the financial markets, notably the stock and commodities markets, which became sources for investment. As profits from industrial output and personal liquidity were channeled into these markets, both the marketing and financial aspects of the business cycle became institutionalized. While these cycles were often severe, the resilience of the dynamics of industrialization carried sufficient momentum to move the cycles from the depression to recovery and prosperity phases.

The Industrial Revolution began in 1776, and with the Congress of Vienna of 1815, Europe enjoyed relative peace for a hundred years, allowing industrialization to flourish. World War I, which engulfed these countries and led to the entry of the United States, resulted not only in tremendous loss of life and natural and industrial resources, but it also left unresolved many domestic and international issues. American isolationism led the United States government to withdraw its support for the League on Nations, which was originally an American initiative. German humiliation, the new and unstable countries in Eastern Europe, and Japan's exploitation of China and countries in Asia perpetuated the postwar instability.

It is a mute point to argue that in the absence of the Great Depression the difficulties of the postwar period might have been resolved. The skills of international politics developed over the centuries may have resulted in another congress similar to that of Vienna in 1815, leading to the establishment of another hundred years or so of peace. But the Great Depression did occur, and as Germany realized, the fastest way out of the economic crisis was to arm itself for war. The resolution of unemployment by wartime production—thereby stimulating the economy and the move to redress the humiliating terms of peace imposed on Germany—provided the necessary political support for the politics of war that were to follow. With these policies there was a sufficient decline in the dynamics of industrialization to maintain the momentum of cyclical motion.

The era of the Industrial Revolution had ended, and the world powers now confronted a new situation in which Germany, Japan, and their allies sought redress through world war.[7]

Our contemporary era of knowledge is the outcome of World War II. While every historical era is unique, delineated and defined by the circumstances that bring it about and by the characteristics and properties that distinguish it, our era of knowledge is perhaps the most dynamic in human history. The Renaissance, with its great contributions to the arts and sciences, attests to the levels of creativity that can be achieved, given the opportunity. We have inherited the works of the Renaissance and the Industrial Revolution, and we are now in a position to exploit the opportunities and possibilities provided in our era. If used wisely and properly, we can lift humanity out of its difficult condition; we can confront the policies of war and resolve those issues that bring about military conflicts, thereby realizing a dream of people throughout history. As we develop our era and our pursuit of knowledge, we must be mindful of an important caveat. Our humanism should not be lost in the wonderment of knowledge. In this context, we should remember the burning of the library in Alexandria which housed the greatest works of antiquity. The library was burned because the wisdom and knowledge it held had little relevance in as much as they were not applied to the social and political issues of the day. The library's wealth was not for the poor. We must not be blinded by wisdom and knowledge, but rather must apply them to our situations. This topic is discussed in the last part of this work in connection with crisis theory, which is formulated and developed in Part II as an alternative to chaos and catastrophe theories. Before these theories can be treated and crisis theory formulated, comments on the social time are in order.

SOCIAL TIME

Social time is delineated by events, processes, and circumstances that impress utility on the eras in which they occur. Individual social times occur in an era, or several such times may take place more or less congruently, depending on the contributions made and the dynamics they generate. There may also be one contribution of such significance that the entire era is known by its characteristics. For example, in the Bronze Age and Iron Age these metals led to developments in construction and warfare, and the prime concern with these eras was the applications of these metals and the search for technologies to improve their qualities. One contribution in social time that had a tremendous influence on its era and that of its successor was Charles Darwin's theory of evolution. The influence of his theory spread from its original domain of biology to the social sciences that remained in its grip. Despite the importance of Lamarckian evolution, to which Darwin acknowledged his debt, it was greatly overshadowed and reduced—wrongly—to insignificance. It was brought to its near-demise because of its misapplications by T. D. Lysenko in the Soviet Union during Josef Stalin's regime as official policy on sociobiological evolution.[8]

It may seem tautological to state that social time is dependent on the era in which it occurs, because only the events unique to that era have their value in the specific era alone. This, however, is not a tautology, for on closer inspection it reveals a historical truth. Just as an era is delineated in part by the demise of its being formed by the events of the past and crystallized into a set of unique experiences, these circumstances are the manifestations of events and contributions of social times that impart to an era its uniqueness. This is the case even though these events may have repercussions and consequences in historical eras in general, and in social times within an era in particular.

An example of this phenomenon is Henri Poincaré's (1854-1912) contribution to mathematics during the Industrial Revolution. Poincarés awareness of the unpredictability of dynamic systems provied the basis for work in nonlinear mathematics, with difference equations providing the foundations for dynamic systems in the natural and social sciences.[9] Economics, for example, relies on difference equations to take into account the time factor neaded to realize the influences of economic policies. However, during the Industrial Revolution there was a lack of conceptualization and equipment for chaos theory to be considered. Knowledge of chaos as such is as ancient as civilization. Earthquakes and snowflakes are familiar to everyone, but even where geological faults have been known, still unknown is the timing when chaos in these faults will result in earthquakes. As for snowflakes, although all flakes come from the same source, it is known that no two flakes are identical. What has yet to be understod is the dynamics of the system of the drop of water that forms each flake, shaping it is a distinct manner. In earlier historical eras, while earthquakes and other uncontrollable events would occur, they were taken as given and were not studied rigorously. In our present era of knowledge, we have developed computer models and can regulate the input into these models so that the dynamics of these events can be simulated and altered accordingly to enhance our understanding still further. While chaos theory is unique in our era, its foundations lie in the previous era with Poincaré contributions. The dynamics of chaos theory are somewhat intuitive and to some extent taken for granted; it is also a combination of the past era's mathematics and this era's technical prowess.

How, then, is our current social time to be understood? To answer this question, further comments are in order. Our era began in the aftermath of World War II with the social time of the reconstruction of Europe, Japan, and other countries damaged by the war. It was also a period when a shift occurred from wartime to peacetime production to cope with the pent-up, demand of the civilians who had been engaged in wartime production and of the demobilized military forces and the citizens who worked to support the war effort. In spite of the breakthroughs in science, such as the development of the atomic bomb and the first stages of the uses of the computer, it was also an age of conformity.

Conformity was necessary to transfer the rigor of military training to industry in order to change the economy from wartime to peacetime production. Market innovations and subsequent imitative products soon led to newness in automobiles, refrigerators, improvements in public transportation, and medical care–all consequences of the knowledge developed during the war.

It was also the age of the Cold War. Countries that had been hostile before World War II became allies to fight the German-Japanese Axis, only to become hostile enemies again after the war, dedicated to the other's moral and physical destruction. The Cold War was fought mainly with military intrigue and posturing, but it was fought on another battlefield as well, that of education. The Soviet Union launched the first successful spacecraft, Sputnik, and initiated the first major social shift in our era. In 1957, when the satellite orbited the earth, the shock to the West's education system was tremendous. The Soviet achievement was hailed as a great accomplishment for humankind and the first real opportunity for space exploration. But it also provided the awareness that the Western education system, with its emphasis on rote learning and secondary and minor emphasis on original thinking, had to change. It was this event in 1957 that finally led to the development of our present era of knowledge.

Computers began to come on-line, revising conceptualizations and allowing the development of model systems for experimentation in space exploration, for research into weather systems, for economic forecasting, for domestic and international political research, and for official communications and transactions.

The emphasis in education had encouraged original thinking, while the necessity of retaining rote learning was still realized. With the explorations into the foundations of mathematics that had begun during the Industrial Revolution, new mathematics were developed. Set theory, for example, had come into its own. With the Cantorial concept of infinity, chaos theory developed, and the nonlinear mathematics provided the time-series concepts that helped explain the evolution of new systems from the older ones.

With the race into space now being conducted in earnest as a result of increasingly refined technological means, the older challenge of maintaining the operative edge in strategy and weapons systems of the cold war was proving to be prohibitive. The establishment of the European Economic Community and the economic challenges it posed for the East European Bloc as it sought to enter fully into the dynamics of our contemporary era–together with the renewed relations with mainland China and the political dynamics this generated–brought that social time to its final stages. Serious international and domestic changes were occurring, and the Strategic Defense Initiative–the so-called Star Wars program–designed to extend the defensive systems into outer space, led the cold war adversaries to recognize that the expense of maintaining the arms race was too great in the face of their tremendous, pressing social problems. The Cold War finally ended by 1990, and cooperation has since replaced the long-standing hostilities. The new social time of our era began with the thawing of Cold War attitudes and moved into a spirit of cooperation. Participation in other countries' space programs, economic cooperation, and reduced reliance on surrogate countries to perpetuate foreign policy indicated that the new social time had begun.

The dynamics of our social time are unfolding, but not without serious domestic and international consequences. Those countries in Africa and Eastern Europe lacking the infrastructure to cope with changes have relied on the age-old tradition of attempting to resolve their difficulties through war. The power bases established in these countries are now being used to repress different opinions due to religious or ethnic differences—all this at a time when greater personal liberty is being given to peoples in countries where the full dynamics of our era are finding expression.

In our contemporary era of knowledge, three types of countries now exist: the future-oriented countries that are taking advantage of the benefits of our era; the present-oriented countries that are in various stages of economic and social development but whose domestic and international policies are geared to entering fully into our era of knowledge; and the past-oriented countries whose leadership is in various states of war with opposing sectors or groups—be they religious, national, or ethnic—as a result of the failure to establish policies to bring them into the present-oriented stage. In the past-oriented countries, social turmoil and war, as destructive as these conditions have always been, are being conducted for more than the traditional reasons of power and conquest. Rather, they are being conducted in order to establish the best form of socioeconomic system both to further the personal positions of those in power and to benefit their countries as they understand it.

The present- and past-oriented countries are being subjected to severe crises as a result of political shifts and changing social conditions. The future-oriented countries are strong enough politically, socially, and economically that all crises can be treated within their socioeconomic political systems without devastating consequences. The extent of these crises for each type of country varies with their causes and circumstances; they can be analyzed and dealt with based n the crisis theory approach, which is developed in Part II and applied in part III of this work.

The present volume formulates crisis theory in contrast to chaos theory and its handmaiden, catastrophe theory, as developed by René Thom. While considering the benefits of these theories, crisis theory possesses a dynamics they lask. Comments on chaos and catastrophe theories are presented in the chapters to follow.

NOTES

1. Jürgen Habermas, "Beyond a Temporalized Philosophy: Jacques Derrdia's Critique of Photocentrism," in *The Philosophical Discourse on Modernity: Twelve Lectures, Lecture VII*, trans. Frederick G. Lawrence (Cambridge, Mass.: M.I.T. Press, 1987), p. 174.

2. St. Thomas Aquinas, *Summa Theologica: A Concise Translation*, ed. Timothy McDermott (Westminster, Md.: Christian Classics, 1989). See also Earnest L. Fortin, "St. Thomas Aquinas," in *History of Political Philosophy*, eds. Leo Strauss and Joseph Cropsey (Chicago: Chicago University Press, 1987), pp. 248-275.

3. See Nicholaus Copernicus, *Complete Works*, trans. Edward Rosen (Baltimore, Md.: Johns Hopkins University Press, 1985-1992).

4. See Galileo, *Two New Sciences* (New York: Macmillan, 1914).

5. See Johannes Kepler, *Kepler's Sonmium*, trans. Edward M. Rosen (Madison: University of Wisconsin Press, 1967).

6. See Sir Isaac Newton, *Mathematical Principles of Natural Philosophy and His System of the World* (Berkeley: University of California Press, 1962).

7. For discussions on the Great Depression and its aftermath, see David Z. Rich, *Contemporary Economics* (Westport, Conn.: Praeger Publishers, 1986), *The Economics of Welfare* (New York: Praeger Publishers, 1989), *The Economics of International Trade* (New York: Quorum Books, 1992), and *The Economic Theory of Growth and Development* (Westport, Conn.: Praeger Publishers, 1994).

8. See J.P.B. Lamarck, *Recherches sur l'organization des corps vivan* (Paris: Millard, 1802), and *Philosophie zoologique* (Paris: Dentu, 1809). Arthur Koestler wrote that Darwin remained all his life half a Darwinist and half a Lamarckian. In 1875, toward the end of his life, Darwin wrote to Sir Francis Galton that "each year he found himself more compelled to revert to the inheritance of acquired characteristics because chance variations and natural selection alone were apparently insufficient to explain the phenomena of evolution." Quoted from Arthur Koestler, *Janus* (New York: Vintage Books, 1979), p. 196. Lysenko's experimentation with Lamarck's theory was inappropriate because Lamarck's theory pertains to the realm of biology and zoology, whereas Lysenko's experimentation was social and sociological. For a discussion on neo-Lamarckianism, see Arthur Koestler, *The Case of the Midwife Toad* (London: Hutchinson, 1971).

9. See Henri Poincaré, *The Foundations of Science* (Lancaster, Pa.: Science Press, 1947), and *Last Thoughts* (New York: Dover, 1963). Poincaré's awareness of the unpredictability of dynamic systems led him to formulate his nonlinear mathematics.

CHAPTER 2

Comments on Science
and Philosophy

Chaos A type of behavior of physical systems in which the evolution
of the system cannot be predicted because of its sensitive dependence on
minor changes in the properties of the system.

Gerald Feinberg,
Solid Clues[1]

ON PHILOSOPHY AND SCIENCE

"A definitive pronouncement of total truth," wrote Benedetto Croce would mean
the burial of thought and all its doubts, and, with them, of man himself, who
would not know what to do with his thought if he did not exercicse it in order to
live a human life."[2] Science is the activity that pertains to the pursuit of truth
about our universe. Historically, this has been the objective of scientists from
the time of the ancient Greek thinkers, who sought to probe the hidden secrets of
their world wite tools of inquiry consisting soley of their observations and their
individual intellects. From the inheritance of these ancient thinkers, those who
have partaken in the pursuit of truth have improved their methods of
observation, and consequently sharpened their theories in their pursuit of their
goal of truth. Both historically and in terms of the contemporary perspective,
with respect to the progress made in the various branches of science, it appears
that final and absolute truth is being approached.

The ultimate goal of scientific inquiry is to find enduring truth, but this goal
has been elusive. Even in our contemporary era with its sophisticated
technologies and advanced theories, we still remain at a great distance from this
truth. Historically, when science seemed to have entered into a period of certainty
and it was almost taken for granted that the ultimate truth was within grasp,
difficulties set in that produced unexpected and new paths of inquiry. This was
the case when the certainty of Newtonian physics, developed from Galileo's earth

physics and Kepler's astronomy, was brought into question by Max Planck–himself a staunch Newtonian–and by the relativity theorists and quantum physicists who followed and developed their theories based on Planck's findings.

Although both historically and ultimately science is the pursuit of truth, the history of this pursuit–the history of science, its theories and developments in its respective branches–has provided us with the disciplines that, even the strict experimental controls demanded by scientists, truth in its absolute remains elusive. Our scientific theories have attained a sophistication never imagined by their Greek forebears, with our methods for testing and challenging theories depending on our intellects, observations, and laboratory techniques. Even so we are not much closer to the absolute truth than were the ancient Greeks albeit, on a different level of understanding, observation, and experimentation.

Therefore, we cannot predict the response to pronouncements of closeness to absolute truth, other than to say, contrary to Croce, that such pronouncements would not mean the burial of thoughts and all its doubts. The physicist, biologist, or zoologist who makes such a pronouncement would have his or her argument met with skepticism, counterargument, and countertesting to weaken the argument or refute it entirely, and perhaps it would be met with religious indignation.

What we understand historically is that the pursuit of ultimate truth is, in practice, the pursuit of knowledge. While we have inherited the notion of truth from the Greek philosophers–and from the world's great religions–over time we have come to concentrate not so much on finding the ultimate truth, as on developing theories and testing them. The pursuit of truth, though still the ultimate objective, is no longer the immediate one.

Truth is wisdom, unchanging and eternal. Once achieved, we can only surmise with Croce that all doubt will be removed. We will not stagnate in our thought, however, but will consider the best ways to comprehend this truth and to work with it. This will surely result in controversy, and through this we will not bury our powers of reasoning and our humanity as Croce indicated, but will remain argumentatively opinionated and therefore very human.

This eternal wisdom has remained far from our grasp. When it seeme that we reached the paradigm of our conceptions, as was the case with Newtonian theory, we thought that we had achieved the end of scientific development and all that was necessary was to continue working out the consequences. But new situations always arise in which significant breakthroughs are made, only to confront us with problems of diffferent and perhaps even greater complexity. These problems have led to the development of new theories to explain and deal with them; from these theories, we have expanded our knowledge, but we have not achieved the ultimate truth.

We have also found that throughout our inquiry for the ultimate truth our knowledge, though workable, is always inadequate or in error, to be refuted by better knowledge which, in turn, has been equally vulnerable to problem shifts and hence to rejection. But we have also found that the sciences develop through changes in knowledge, while the pursuit of truth tends to the more religious aspects of the human condition.

Although traditionally the ultimate objective of the sciences is the pursuit of truth, in practice, science has become the pursuit and development of knowledge. It is in this practical sense–and indeed historically–that science, as a body of knowledge, is in error. This error may be universal in form, as was Aristotelian physics, even though it provided explanations for natural phenomena.[3] Scientific advances may render a theory that was once stated as universal to be particular. This is in the case with Newtonian theory, relegated to the limit-case of three dimensions by and hence deemed irelevant to the broader-based physics of Einsteinian relativity and quantum physics.

Philosophy, on the other hand, is the love of wisdom, and just as with scientists, philosophers seek eternal truth and its wisdom. With regard to their approaches to this pursuit, both philosophers and scientists seek the best approach to this pursuit, the one that will eliminate as many ambiguities as possible and move the search for eternal truth and its wisdom that much faster and more surely

Because of their common ultimate pursuit, the important treatises and debates in philosophy concerning science cannot be dismissed. This is because scientists are subject to the very same considerations that philosophers have dealt with since Descartes, Leibniz, Hume and Kant among others. Philosophical speculation is important because it provides the conceptual framework, developed over the long history of ideas, that allows scientists to step back, as it were, to view their works from viable philosophical and scientific perspectives.

Although Isaac Newton (1642-1727) demonstrated that the demarcation between science and philosophy is unclear, in our contemporary era this demarcation has become sharpened. Granted that the ancient Greek philosophers raised questions about the atom, about infinity in mathematics, and about eternal truth, contemporary scientists are concerned with matters of atoms, relativity, and the expansion of knowledge. Aristotle provided the basis for the study of biology, but the genetic code was broken by contemporary chemists and biologists, with their work paving the way for genetic engineering. Given the current specializations and the divisions in the sciences, philosophers help the theoretical and practical scientists better understand their fields and the basis for their procedures, as well as the development of their theories. This is the reason and the very one that Newton recognized–why philosophy and science are more than handmaidens both historically and practically. This is more so the case in our era, for each is necessary to the development of the other: as science develops, so does philosophy, and as philosophy develops, so does science, as the theory of chaos attests.

TRUTH–REALISM AND ANTIREALISM

In contrast to the of truth as enduring and as the goal of philosophical and scientific pursuit, there, is the doctrine that truth is what exists. This is the realistic theory of truth and differs from the pursuit of philosophy and science because it is not historical in its perspective, nor is ultimate in its goal. Rather, it describes conditions and situations as they are considered to be–as objective, nonhistorical, and with a truth-value independent of our observations. In terms of this doctrine, conditions and situations are true without our subjective influences on them, but our description of them as true means that our descriptive statements correspond to these conditions and situations with each statement having a corresponding truth-value. These events therefore possess a reality independent of our subjective interpretations, and if for whatever reasons we question their validities, it is our judgment that is in error and not the reality. This approach to truth is descriptive, based on the attempt to understand reality as it is. In this sense it is a diminutive form of truth as ultimate and enduring. Moreover, since it is independent of human observation, we cannot affect its value in any way.[4]

There is yet another position concerning truth; this is the antirealist position, which is not a counterargument to the realist argument concerning truth, but a variation of this argument. The realists describe conditions and situations as they exist during the duration of their observations. Indeed, this is the strength of their position. The antirealist approach, however, is based in our contemporary era of knowledge. While in previous historical eras, given their developments in philosophy and science, attempts to posit an antirealist approach to truth would have been criticized, perhaps dismissed out of hand, in our era of knowledge this cannot be the case. The situation today is such that the dynamics of knowledge renders conditions or circumstances true in its nonenduring sense–for a limited period of time, while being false for other times. This does not conflict with the search for the ultimate and enduring truth, but pertains to the flexible conditions that exist in our dynamic world and the knowledge systems (that is, crisis theories as to be developed in this work) that have become integral to our era.

The philosopher dealing with science has thus to consider truth in relation to the problems being investigated and analyzed, with truth in this respect being relevant as long as the circumstances of the problems and the theories developed to work with them retain their validities. The antirealist approach argues that truth exists and is significant as long as the circumstances of this truth remain valid. As these circumstances are altered, so is the truth of the situation changed to the extent of perhaps being negated, depending on the nature and degree of the alterations. This does not conflict with the ultimate truth that is the object of scientific and philosophical pursuit, but places within the general concept of truth its diminutive form of antirealistic truth. The antirealistic truth is thus relative to its circumstances and holds as long as the problems and the theories for dealing with them are maintained. In our contemporary era, these truths are of limited duration–some longer than others–as inquiry proceeds and knowledge is altered.

COMMENTS ON HERMENEUTICS AND EPISTEMOLOGY

"What science and the quest for knowledge are after," wrote Hannah Arendt, "is *irrefutable* truth, that is, propositions human beings are not free to reject–they are compelling."[5] The quest for knowledge is the contemporary pursuit of the ultimate truth. Given the antirealist approach of our era, both philosophers and scientists have described truth in antirealistic relativistic terms, with the understading that while the objective is to achieve permanent and enduring truth, the relative truths of conditions and situations will eventually be demonstrated to be incorrect, to be replaced by other such truths.

As both philosophy and science share this common objective, we should comment on Richard Rorty's position that the eventual demarcation between philosophy and science was made possible by the notion that philosophy's core was, "'*theory of knowledge*,'" which is distinct from the sciences because it serves as their foundation."[6] He maintains that the idea of the foundation of knowledge is the product of perpetual metaphors, as knowledge is a relation to propositions and thus is "of justification as a relation between the propositions in question and other propositions from which the former may be inferred."[7] This is the principle of axiomization, in which a system of knowledge is structured with statements or propositions from which other statements or propositions may be inferred. Every scientific and rigorous philosophical system functions in this manner, enabling statements of the various theories composing each problem area to be tested for their validity.

Rorty discusses what he calls "epistemolgical behaviorism," which he maintains is a species of holism but one lacking in metaphysical underpinnings. He states that if we understand the rules of a linguistic game (or mathematical or logical system, for example), we understand all there is of the game and why the moves of the game are made.[8] He then raises the question of whether we can treat the study of human knowledge just by studying the ways in which humans react, or whether this study involves a specifically philosophical way of describing human beings with the assistance of biology, history, and other natural and social sciences. In this case Rorty's position on philosophy is that for epistemological behaviorism, philosophy will have no more to offer than common sense.

Instead, Rorty posits hermeneutics, which he views as the expression of hope that the demise of epistemology will not be realized, and that the previous constraints on epistemology will no longer be required. Indeed, Rorty maintains that epistemology proceeds on the assumption that all contributions of a given discourse are commensurable. The term "commensurable" is used in the sense of being able to be brought under a set of rules that inform how rational argument can be reached on conditions that will settle the issue on each point in which statements seem to conflict, such as the rules of logic in debate, or the derivation of theorems from axioms of a system of science. Such theorems are consistent, and yet subject to debate concerning their validities and their applications to their problem areas.

Rorty believes that a struggle necessarily exists between hermeneutics and epistemology. To resolve this conflict, he advocates the use of hermeneutics as being philosophically free, and thereby relegates epistemology to a lesser order of significance. However, Rorty's argument can be countered on four grounds. First, epistemology is the discipline concerned with knowledge, its philosophical foundations, and its relationship to systems of philosophy and science, whereas hermeneutics is the study of interpretation, originally conferned with biblical scholarship, but as concept applicable to all disciplines of inquiry. Hence, one ground for contention is Rorty's position that a struggle necessarily exists betweenn hermeneutics and epistemology. Since epistemology is the study of knowledge, and hermeneutics in the study of interpretation, when investigating philosophical or scientific problems, agreement must be found between the system in question and the interpretation its uses. If not, a problem arises that can be resolved only by further searching and establishing knowledge. "Behavioral" epistemology and epistemology as such are identical because every theory of knowledge has its rules of procedure–its axioms–that state the system's "behavior," or how it is to be used. The interpretation of the system and the application of its rules to derive theorems and the moving of the system into unchaertered domains by the use of its rules (Planck's radiation experiments, undertaken from a Newtonian perspective, which nevertheless led to relativity and quantum theory is an example) are applications of hermeneutics, that is, the interpretation of the system. This is completely compatible with epistemology, for epistemology is the construction of knowledge theories, and hermeneutics is the interpretation of these theories and the information so derived from them within their contexts and domains.

The second ground of contention revolves around Rorty's claim that behavioral epistemology has nothing more than common sense to offer. This is certainly not the case, for common sense as such is unrigorous in that it is acquired from life's experiences, but is not the domain of academic philosophical training. The only "common" sense that has relevance to epistemology is the common understanding of the philosophers and scientists who work with their respective theories, The commonness here is the acceptance of specific philosophical and scientific theories, or their rejection, and this for reasons made available to the public concerned with them. This is certainly different from the general usage of common sense in its social and cultural settings.

A third ground of contention concerns the incompatibility of epistemology and hermeneutics because epistemology deals with commensurability, and hermeneutics, as interpretation, stands in opposition to this. Theories of knowledge have to relate to the real world and be commensurate with their problem areas, with the extent of this commensurability subject to debate; if they do not, they are unacceptable. Hermeneutic interpretation, as an extension of the knowledge system, must therefore relate to the problem area for which the theory is constructed if not, there would be total theoretical anarchy. This does not negate the subjective interpretations of theories, the significance of which is obtained only when made public to the relevant audiences, either through debate or in journals, or in its applications for others to review. The subjective aspect of interpretation, the hermeneutics, is thus necessary for both philosophers and scientists to analyze theories for their consistency, logical clarification, and ability to be moved into domains not accounted for in their original formulations. Although scientists may apply the scientific method to test the ability of theories to perform in their domains as stated, both philosophers and scientists will evaluate the theories and methods of investigation used to determine whether the theories are accepted or rejected as the case may be.

The fourth ground of contention is that epistemology deals soley with commensurability. This is an important aspect of knowledge, but it is not the entire role of epistemology. Granted, with advances made in mathmathics and statistics, and with our highly refined measuring techniques, the theories can be tested rigorously for their commensurability within their domains. This, however, can be refined further, with even greater accuracy obtained by applying these theories to their domains, and this requires the dynamics of epistemology in the testing, The interpretations of these theories, and indeed the ways in which they are used, make up the hermeneutic aspect.

With regard to the distinction between philosophers and scientists, Newton demonstrated that in his time the distinction was neither clear nor important. Moreover, philosophers and scientists move very well in each other's fields. For example, Albert Einstein (1879-1955) was a probabilistic determinist, whereas Werner Heisenberg (1901-1976) was an indeterminist. Both positions are strongly rooted in the traditional arguments concerning free will versus determinism, and in probability theory which developed from observation and philosophical investigation. Scientists such as Poincaré and Pierre Duhem did important work in both disciplines,[9] and Newton demonstrated the enduring relationship between science and philosophy, which was forged by the ancient Greeks and is valid in our contemporary era.

Chaos theory, though scientific, has its foundations in philosophy. For example, Georg Cantor's (1845-1918) triadic set, in which regions are broken down infinitely, results in the Mandelbrodt number of .6309. The concept of infinity was enriched by the Greek Zeno whose paradoxes of infinity still haunt mathematics in such forms as Cantor's triadic set extension and the nonstandard analysis that is engaging the efforts of many contemporary mathematicians and logicians. Moreover, Gerald Feinberg's definition of chaos as the type of physical bahavior in which the evolution of the systems cannot be predicted because of its sensitive dependence on minor changes in the system's properties demonstrates another aspect of chaos theory's philosophical foundations. The search for stability out of chaos, for order out of disorder, is one aspect of chaos theory. Although the chaotic system's evolution cannot be strictly predicted, there is a degree of determinism in the terms of Poincarés stable limit cycles, in which a differentiation of two variables produces a disturbance in the cycle's oscillation, which is eventually restored during the continuing phases of the cycle's oscillation.

Two philosophical issues are involved here: one concerns the evolution of a physical system and the extent to which such, evolution exists; the other concerns the oscillation around a static point in the dynamics of a system—according to Poincaré's stable limit cycles, which, though applicable to mathematical systems, is also applicable to physical systems.

Do all physical systems evolve? Some, such as snowflakes, evolve necessarily as a result of their inner dynamics and continue doing so until their inner dynamics ceases or until an interference interrupts this process. This, however, is not the same evolution that occurs in biology, with new species evolving from existing ones and with species not effective in long-range survival being rendered extinct. For physical systems, such as the snowflake, the evolution is structured within the system; once the system's potential is realized, the evolution ceases. The question we must ask is whether external physical stimuli can influence such an evolution. If so, is this still chaos, or is it a different approach to the same problems?

As for the other issue, whether physical systems oscillating around a fixed point in the sense of Poincaré's stable limit cycles meet the criteria of chaos, and if so, how can this contribute to our understanding of these systems? To program a mathematical system to oscillate around a fixed point provides us with interest only for their limited uses. We can adjust the system's parameters to achieve different oscillations with such cyclical depth, width, and duration of the cycle's phases. These movements will still be around a fixed position that, even after adjustments are made, is maintained.

Thus, there are two types of physical system, with one type conforming to chaos theory and the other most definitely not. The type of system that does conform is that of the snowflake or gas in a container.

The snowflake begins its journey through the atmosphere as a droplet of moisture, being formed to its final and unique shape as it comes into contact with the effects of the weather. It achieves its shape as it falls to the ground, taking from the weather those forces that are necessary for its development. That the weather affects the droplet in its formation into a snowflake demonstrates that this external condition is necessary for the snowflake's evolution from one form of moisture to another. This dependence on the weather is built into the flake's evolutionary dynamics, so that the droplet takes from the atmosphere but does not in turn give to it.

Unlike the snowflake, gas does contribute to the atmosphere but does not take from it. The gas is contained under pressure sufficient to prevent it from escaping. Once released from the container, it escapes from it at a rate determined by the pressure. It enters the atmosphere and first expands at an accelerating rate and then at a decelerating rate, until it is at a state of equilibrium with the atmosphere, to be ultimately dissipated in the atmosphere, losing its identity and its existence.

These systems conform to chaos theory in the sense that they cannot be predicted: the shape the snowflake will finally take cannot be known in advance, nor can the movement of the gas in the atmosphere be determined. While computer models can give conditions in order to direct the snowflake's development and the movement of the gas, such controls in the real world do not exist. Releasing the gas in front of a fan while providing general movement to the gas, but determining the position of a certain molecule at a certain time is impossible.

In both cases, changes within the systems were brought about because of their internal dynamics, given the influences of the environment in which they exist. Their relationship to their environment is one-sided in the sense that the snowflake takes from the environment, whereas the gas contributes to it. In these chaos-conforming situations, there is no mutual reliability in the sense of two or more fairly self-contained systems getting together to form a working unit. In this sense, then, chaotic systems are static, because their reliance is always constant, with the consequence that snowflakes will always be unique individual systems, and gas, when released into the atmosphere, will always dissipate.

The type of physical system that does not conform to chaos is that of a theory that, through applications, has become a working system. Take, for example, Werner Heisenberg's uncertainty principle in quantum theory.

Heisenberg's uncertainty relations pertain to the atomic and subatomic universe, that of the atoms and their waves or particles in their orbitals. Because of the magnitude of the atoms and their substructures, the uncerttainty relations pertain to a realm far different from that treated by classical Newtonian physics. For example, if x is an expression of the accuracy in which the position of an object greater than atomic proportions moves along a straight path, and p is the value of accuracy of the momentum for the same object along the same path, the object's continued travel can be computed. Should there be interference along the path of travel, the effects of this interference can also be computed and the object's future position can be determined according to Newtonian theory. Hence, both position and momentum are known, and the process of observation has no effect on the object's final destination.

For the atomic and subatomic realms, however, the situation is vastly different. In his treatment of the uncertainty relations, Heisenberg first discussed the particle theory of matter. He explained that the position of an electron is known within a certain accuracy c at rime t, visualized by a wave packet (showing the duality the problem in terms of particles generating wavelike activity) in a proper position with a proper extension of Δx; by a wave packet, it is meant as a wavelike disturbance whose amplitude is appreciably different from zero only in a bounded region. This region is generally in motion, changing in size and shape, As the velocity of the electron corresponds to that of the wave packet, the diffusion that occurs hinders the ability to achieve an exact definition of this velocity with respect to the wave interference.

Following Heisenberg's reasoning, this indeterminance is an essential characteristic of the electron, and does not constitute evidence of the inapplicability of the wave argument. Heisenberg defined motion as $px=mvx$ with m as mass of the electron and v being equal to its x component of its velocity. The uncertainty in the velocity computation results in the uncertainty in px to the amount of p. He further argued that from the laws of optics, together with the empirically established law $\lambda = h/p$, with the small case lambda being the wave packet of electron, $\Delta x\,\Delta p \geq h$. If the wave packet is made up by the superimposition of sinusoidal waves, with all the wave lengths being near λ_0, then the general number of crests and troughs in $\Delta x\,\lambda_0$ falls within the boundary of the wave packet. Outside this boundary the wave plane must cancel by interference, which is possible only if the set of component waves contains some waves for which at least n+1 waves fall within this critical range. This provides $\Delta x/\lambda_0 - \Delta\lambda \geq n + 1$, with $\Delta\lambda$ being the approximate wavelengths necessary to represent the wave packet. Therefore, $\Delta\lambda/\Delta\lambda^2 \geq 1$. However, the velocity of the wave packet is $v_w = h/m\,\lambda$, so that the spreading of the wave packer is characterized by the range of velocities $v = h/m\,\lambda^2_0\lambda$. As by definition, $\Delta p = m\,\Delta v_w$, then $\Delta x\,\Delta p \geq h$ with this uncertainty relation specifying the limits w within which the parti cle picture can be applied.

Heisenberg's argument is more than a position based on the shifting from a particle concept to a wave concept. Making strict use of the particle concept, given the quantum position position of the q-coordinate of an electron, we can assess the probability of the coordinate's numerical value as lying between q' and $q'-dq$, with d being the differential operator. Heisenberg's argument involves Hilbert space and diagonal diagonal matrices, and he concludes that the electron's velocity and its position cannot be determined accurately.

Either the wave amplitudes can be known or the probability of the electron's position can be assessed, but neither can the position and the velocity nor the amplitude be known at the same time. In Heisenberg's words: "This may be expressed in concise and general terms by saying that every experiment destroys some knowledge of the system which was obtained by previous experiments."[10] Heisenberg's uncertainty principle thus states that for every atomic system in which either the particle's velocity alone or its position alone is known every subsequent observation will alter its momentum by an unmeasurable amount. This formulation does not refer to the past, so if the particle–say an electron–is in an exactly measured position, with its initial position known, its position for previous times can be calculated, with $\Delta p\,\Delta q$ being smaller than the limiting value. This past knowledge–unlike in Newtonian physics–cannot be used in the calculations in any future experiments concerning the progress of the electron and hence is outside the domain of experimental verification or refutation.

In the application of his uncertainty principle to waves, Heisebnerg discussed wave amplitude. Every measurement of amplitude can yield only an average of its value in a small region of space and during a short interval of time. Assuming that measurements always give average values over a small area of volume, then δv-$(\delta 1)^3$, depending on the experiment and measurement. Light waves of length λ, much less than the extremely small v, will not be detected by experimenting. With the measurements giving the values of E–the total energy of the system–and H–the Hamiltonian $H(q,p)$, that is, the q-coordinate and the geodesic position-the field strengths everage over the range of ± 1. Thus if these values were exactly known, there would be a contradiction to the particle theory. This is so since the energy and momentum of the small volum δv are: $E = v1\pi/8$ $(E^2 + H^2)$ with momentum = $\delta v1/4\pi$ $kExH$, with k being an arbitrary constant as a measuring reference. As the right-hand members can be made increasingly small by making v increasingly small, this is consistent with the particle theory inwhich energy and momentum in the small volume are composed of discrete and finite amounts of δv and hv/k respectively. Heisenberg maintained that as for the highest detectable frequency $hv \leq hk/ \delta 1$, it is clear that the right-hand members of E and momentum must be uncertain by the order of quanta hv and hk for there to be no conradiction with the particle theory. Thus, the particle's momentum is associated with wave propagation, with the wave picture predicting correctly the particle's possible motion.[11] Therefore for every subsequent observation of an atomic system, either a particle's velocity or position can be assessed, but not both. Because the wave theory predicts correctly the particle's possible motion, it too is subject to the linitation of assessing either the particle's velocity or position, but not both.

Even with the highly refined electron microscope. Heisenberg's situation still prevails, The observer of the particle and its wave dynamics will inject into this system energy through observation, thereby disturbing the system and causing it to behave in an uncertain manner. For example, locating an electron accurately requires a large microscope lens and a short light wave, and this affects the recoil of light on the electron. Computing the recoil accurately requires a narrow base of angles to allow the electron to move; it also requires long-range photons for the energy required for observation. This, however, destroys the knowledge of the electron's position. Therefore, the very processes of observation interfere with the electron by bringing into view a fuzzy and inaccurate picture. The physical observation so necessary for experimentation cannot, therefore, determine precisely the particle's position and motion. Heisenberg's uncertainty for the problems of particles and waves, raised by Newton and Christian Huyghens (1629-1695) and brought over into quantum physics, pose problems for both scientists and philosophers as they continue their search for the enduring truth.

This argument demonstrates that, although chaos theory is relevant for some physical systems, it is irrelevant for others. Of course, it can be claimed that a theory such as Heisenberg's uncertainty principle is in fact a meta theory in the sense that it sets limitations on atomic and subatomic structures independent of these structures' inner dynamics. The uncertainty principle is universal and has no specific nuances for a specific system. The description of the snowflake's development, while universal, does not detract from the uniqueness of each snowflake. Moreover, the influences of the weather, though uncertain, can be regulated in computer models to shape the computer-generated snowflake accordingly. For Heisenberg's theory, apparently no method to overcome this problem has been found so that either motion or position can be known but not both. Indeed, this is not a meta theory, but a general theory, applicable under all circumstances, until we can find ways around its barriers.

Chaos theory, then, pertains to the evolution of systems. Its applications were originally in the fields of the natural sciences, but with the development of nonlinear analysis, it has been applied to the social sciences as well. Economic systems evolve, social systems evolve, and international systems evolve; such evolution is subject to the nonlinear analysis as time series are always necessary in their dynamics. However, while chaos theory pertains to evolution, another type of theory, that of crisis theory, also pertains to evolution and is more flexible in its treatment. Crisis theory, as an alternative to chaos theory, is discussed in Part II of this work.

NOTES

1. Gerald Feinberg, *Solid Clues* (New York: Touchestone Books, 1985), p. 264.

2. Benedetto Croce, "Discourses on Philosophy," in *My Philosophy*, trans. E. F. Carritt (New York: Collier Books, 1962), p. 1.

3. See Aristotle, *Physics*, trans. and ed. by W. David Ross (Oxford: Oxford University Press, 1936).

4. See Michael Dummet, "Realism," in his collected essays, *Truth and Other Enigmas* (Cambridge Mass: Harvard University Press, 1980), pp. 145-165.

5. Hannah Arendt, *The Life of the Mind* (New York: Harvest/HJB Books, 1978), p. 59.

6. Richard Rorty, *Philosophy and the Mirror of Nature* (Princeton, N.J.: Princeton University Press, 1980), p. 132.

7. *ibid*, p. 159.

8. "All," he adds, "that is, save for the extra understanding obtained from inquiries nobody would call epistemological–into, for example, the history of language, the structure of the brain, the evolution of the species, the political or cultural ambience of the players" (*Philosophy and the Mirror of Nature*, p. 174).

9. See Henri Poincaré, *Science and Hypothesis* (New York: Dover, 1906), and *The Foundations of Science* (New York: Macmillan, 1914); see also Pierre Duhem, *The Aim and Structure of Physical Theory* (Princeton, N.J.: Princeton University Press, 1954).

10. Werner Heisenberg, *The Physical Principles of the Quantum Theory*, trans. Cark Eckhart and F. C. Hoyt (New York: Dover, 1949), p. 20.

11. See A. d'Abro, *The Rise of the New Physics* (New York: Dover, 1951), Vol. 2, pp. 654-656 and 670-673 for a discussion of this point.

CHAPTER 3

Further Comments on Chaos Theory

Chaos theory shows that a simple relationship that is deterministic but nonlinear, such as a first order nonlinear difference equation, can yield an extremely complex time path. Intertemporal behavior can acquire an appearance of disturbance by random shocks and can undergo violent, abrupt qualitative changes, either with the passage of time or with small changes in the values of the parameters.

William J. Baumol and Jess Benhabib,
"Chaos: Significance, Mechanism, and
Economic Applications"[1]

Intertemporal behavior, with its acquired appearance of disturbance by random shocks resulting in violent qualitative changes, is responsible for the uniqueness of each falling droplet in its conversion into a snowflake. It is also responsible for the dispersion of gas when released from its container. Intertemporal behavior is thus necessary for the development of this snowflake and for the form that the dispersed gas takes. When this intertemporal behavior is necessary for the system, the system reaches its equilibrium position and then ceases to exist in its finalized form. The snowflake, having achieved its final form, either melts or is destroyed by forces of nature; the gas achieves an equilibrium position with its atmosphere when it is fully absorbed into the atmosphere, until it ceases to retain any of its unique identity as the original gas.

The question that has to be considered is whether chaos theory can be replaced by another theory, one of greater utility. To treat this question, a discussion of chaos theory is in order.

While Poincaré with his contributions to nonlinear analysis established the early foundations of chaos theory it was only in our era that chaos theory was formulated. Chaos theory deals with the evolution of systems. Although the theory was originally applicable to physical systems, nonlinear analysis was applicable To the social sciences, for example, with difference equations in economics reflecting the dynamics of policies on the economy and the influences of regional development on demographic dynamics. Regardless of their inner evolution, chaos systems revolve around what is termed "strange attractors." A strange attractor is a set of points **P** to which any point **p** within **p**'s region approaches **P** as time approaches infinity. Hence, **P** attracts all such **p**'s over time and is termed "strange" because its geometries of motion are such that these points move into **P** while the system is evolving. As a result patterns are formed that are often erratic, as in various markets during long-run business cycles.

As the parameters of the evolving system change through expansion, bifurcations, that is, changes in the qualitive dynamics of the system result, leading to changes in its evolution–hence, the differences in snowflakes and the patterns of gas expansion. Each value of a changing parameter is a bifurcation point, and the system is said to be undergoing bifurcation. A change from a system that is steady to one that begins oscillating is in a Hopf bifurcation; from such bifurcations, new systems evolve with chaos dynamics. This process continues until the dynamics of the system ceases.

Fractals are parts of systems that have been broken down into smaller parts. When we look at a map of a coast line, the indentations and protrusions seem finite, but when we are walking along the same coast, its area can be broken down into smaller lengths. These lengths can be broken down into still smaller lengths, and so on. The Cantor triadic set is a fractal set, for it can be broken down infinitely.

Fractals are significant because in the dynamic evolution of chaos systems, they frequently lead to bifurcation and the development of new systems. Fractals can also act as strange attractors in these bifurcations because by branching off into new systems, the evolution of these systems tends to be centralized around their origins before developing and spreading out, just as a falling droplet of water remains within itself until weather conditions operate on the droplet as it falls, providing the basis of its evoltion into a snowflake. The fractalized snowflake continues its development until its evolutionary processes are halted and the snowflake remains in its final form until it ceases to be. Once a chaos system's evolution comes to an end, its fractalization is terminated. Hence, the coast never ceases to exist as it is changing due to the erosion from the motion of the water and the deposits of vegetation and animal life which maintain the soil's composure.

Associated with the development of chaos systems are hard and soft excitation. A system is in hard excitation when, for an increasing parameter, a steady state suddenly becomes unstable with large-amplitude oscillations being observed. A decrease in the parameter leads to an abrupt loss of oscillation. A systems is in soft excitation when a parameter increases, and a steady state becomes unstable with low-amplitude buildup; a decrease in the parameter leads to oscillation loss with its path slowing down and with no disruptions. Chaos systems are deterministic, with their evolutionary patterns preestablished and their development dependent on both their internal dynamics and their relationships with their environments. In contrast, random stochastic influences–"noise" in the language of chaos theory–may or may not affect the systems' evolutionary development.

This brings chaos theory into conflict with real environmental situations, for even when such a system is undergoing excitation, be it hard or soft, the impact of influences incongruent with chaos systemic development can bring about unexpected disruptions. It is not that the flapping of butterfly wings in Spain will influence California's weather;[2] for chaos theory, given the existence of an unexpected influence–for example a sudden rainstorm in Spain–its effects in California can be assumed but not predicted. Weather conditions influence geographical regions and are in turn influenced by them. Moreover, the shifting layers of crust within the earth affect climactic conditions in Asia and the American West Coast. Just when these shifts will occur and to what extent the climate will be affected have yet to be understood.

What is clear is that noise and the evolution of chaos systems seem to be in genuine conflict, for noise, being unrelated to these systems, interferes with the development of the systems and perhaps disrupts them totally. Within the context of chaos this is real, but it will be resolved within the framework of crisis theory, which is discussed in Part II.

NOTES

1. William J. Baumol and Jess Benhabib, "Chaos: Significance, Mechanism, and Economic Applications," Journal of Economic Perspective, 3 (1989): 77-105, 79. On page 80, they state that "It warns us that apparently random behavior may not be random at all." Quoted here from Brian J.L. Berry, *Long–Wave Rhythms in Economic Development and Political Behavior* (Baltimore, Md.: Johns Hopkins University Press, 1991), pp. 14-15.

2. The concept of the butterflies travel in groups. The impact of the movement of butterflies' wings on plant and insect life can also result in disturbances on the other side of the globe according to this approach. It is an interesting concept but one more prone to making a point than being a point.

CHAPTER 4

Chaos and Catastrophe Theory— A Critique

Where chaos begins, classical science stops. For as long as the world has had physicists inquiring into the laws of nature, it has suffered a special ignorance about disorder in the atmosphere, in the turbulent sea, in the fluctuations in wildlife populations, in the oscillations of the heart and the brain. The irregular side of nature, the discontinuous and the erratic side these have been puzzles in science, or worse, monstrosities.

James Gleick,
Chaos[1]

FURTHER COMMENTS ON CHAOS THEORY

Nature, despite its apparent regularity, has always been irregular. This is manifested in the early investigations of nature, such as the seasons. Winter is supposed to be cold, and summer not. There have been cold winters with warm spells, while summers have been hot and yet still cooled by breezes. The motions of the stars that have intrigued us since the ancients are also irregular; hence, the heavenly constellations shift from the beginning of the months toward their ends. The regularity of nature has been subject to human will; the common calendar, for instance is based on twelve months and not on ten as was the case in ancient times. October is based on the number 8, November on 9, December on 10–but these are the tenth eleventh, and twelve months, respectively with July and August named for Julius and Augustus Caesar. Perhaps it was recognition of the apparently regular side of nature in the early periods of civilization that provided the basis for considering the absence of regularity in nature. The inquisitive person would seek not only the familiar and the similarities, but also the unfamiliar and the different. The seasons impose themselves on us, and we impose ourselves on the seasons. We protect ourselves when cold by adding coverings such as heavy clothes and by installing heating systems; we protect ourselves when hot by retreating to shade and purchasing cooling systems. Although we are at the mercy of natural weather sources, we have learned to gather water together and to store it for consumption and agriculture.

The irregularities are far from new to humanity; they have been recognized for what they are ever since civilization was formed and the necessity to control nature was recognized. Seafarers sailed the turbulent seas and learned to navigate their ships through troubled waters by using star charts and the sailing and reckoning techniques that were passed down from one generation of sailors to the next. With regard to disorder in the atmosphere, weather charts have been compiled to assist in navigation and in other forms of activities. The fluctuations in wildlife population have been considered ever since the establishment of farming and agriculture; the encroachment of unwanted wildlife on farms led to the placement of controls, some of which have been successful, while others have been less so. The consideration of fluctuations in wildlife population has been incorporated into general ecology and control. As for classical science suffering a special ignorance about the oscillations within the heart and the brain, the great strides made in contemporary biology and especially pathololgy have led to advances in neurosurgery, and to tremendous advances in open-heart surgery and transplants where genetic differences cause the heart cells to oscillate at different levels, therefore remaining unrecognized by the body's immune system and requiring medication to prevent the heart's rejection and to allow its cells to shift into proper oscillation.

With the development of civilization, the puzzles and monstrosities that science revealed over time provided the very challenges for science to understand. From the flat earth and the dangers of falling into the depths of infinity for all who ventured too far from the horizon, to the searching of the heavens for revelations of the future, to the exploration of territories and the oceans' depths and the searching of the heavens to understand the origins of our universe, the challenges of science have always been met by those who probe nature's apparent regularities and obvious irregularities. Throughout history, then, nature has harbored the puzzles and monstrosities of nature only until they have been resolved and understood.

Moreover, Gleick's statement is far from clear: classical physics ended with Newton's *Principia*, and neoclassical physics ended with Max Planck's contributions, which resulted in the works of Einstein and the modern atomists.[2] Classical biology began with the works of Linneas and his botanical classification in the tradition of Aristotle, whereas neoclassical biology began with the works of Jean Baptiste Lamarck, Charles Darwin, and his associate R.A. Wallace, and modern biology with the works of R.A. Fisher and the neoevolutionists who followed.[3] Neither classical scientists nor our contemporaries have doubted their ignorance but neither have they wavered in their search for understanding and their pursuit of truth.

The theory of chaos is no different in this respect from any other theory of contemporary science, whatever the field. The puzzles and monstrosities that brought about chaos theory are as bewilderng as those issues confronting contemporary physics and biology. In contemporary physics there is a coming together of Eastern contemplation and Western dynamism, as physicists seek to understand the strange phenomena of black and white holes, of the wormlike minute space of Jiffyland, of the subatomic particles of the atom and their influences on each other, and the seemingly insurmountable barrier of Heisenberg's uncertainty principle in understanding the conditions of micro physics.[4] In biology, models are being constructed in which nonlife yields life according to variations in the spontaneous generation of life theory, the concept of spontaneity takes on meaning as occurring in a catastrophic situation that is, in terms of catastrophe theory–when conditions come together making life possible.[5]

Chaos theory, for all its clarifications of the workings of nature, is not without its difficulties. For example, consider Feinberg's definition of chaos as being the type of behavior of physical systems in which evolution can not be predicted because of their sensitive dependence on minor changes in the system's properties. Expanding this definition to include all dynamic systems in which evolution is inherent in them (such as economic cycles as described by Brian Berry, and the dynamics of economic systems as treated by William Baumol and Jess Benhabib, and the socioeconomic systems discussed in the last part of the the present work), we can see that the concepts of evolution and equilibrium present a problem. For example, the snowflake evolves from a droplet of water falling from the sky during given weather conditions. It reaches equilibrium as a system in accordance with the conditions in which it exists; when its final form is achieved, its equilibrium is also achieved, but here evolution ceases. The snowflake will then be destroyed and its evolutionary process terminated. The same observations pertain to gas: when released from its container, gas expands rapidly, but it reaches equilibrium with its surrounding atmosphere, only to be dissipated and lose its existence as a gas. With its evolution terminated, the gas no longer exists as such.

In economics, the business cycle's motion is dependent on political events, just as to some extent political events are dependent on the business cycle. For example, the Great Depression created the conditions for World War II, although their foundations were laid in the Versailles Treaty that ended World War I.[6] Moreover, in our era, the policies of business leaders concerning investing and profit-taking eventually bring small investors into the market, sometimes with devastating consequences. The severe overheating of the markets in October 1987 and the profit-taking that began early in that month led to the crash of October 19, which, while beginning in the United States, soon brought the world's markets tumbling downward. The "paper chase," the seeking of stocks and bonds for profit, is a phenomenon as old as the stock exchanges. When the demand for paper becomes overextended, the markets tend to rise and fall sharply, affecting aggregate liquidity, thereby limiting monies available for investment in productive assets. The influences of policy on the cycle and the cycle's influences on policy make this relation symbiotic, for each depends on the other.

Berry's claim that chaos explains the long-term business cycle is, therefore, somewhat problematic. Economic systems are evolutionary, with the extent and degree of their evolutionary processes being maintained depending on the strengths and durability of the governments. For example, in the previous social time, the Soviet Union economic system collapsed together with the governing system on which it was based and by which it had evolved. The evolution of this economic system had been hindered by "noise" to such an extent, with inefficiency becoming the norm and efficiency being the exception, that in light of the European Economic Community and the challenges of the United states Strategic Defense Initiative as well as the costs of maintaining its satellite countries, the regime in Moscow began to be overwhelmed. As a consequence the Soviet leaders reconsidered the Cold War and took into consideration their country as position the context of the changing world and the new challenges that had to be confronted. The Soviet economic and government and system were abandoned, resulting in both the dynamics of a social time of peace among the superpowers and deadly conflict among the samaller nations, some of which were previously under the domain of the now defunct Soviet system.

The Soviet system was deliberately altered, and its evolution intentionally terminated. This was because as the system existed and was evolving, it was incapable of surviving the challenges of the American investment in a new defense system that would also provide a potential for a first-strike attack. It was also unable to cope with the new challenges of a united Europe operating as a customs union, confronting the Soviet-based Comecon customs union with all its inefficiency and corruption. However, the equilibrium points in the economic system as it was then configured were those periods when the production quotas were met, and when the goods and services available were those that were consumed. But even in this system these equilibrium points lasted only briefly as the new economic planned programs set in and the entire process began all over again.

The long-term cycles that Brian Berry discussed (Part III of this work) differ from those of the Soviet economy, first, because they concern cycles that were recorded prior to the founding of the Soviet Union; and second, while each business cycle during the latter part of the Industrial Revoiution, and most certainly in our contemporary era, did reach an equilibrium point, it was a fleeting moment in the dynamics of the cycle. Equilibrium in economics is momentary, as the supply and demand in specific markets tend to the position of equality. However, peoples' tastes are not consistent and market planning for a specific product can never be accurate. When equilibrium does occur it is not the kind of equilibrium depicted by Berry in which supply and demand in the aggregate tend toward equality. The point is that with each business cycle the economy is on a new footing, with different products available and with market compositions different from all previous cycles. The long-run business cycle with respect to chaos and crisis theories is discussed in the last part of this work. Let it suffice here to mention that, in terms of chaos theory, the strange attractor **P** which is the equilibrium position attracting the **p**'s which are the specific markets in a dynamic, would indeed reach equilibrium. In terms of crisis theory, when viewing the economy, the continuation of its dynamic cyclical evolution, results in a different foundation of a sufficiently unique industrial base to make the cycle move in a distinctive evolutionary pattern, with newness coming from the old.

According to chaos theory, equilibrium is an essential position in the business cycle's movement, with each cycle, either during its process or upon completion, having been in an equilibrium position. In the real-life dynamics of business cycles, however equilibrium is a rarity, and should it occur, it does so in specific markets for limited periods of time. This is far different from the strange attractor equilibrium positions demonstrated by Berry. These equilibrium positions have to be interpreted according to the economic conditions at the time. They must be understood as referring to new cyclical positions in an economic base distinct from the previous cycle, but, again, this discussion must await the last part of this work.

Referring again to Feinberg's definition of chaos, the system's evolution cannot be predicted because of its sensitive dependence on minor changes with in it. As with the snowflake and the released gas, these changes depend on conditions outside the system; with economics, it is also the case that an economy is dependent on its country's politics, and the politics are, in turn, dependent on the economy. Such systems, be they physical or socioeconomic, cannot be considered totally in isolation, for their very dynamics of evolution depends directly on external circumstances.

In this context, therefore, consider Leon Glass's and Michael C. Mackey's comment about chaos:

> Technically, chaos refers to randomness or irregularity that arises in a deterministic system. In other words, chaos is observed even in the complete absence of environmental noise. An important aspect of chaos is that there is a sensitive dependence of the dynamics to the initial conditions. This means that although in principle it should be possible to predict future dynamics as a function of time, this is in reality impossible since any error in specifying the initial condition, no matter how small, leads to an erroneous prediction at some future time.[7]

The difficulty with this opinion is obvious: every evolutionary system has a sensitive dependence on its initial conditions, but evolutionary systems do not exist in isolation. Consider the snowflake: in an isolated existence, the snowflake would not develop, for the external factors necessary for its development are not functioning. Snowflakes designed by computer graphics are fulfilling the program's requirements, and to this extent this development is evolutionary. But this type of evolution is unnatural, strictly determined, and in terminated when the computer is turned off or when the program ends. Snowflakes in the real world are not isolated from the external conditions necessary for the realization of their natural evolution. Even though there is sensitive dependence on their initial conditions, their evolution, while not predictable, results in unique entities each time. The point is that every evolving system–be it socioeconomoic, political, biological, or even ideological–has a sensitive dependence on its initial conditions, while evolving in dynamic environments with outside influences penetrating it. Hence, in contrast to Glass and Mackey's sentiment, even in principle it should not be possible to predict the future dynamics of a system as a function of time, because the external conditions are necessary for each system's evolution, as evolution does not exist in isolation.

It is for the reason that such systems display aperiodic equations. Their growth is irregular, and so the mathematics for treating them must also be irregular, showing the changes that occur as these systems evolve as a function of time. In physics, for example, accepting this notion was difficult because of of the impact made by Newtonian physics, which is strictly deterministic, for which difference equations are only a mathematical concept. Einstein was a determinist, but a probabilistic determinist, and based his concept on the real-world geometry as Riemannian, with time-space curving back on itself as objects move through space-time. Einstein could not accept Newtonian determinism because of Planck's findings of radiation being pulsated in small packets of energy or quanta at rates different from those predicted by Lord Rayleigh and Max Wein.[8] In the Newtonian framework, nonlinear equations are only conceptual; in the framework of Einsteinian relativity and quantum physics, these equations gain practical significance in time-series calculations for dynamic events in a probabilistic deterministic and strict indeterministic world respectively.

This would seem to demonstrate the relationship between relativity and quantum physics to chaos theory. Indeed, the time-series equations to describe the radiation of the oscillators in quantum experiments within atomic structures are the same types of equations used for dynamic economic analysis. The difference is, however, that for relativity and quantum theory as they are generally understood, there is no evolution within their systems, and hence they are not subject to the influences of other systems on them. However, the emphasis is on general understanding, and only now are we beginning to comprehend the concepts of micro and macro infinity and the interrelations that these two concepts–indeed systems–have on one another.[9]

COMMENTS ON CATASTROPHE THEORY

Catastrophe Theory A branch of mathematics used to describe how quantities may change suddenly when some parameter that they depend on changes slightly.

Gerald Feinberg,
Solid Clues[10]

In his chapter on "Kinematics of Forms: Catastrophes," René Thom discusses the morphology of a catastrophic process. Assuming that a natural process of any kind whatsoever occurs in an area designated as box **B**, and then consider that **B** X **T** is the domain on which the process is defined, with **T** being time. Assume that an observer has probes or other means to investigate the neighborhood of each point **x** of **B** X **T**. If the observer detects no irregularity for point **x**, with respect to all other points, then **x** is a regular point in the process. The regular point forms an open set on **B** X **T**, and the complementary set **K** is closed and is the set of catastrophe points, thereby having some discontinuity in every neighborhood. Something happens in every grouping with center **c** when **c** ε**K**. The set **K** and the singularities of each of its points, Thom maintains, constitute the the morphology of the process. Furthermore, he maintains that the distinction between regular and catastrophic points is somewhat arbitrary, for it depends on the fineness of the observation used, leaving open the argument that each point is catastrophic in response to sufficiently sensitive observational techniques. This distinction, Thom states, is an ideation that in made precise by a mathematical model.

For Thom, catastrophe is associated with discontinuity. Hence, for him, it is natural to say that a point (**x**, **t**) ε**K** in **B** X **T** is a catastrophe if at least one of the functions q (**x**, **t**)–or one of its first or second derivatives–has a point of discontinuity. Supposing that **K** is not locally dense, for then the neighborhood of some points would not be chaotic and turbulent, with the idea of structural stability losing most of its relevance. Thus, with the mapping of box **B** onto **B**', the closed catastrophe sending **K** onto **K**' will correspond under strict mapping for **B** X **T** , and the boxes will be of the same topological type and have the same form in the two boxes.

Under the section heading 2.3. "Structural Stability and Models," Thom discusses formal and continuous models. Formal models are those of formal systems that have the following advantages: their description is simple, being axiomatic or combinatorial, with deduction within these systems possibly mechanized. The formal model is compatible with some indeterminacy of phenomena inasmuch as deduction is an intermediate operation. In formal models, questions are undecidable within a system in the sense of knowing whether a proposition is the consequence of a set of propositions. Thom also maintains that no dynamic is possible for them.

Continuous models, on the other hand, admit a dynamic, and the use of different models provides strict determinism. Even qualitatively different models may be described by structurally unstable dynamic systems. These models are difficult to describe. Moreover if explicit differential equations are used, only a small number of sufficiently simple algebraic or geometrical forms can be used, conflicting in general with the a priori need for structural stability when dealing with a process that apparently is empirically stable.

René Thom's work is not only fascinating, but it is also important in the biological aspects of morphogenesis in embryonic development and multicelluar organisms. Indeed, it is important in the general theory of evolution, for development is one of the outstanding issues of biology, botany, and zoology.[11] For chaos theory, it is also important, especially for dynamic systems.

Consider the snowflake again; two droplets of water falling under identical conditions, and with the same external conditions affecting them, evolve into two distinct and unique snowflakes. Taken as formal systems, each droplet isolated in space and time has its own structure whose description is simple, and in its isolation being axiomatic or combinatorial, it conforms to standard three-dimensional geometry in the space time framework. From its standard form in isolation, no prediction concerning its situation can be made, because its formal situation is static. The process is also continuous, as snowflakes are transformed from droplets to the final form of the flake itself. This transformation is due to the effects the external environment on the droplet as it descends. The qualities of the droplets change suddenly as the parameters of the environment change, no matter how slightly.

This situation is identical to that of chaos. The evolution of a system cannot be predicted because of its sensitive dependence on changes, however minor, in the properties of the system. These changes are sudden, whille the generators of the changes nay be ever so slight. What René Thom has described and dealt with are, therefore, the mathematics of chaos theory. Chaos systems undergo rapid quantitive changes when a single external parameter change occurs–and more so, when many parameters change–bringing changes within the system, as with the snowflake and indeed with the dispersion of gas as it is affected by its environment in the form of alterations in wind direction and force, and the influences of other conditions within the area.

With respect to the set **K** in **B** X **T**, the distinction between regular and catastrophic points is not as Thom maintains, but between static and dynamic conditions within the area. Equating the static condition to Thom's definition of formal, then the static condition has a simple description, being axiomatic and combinatorial in composition. Deduction within these systems may be mechanized, but is determinate. The formal condition in a thriving **B** X **T** domain–the nature of the domain is not important here–will not remain formal or static for any significant duration owing to the continuous or dynamic conditions within the same domain. As the continuous situation is dynamic, there will be discontinuity within this continuous situation.

Consider the situation for this perspective: discontinuity tends to occur in this domain (and indeed, in every domain that is to some extent dynamic) in a random, yet fairly persistent manner. Discontinuity is therefore expected, even though the general domain is believed to be consistent. Hence, point $(\mathbf{x}, \mathbf{t})$ $\varepsilon \mathbf{K}$, whether continuous or changing at its first or second derivative, will be discontinuous over time $\mathbf{t}$ owing to the impact of the dynamics within the domain. The catastrophic situation that Thom discusses is therefore to be expected for each part of the domain, no matter how small, over time.

Each $\mathbf{B} \times \mathbf{T}$ domain is, in fact, dynamic. Its formal or static setting may have been its initial position captured in the instantaneous moment in time. Every domain is evolutionary, developing according to its internal dynamics and effect that the external environment exerts on it. Therefore every domain can be considered a system, with its parts subject to the statics of its initial position and the dynamics within it foisted upon it from other parts of the domain as they change, and by the influences external to the domain. In other words, each domain operates according to the laws of chaos, with catastrophic situations being identical to those that bring about changes in evolving systems. Every domain (=system), when in use, is dynamic and subject to chaos considerations when considered in terms of catastrophe theory. The association of catastrophe theory with chaos theory is valid because chaos systems tend to equilibrium as demonstrated by Berry's treatment of the business cycle, and by the strange attractors in chaos theory bringing the system into equilibrium even though evolution is occurring. Catastrophe theory describes the discontinuous changes within the domain during the continuous bevelopment of the chaos system. But just as the system tends toward equilibrium as with the snowflake and the dispersed gas–the discontinuous changes within the system increase, first at an increasing rate as the business cycle heats up, as the droplet of water begins changing shape into the snowflake, and as the initially released gas begins its expansion. Then it tapers off, decreasing at an increasing rate as the system moves toward equilibrium.

For chaos theory and catastrophe theory on which chaos relies for development of systems, there are difficulties. Chaos pertains to the evolution of systems, and catastrophe shows the direction that the systems' evolutions take. The she snowflake's design is based on the catastrophic changes that the falling droplet undergoes as its internal and external dynamics meet and clash–as is necessary for its evolution. The released gas is also dispersed in terms of catastrophe, for there is no smooth path that the gas takes. It has its various directions altered owing the pressure of its environment and the impact of the environment on its development.

Both chaos theory and the dynamics of catastrophe theory are therefore in a paradoxical situation: evolution ceases when equilibrium is reached, yet evolution as such does not cease but takes differing paths. This paradox can be resolved by distinguishing between evolution and development. The snowflake develops according to its internal dynamics and the dynamics exerted on it by its environment; released gas develops according to the force of its pressure when escaping and to forces on it when it disperses. The development of chaos systems ceases when equilibrium is reached–that is, when no further internal dynamics exist and no external dynamics can bring about alterations.

Evolution, however, does not cease; only strains of the evolutionary process are terminated owing to interferences of external dynamics and the lack of sufficient internal dynamics to regulate the external influences. Although the problems of evolution theory as such must wait for a later work, a theory for treating systems and their evolution, with both internal and external changes within the system treated, is formulated and discussed in Part II. This is crisis theory. It incorporates situations explained by chaos and catastrophe theories, with equilibrium being considered in a different context and without the paradox of evolution.

NOTES

1. James Gleick, *Chaos* (New York: Penguin Books, 1988), p. 3. Nature has always been irregular, and since this irregularity has been noted by scientists throughout history, it has been a source of arousing curiosity. Scientists today engage in research into the fields mentioned by Gleick. Just to give two examples, for weather research, see Philip D. Thompson's book, *Numerical Weather Analysis and Prediction* (New York: Macmilan, 1961), and for research into the brain, see "Scientists Who Pick Dead Brains Living," *Jerusalem Post*, May 15, 1995, p. 7, issued by Reuter News Agency.

2. See Max Planck, *Scientific Biography and Other Papers*, trans. Frank Gaynor (Westport, Conn: Greenwood Press, 1968). See also Albert Einstein, *The Meaning of Relativity*, 5th ed. (Princeton, N.J.: Princeton University Press, 1953). For a discussion on Nelis Bohr and the atom, see A. d'Abro, *The Rise of the New Physics* (New York, Dover, 1951) Vol. 2 Chapter XXXVI, pp. 488-583. See also Niels Bohr, *Collected Works* (New York: Elsevier, 1972).

3. See, for example, Richard Dawkins, *The Blind Watchmaker* (New York: W. W. Norton, 1987), and Robert Jastrow's discussion on evolution and natural selection in his *Red Giants and White Dwarfs* (New York: Warner Books, 1980), pp. 188-262.

4. For example, see Gary Zukov, *The Dancing Wu Li Masters* (New York: Morrow Quill, 1979), and Paul Davies, *Other Worlds* (New York: Touchstone Books, 1980).

5. See, for example, Stuart A. Kauffman, *The Origins of Order* (New York: Oxford University Press, 1993).

6. For a discussion on the economics of trade during the Great Depression, see David Z. Rich, *The Economics of International Trade* (Westport, Conn.: Quorum Books, 1992), chapter 2, pp. 13-28.

7. See Leon Glass and Michael C. Mackey, *From Clocks to Chaos* (Princeton, N. J.: Princeton University Press, 1988), pp. 6, 7. The authors state further on p. 33 that two main features characterizing chaos must be fulfilled:

(1) For some parameter values, almost all initial conditions give rise to aperiodic dynamics; (2) arbitrary close initial conditions display independent temporal evolution as time proceeds. Thus there is a *sensitive dependence on initial conditions*. [italics in original]

8. Rayleigh's law of radiation is $i_v = v^2/c^2kt$, with i_v being the intensity y of the radiation of frequency v, c is the velocity of light in vacuo, k in the gas constant, and T is the absolute temperature of the gas enclosed. This does not, however, satisfy the displacement law stating that the frequency of the radiation of maximum intensity is directly proporionate to the absolute temperature. Wein's relation is $i_v = v^3/c^2 f(v/T)$. D'Abro comments that not all the conceivable laws that satisfy Wein's relation entail a radiation of maximum frequency and lead to the displacement law. But this relation is not inconsistent with the displacement law as we can imagine laws that satisfy Wein's relation and also the displacement law. See A. d'Abro, *The Rise of the New Physics* (New York: Dover, 1951), Vol. 2, pp. 447-471. It was only when Planck eliminated this difficulty with the understanding of radiation that Einstein could accept the quantum theory of radiation, as well as the probabilistic determinism that was consitent with the world-view of Riemannian geometry and the probability associated with quantum physics.

9. As our world seems to be evolving, perhaps it is the interaction between the micro and macro spheres that brings about evolution. This subject will be treated in a later work.

10. Gerald Feinberg, *Solid Clues* (New York: Touchstone Books 1985), p. 264.

11. See René Thom, *Structural Stability and Morphogenesis*, trans. D. H. Fowler (Reading, Mass.: Addison-Wesley, 1989). For a discussion on catastrophe theory see chapter 2-5, pp. 12-100 with respect to three-dimensional space and time, associated with conflicts of regimes as expressed by conflicting geometries in the space-time continuum. These situations are dynamic within the Riemannian conceptualization and indeed, could be applied to other non-Euclidian geometries. The either-or aspect of catastrophe theory, in terms of the sudden changes of systems in response to slight changes of a parameter on which they depend has significance for chaos theory.

PART II

CRISIS THEORY

CHAPTER 5

Introduction

There are times in any science when one senses that a transformation to a deeper understanding is pressing upward in some as yet poorly articulated form.

Stuart A. Kauffman,
The Origins of Order[1]

In the discussion of chaos and catastrophe theory in Part I, regardless of the critique of these theories, there was nevertheless the understanding that chaos theory deals with a wide range of problems outside the general scope of traditional science, and catastrophe theory operates in the development of chaos systems.

Indeed, there is a need for a theory that can handle unique weather conditions and that can describe the development of snowflakes and the dispersion of gases. The oscillation of cells, the cell's strange attractors specified in the combinatorial gene code, and the bifurcation of cells into various organs as determined by the overall genetic program require a theory such as chaos to describe its dynamics. For biology, chaos theory seems appropriate because it deals with the development and, to some extent, the evolution of life forms. The evolutionary aspect is the combinatorial gene pattern that forms a unique being. The development aspect is the formation of life forms from conception, in which male and female cells are joined, to the fully formed adult life at which no further physical development, occures; with the cessation of physical development, physical decline sets in, with death the ultimate consequence. In biology, catastrophe theory explains the direction of evolution that cells take in their bifurcation–processes that, once having been made, cannot be reversed, for they are controlled by the information contained in the combinatorial gene code. The uniqueness of each individual is due to the uniqueness of the combined genetic material that composes the individual. Thus, even for identical twins the genetic code differs sufficiently so that people who know these twins (and this refers not only to humans but to all life forms) can distinguish between them not only by their personalities, but also by their appearances.

Chaos theory, and by the definition of purpose, catastrophe theory, are nevertheless insufficient to explain biological development and evolution. Although both occur in the formation of a new individual, no real equilibrium is reached, but only the cessation of growth and the physical decline that follows.

Another difficulty here pertains to catastrophe theory. This is the subjective delineation of catastrophic points in Thom's **B X T** domain. As Thom states:

> The distinction between regular and catastrophic points is obviously somewhat arbitrary because it depends on the fineness of the observation used. One might object, not without reason, that each point is catastrophic to sufficiently sensitive observational techniques. This is why the distinction is an idealization, to be made precise by a mathematical model.[2]

If the distinction between catastrophic and noncatastrophic points in the **B X T** domain is somewhat arbitrary, then how can catastrophe theory be applicable? More than a mathematical model is needed to explain this, for models relate to reality only when necessary adjustments are made. Without these adjustments, catastrophic conditions occur that conform to Thom's conceptualization without the subjectivity and arbitrariness that he discusses above. However, given Thom's arbitrariness, as catastrophic situations are arbitrary, and as they are the motivators for chaos, then chaos seems to be arbitrary as a condition. Hence it exists as perceived, given the internal and external dynamics of the situation.

Since the consequence of catastrophic situations is arbitrary, and the systems for which they are formulated are also arbitrary, these formulations are at the discretion of the people who conceived them. The equilibrium conditions would then be arbitrary, with the influences of both internal and external dynamics being conditional, rendering the entire direction of development and evolution arbitrary. The point is, however, that as Kauffman expressed it, there is a transformation to a deeper understanding that is pressing upward; this has found expression in chaos theory with its difference equations. This type of mathematical reasoning is incorporated into chaos theory because it is useful in analyzing different stages of development and evolution of the chaos structure. Difference equations do not necessarily relate strictly to chaos theory. Indeed, they are useful in the inquiry into all dynamic systems, whether undergoing development and evolution or in the temporary static phase of equilibrium.

As a branch of mathematics, nonlinear difference analysis describes conditions in systems, showing their changes. This type of analysis is used in chaos theory because it describes these systems and their catastrophic dynamics, to the point where development and evolution cease and equilibrium sets in.

Nonlinear analysis does not, however, clarify why development and evolution cease and equilibrium sets in. Although this is the teleological conclusion of every chaos system, it is not so in the mainstream sciences. In physics, for example, the introduction of Eastern attitudes to physical events has shown that the discipline remains open to different approaches that can yield new knowledge. Moreover, subatomic physics is indeterminate and its systems do not reach equilibrium. Those systems that do are within the Newtonian framework and rely on conditions being maintained over the very long run, which, given our comprehension of quantum physics, is impossible.[3] In biology, although cells oscillate in equilibrium, they do so only for the duration of the cellular systems being static. Given the growth of the organism through the multiplication and expansion of cellular tissues, these oscillations take on different frequencies. It is only when the organism's growth is maximized according to its genetic code that its equilibrium position is reached, after which the organism declines and dies. However, the species continues to thrive, unless conditions exist that pose a serious threat to the species' existence and evolutionary survival. This is evolution nevertheless, and while individual members of a species die, if left unhindered the species survives and its evolution continues. But, as was stated earlier, this must await another work. In must be clear here, however, that the frequencies of cells in oscillation are maintained in equilibrium only for the duration of the equilibrium of the systems. For a living organism, this duration is very short, for even when growth ceases and equilibrium is reached, the organism undergoes a rapid decline into disequilibrium, resulting in death.

Kauffman's sentiment must be generalized to include all sciences. The transformation to a deeper understanding has resulted from the search for a mechanism, for a scientific device, that is universal and applicable in all the sciences. In the twentieth century, the mechanism of Cartesian-Newtonian determinism gave way to the probabilistic determinism of Einstein and the uncertainty of the quantum physicists. Yet, when examining chaos systems, determinism has been seen to be restored. This is so in physical, economic, meteorological, and biological and chemical systems. The bifurcations and fractals that generate them are still moving in the direction of the strange attractor, with all systems eventually resulting in the recurring graphic shape of the "butterfly wings" that Edward Lorenz described. The mechanism of chaos is eventual equilibrium and stability within systems, so that it can be controlled and worked with, and so that a new philosophical order can be established, one of ultimate stability and permanence that is associated with truth.

This is a desire to return to a time that never was, to a period of tranquility that has evaded humanity throughout history, to an ideal but highly unrealistic situation, given our current state of knowledge of the sciences. Our historical era of knowledge goes against this attitude, as the achievements in our era–and throughout the developments in the arts and sciences–have been attributable to solutions to problems in the domains in which the contributions have been made.

In the arts and sciences, as Kauffman states, we have achieved a transformation to an upward pressing to a deeper understanding. This understanding is not within the mainstream of the development of ideas, but rather is a new approach that allows for the development of new concepts. Chaos theory was one such approach, but because of its difficulties, it has to be replaced by another approach, one that is more realistic and of greater utility. This is crisis theory, and it is discussed in the chapters that follow.

NOTES

1. Stuart A. Kauffman, *The Origins of Order* (New York: Oxford University Press, 1993), p. 3.

2. René Thom, *Structural Stability and Morphogenesis*, trans. D. H. Fowler (Reading, Mass.: Addison-Wesley, 1989), p. 38.

3. It is impossible to maitain physical conditions over the long run because of the changing micro and macro conditions within a physical system and outside it. Micro conditions are changing as subatomic particles move around their nuclei, for quantum physics has shown that the atom is far from being a stable structure. The external influences are due to the earth's motion, the magnetic fields generated around each system, and the effects they have on the systems. The concept of closed systems is no longer of utility; this point, however, is discussed later in this work.

CHAPTER 6

Crisis Theory—
The Formal Statement

One must think the thought: one must question an argument's logical connections and relations to the world in order to follow it.

Nathan Tarcov and Thomas L. Pangle,
"Epilogue: Leo Strauss and the History of Political Philosophy"[1]

INTRODUCTORY REMARKS

Two issues are involved in Tarcov and Pangle's statement. One is to think the thought, to explore an argument's logical connections, its interrelations, to determine its strengths and to seek out its contradictions. This requires an intellectual detachment concerning the argument, even though we are all too human and too often attach our identities to the position, letting our basic irrationality control our reasoning. Often in these situations, in the heat of debate, arguments based on authority are used to belittle the opponent's view. The terms "debate" and "opponent" are used intentionally, for in the debating situation reason is often cast aside, to be replaced by emotion. When reasoning out an argument alone, however, errors in reasoning may be made, however unintentionally, that could perhaps be avoided during argument. Considered in these terms, an argument is a reasoned position undertaken to understand a situation, a concept, and how it relates to the area for which it is stated and presented. This may provide an understanding of the position and how it relates to the world, but its status in relation to the world is static, and this is the second issue.

Following an argument's logical connections is one thing, and relating the argument's premises, middle points, and its conclusions to the real world in order to follow it is another. Again, this attitude assumes that the domain for which the argument is considered is static, that neither the domain nor the real dynamics of the argued position changes.

Of course, change is neither instant nor constant. When quantum physics first appeared, the argument was about the nature of the atom and the subparticles that circle its nucleus. The movement of these subparticles into differing orbitals, and the considerations of the gravitational force that holds this complex entity together, were the issues of that argument, with each point being argued along the way.

Since the early days, however, changes have occurred. Heisenberg's uncertainty principle altered the way the argument was conducted. Prior to Heisenberg's principle, the atom was considered to be an entity like all others, subject to the principles of observation and testing. Heisenberg demonstrated that this is not the case, that observation exerts energy and that this energy influences the positions and motions of subatomic particles. The composition of the atom has changed with our understanding of it, and arguments have been advanced concerning its final composition, whether the final building blocks of nature and the energy forces that control these blocks have indeed been found. That domain of the world that is concerned with quantum physics has changed, and so have the arguments.

This, of course, does not mean that all arguments are as such, subjected to the dynamics of the world as it changes in its various domains. Arguments such as those pertaining to issues of history, past issues in the sciences, in philosophy–in all intellectual activity–are static in the sense that the situations already occurred and what is being argued is the clarification of the position. This can be enhanced should new material be brought into the discussion, changing the opinions of the participants. These are static issues, situations that have already occurred, and the discussion is involved for the clarification of the situation.

Every argument has two phases in time sequence. The first phase is the formal or static statement, which shows how the position is set up, how its terms are defined and delineated, and how it relates to its domain–to the world according to Tarcov and Pangle–according to its terminology and the rules incorporated for its use. The second phase is continuous in the sense of its being used, and as such, being changed as it relates to a dynamic domain. Crisis theory is a generalized form that is applicable to a range of issues that are evolutionary and hence dynamic. This theory uses difference equations as they relate to time changes within each specific domain. It is noncatastrophic in the sense of either-or as Thom expressed his theory, but it is dynamic, changing, and subject to alterations to maintain its viability in its applications. In order to understand crisis theory in its continuous setting, it must first be explained in its formal setting; this is the task in this chapter.

THE FORMAL STATEMENT: A SCHEMATIC

Each crisis theory is composed of two interrelated languages. One language delineates and defines the area of concern for which the theory deals; the other defines the working operations of the first language on the problem area. The area language, as constructed according to the designs of its formulator and those who employ it, tends, in its static form, to be complete, for at this stage the defined area is restricted by the problem for which it was constructed. Hence, the operational language also tends to be restricted as the types of, and procedures for, operations allowed by the theory's innovator and those who work with the construction, as determined by the area's lanaguage. The schematic for a crisis theory C^*_t takes the form: $C^*_t = \Sigma\,(O_d A)$, with O the operational language, A the area language, and the subscript "d" the defining relationship. The sigma sign is the summation operator of the theory's operational and area statements. The time-signature "t" indicates that the theory is either static or dynamic, depending on the duration of its use. When static, the theory relates to the domain as is; when dynamic, there is no guarantee that the same operational and area statements will exist in time period $n + 1$ as in period 1. The reasons for differing time periods are that different contributions have impacts on the domain that may induce changes within a specific C^*, that nuances have infiltrated the languages, or that competing theories may render some statements entropic.

For C^*_t, if there are n statements for A, there will originally be a corresponding number of statements for O, so that the a elements that compose A are matched isomorphically with the o statements in O. This is the formal statement of a crisis theory. As during its uses, the theory is far from static but is changing; C^*_t is a highly dynamic system, the viability of which depends on the conceptualizations of those who work with it. Its evolutionary development is thus not axiomatic but requires active participation in the theory's functioning. The meaning of terms may be altered–perhaps ever so slightly–and this affects their utilities as the changes in nuance are incorporated into the theory's performance.

The formal schematic of crisis theory can be contrasted to Thom's formal model for catastrophic situations. Thom's formal model is described as simple, being axiomatic or combinatorial, with deduction within the model being formalized and theoretically mechanized. In addition, Thom maintains that his deduction is an indeterminate operation. Moreover, some questions may be undecided within the model in the sense of knowing whether a proposition is the consequence of a set of propositions. Thus, he maintains that no dynamic is possible for them.

In contrast, the formal schematic of crisis theory may or may not provide a simple description of the domain for which it is constructed, for this depends on the domain and the complexity of the information involved. The axiomatic aspect of the model is its operational language, which is usually combinatorial. Deductive reasoning for these types of models is in accordance with the axiomatic uses of the operational in the area language, and this, with respect to the domain. Within the formal schematic, no questions are undecidable because of the isomorphic mapping of the operational onto the area statements. As the area statements describe the real domain for which the theory is stated, in its static form no crisis theory has statements that cannot be determined or decided within the theory. Deduction has a limited role in such theories, being important only for formulating the theory, checking for its inconsistencies after the theory is finalized. As the object of the theory is in its dynamics which are derived in its final form, deduction is for examining the logical structure and not for working with the theory as such. For this schematic, it makes no difference whether a proposition is a consequence of a set of propositions. The only significant point is how a proposition in one language relates to its corresponding proposition in the other language, and how these languages relate to the real-world domain. The terms of other theoretical languages may or may not be incorporated into the theory's languages, but once incorporated, they must take on the theory's nuances.

As an example of crisis theory, consider the Big Bang theory of the origins of the universe. The terms of reference are the **A** statements, and the procedures for working with these statements are incorporated within the **O**. **A** describes the predicament of an initial big explosion, spewing cosmic dust in all directions. After a great length of time this dust fell into gravitational relationships and began to form galaxies, with their solar systems and all that we know about the dynamics of the universe. On the basis of **A** and its statements, **O** is employed to build models, construct computerized languages that are able to handle stellar observations based on the Big Bang theory, and offer explanations for both observed and predicted phenomena.

When in use, a crisis theory remains in its formal position for the duration of its usage for the situation for which it was constructed when the area remains described and fixed according to the understanding of those who work with the theory, as long as its operational language relates to its area language. Thus, if there is no difficulty, and none is conceived, the theory works smoothly, as it was initially designed to function.

CRISIS THEORY AND UTILITY

A difficulty with constructing a crisis theory can be detected, for while the general problem area may be very broad, encompassing the activities of several disciplines, a theory seeks to limit its range by its rigorous definitions. In this way, the theory attempts to remove or lessen as much as possible the influences of those parts of the general domain that are not considered to be within the theory's realm. The theory's construction must be such that all extraneous influences are eliminated or kept to a minimum, so as to allow for the maximum effect of the utility prescribed to the theory.

Utility, therefore, is a measure of the theory's effectiveness, as determined by the theory's objectives within the delineated domain of the problem area and its ability to incorporate influences that are not part of the original construction. A theory C^*_t is constructed to be measured between two limits. The lower limit, zero, is a boundary that is never reached because the theory's system breaks down before and is not subject to restoration. In this condition, its elements are incapable of reaching this limit because of the information that has entered C^*_t, thereby rendering it unworkable. Hence, it is abandoned.

The theory's languages comprise its elements, which contain and convey information. The area language describes the range and contents of the theory, while the operative language determines and describes the working of the area. When these languages perform as they are supposed to according to the theory, the upper limit of 1 is approached; like the lower limit, this upper limit is never reached. The quantity and content of information within the general area is in a fairly continuous state of movement, being increased and altered with new contributions, changing and being reformulated as theories are phased out and as others enter the area. Thus, maximum utility can never be attained because the theories' languages are changing and the area does not remain fixed. The maximum limit can be approached, however, for this is the intention of those who work with the theory, and indeed its innovator.

The limits–or boundaries–are thus determinants, indicating the theory's health at any specific time. Thus, $0 < C^*_t < 1$ is the general position of a working theory. Its proximity to these limits determines the theory's viability, so that as C^*_t approaches 0, it is becoming entropic; as it approaches 1, its utility is increasing.

Utility is assessed according to the theory's objectives, its problem area, and its ability to work with the area. The theory's innovator states the position and presents the theory, demonstrating its workability. The theory's information content and viability are determined by the ability of its languages to relate to its area. This determination is probabilistic because maximum utility is unobtainable. Utility tends toward the maximum limit when the theory functions according to its requirements, so that it relates to its area at the given time stated, with its operational and area languages performing as formulated. The theory's languages function according to their information content and the conditions of its problem area. Thus, the area language must be so formulated that it allows the nonrestricted ability to work with its operational language and with the problem area.

All information within the theory that does not pertain to its structured languages is either for clarification or for embellishment, thus relegating this information to the status of metalanguage, which is relevant in that it relates to the working languages and seeks to improve on them conceptually. The metalanguages cannot, however, assist in the workings of the operational and area languages.

In its formal statement, a theory's utility is assessed according to how well it relates to its domains, as set out in its languages. Because maximum utility is impossible to achieve, so that the theory functions according to a probabilistic relationship between the workings of the languages and the actual designated domain, utility can be stated thus: $U_t = [P(O_dA) = I(O_dA)]_t$. That is, the theory's utility at a specific time is identical to the equality between its probability measure and its information content, with "d" being the defining and delineating operator of **O** unto **A**, with the probability measuring the information of **O** and **A** as they relate to the area and measuring every **o** and **a** of the theory. Because these languages contain information, the probabilistic measure determines the validity of the statements, that is, their information, **I**, as they relate to the domain so that the closer these statements relate, the greater their probabilities, and hence the greater utility for $C*_t$. Of course, the innovator seeks to formulate a theory whose utility approaches the maximum 1, while both the innovator and the theory's followers, imitators, seek to maintain the high utility level by attempting to reconstruct those elements that are reduced in their utilities owing to area shifts in the domain or to language changes. The lack of treatment in these circumstances results in further erosion of the theory's utility, which may eventually bring it into a condition of entropy.

CRISIS THEORY AND ENTROPY

Utility is a measurement of the theory's ability to perform as required in its full formal statement, thereby yielding results as required by its operational and area languages. Utility, then, is a measurement of how well the theory achieves its purpose, how significant its information content is in its defined and delineated domain and specific problem area, and how effective the operational language is in relation to the area language.

Entropy, on the other hand, is both a measurement and a condition of the theory's decline as assessed by its lack of effectiveness in performance according to its languages and objectives. As a measurement, it indicates just how far the theory has deviated from the original problem area it defined and delineated and hence from its operational abilities. Usually, this entropic condition can be removed or at least alleviated, so that utility can be restored, perhaps not to its formal level but to the extent that the theory can continue to be employed without too much difficulty.[2]

As is true of utility, the determination of entropy relies on the theory's information content, which is assessed with respect to the information's probability as its operational elements relate to its area. The decline in information is the direct result of the lack of effectiveness in the theory's elements, resulting in the probability that these statements tend toward the lower limit. Altering these defective statements changes their meaning and may affect the original intention of the theory as it was constructed. In the attempt to remove the entropy if the change is not too extensive, the theory regains utility and most likely continues to be used as a working formulation for the problem area it delineates and defines. If such reconstruction is not undertaken, the theory in its original form will decline further until the extent of entropy becomes so pervasive that the theory cannot be saved.

One way this decline occurs is that alternative theories are introduced as competitors. Under competition, these theories maintain their utilities to a large extent, thereby rendering the weakened theory of little or no utility. This means that the theory is either approaching entropy or has become entropic, as the case may be.

Should alterations be initiated because of the need to correct the entropic statements, the theory will most likely continue to be used, employed in a somewhat different approach owing to the changes from its original position. This situation will continue until finally changes in the problem area are not dealt with by the corresponding alterations in the statements, continuing until the entire theory is brought into decline. The entropy measurement will show that the theory is approaching the lower limit. As a result, either the theory is replaced by one of vastly higher utility, or the theory is abandoned and falls into disuse.

One further point must be made here, and this concerns the use of the thermodynamic term "entropy." Sadi Carnot, Rudolph Clausis, Ludwig von Boltzmann, and others who worked with the principle of entropy in physical systems were not concerned with information as such, but with the functioning of these physical systems and their eventual breakdown.[3] Since the pioneering work done on the second law of thermodynamics, this law has attracted attention in other fields of inquiry. Theories do not have to pertain to the physical realm, and entropy does not have to relate specifically to the decline of physical energy. Theories are abstractions, stated as formulations and conventional methods for working with problem areas. While they are valid, they have utility; they are used and examined, accepted and applied, until better theories replace them, or until new information pertaining to the problems for which these theories were developed renders the accepted theories inadequate. Entropy is thus a condition produced by the theory's information to relate to its designated problem area, rendering it appropriate, though in its diminished capacity. The extent of this diminution depends on the availability of better alternatives.

Throughout history, all theories eventually decline, become entropic, and are abandoned. All theories have utility; otherwise, theory would lack any semblance of a working body of knowledge. Theories encounter entropy in small amounts, as their elements lose some of their utility owing to area shifts or to changes in their languages. To maintain the utility of theories, entropy has to be corrected.

Changes in theories have been more rapid in our contemporary era of knowledge then in any other historical era. Hence, although theories in their original constructions are the basis for the development of knowledge, they are also subject to changes through their uses. As a theory maintains its integrity through its use, it also undergoes changes in its languages and perhaps even in its area as the dynamics of its uses influences both its languages and the problem area through use, for which the theory was formulated and applied. With respect to chaos, theories as they are discussed here are evolutionary only in the sense that they are dynamic and unstable, adapted through use to cope with their problem areas and the changes that occur within them. There is no equilibrium, however, and the theories fade into disuse when they become too entropic to salvage. This includes situations when theories of greater utility are formulated, resulting in those existing and worked with previously to be abandoned. This topic is discussed in further detail in the next chapter. As is demonstrated there and in the chapters to follow, all theories comply with the dynamics of crisis theory, and chaos theory is inadequate, with respect to crisis theory, for explaining the phenomena for which it was developed. The statics of crisis theory have been discused, and now crisis theory has to be placed in it dynamic setting, after which further comments on crisis theory and chaos theory are presented.

NOTES

1. Nathan Tarcov and Thomas L. Pangle, "Epilogue: Leo Strauss and the History of Political Philosophy," in Leo Strauss and Joseph Cropsey, eds., *History of Political Philosophy*, 3rd ed. (Chicago: University of Chicago Press, 1987), p. 913.

2. In this context, the general definition of entropy is $HC^*_t = -\Sigma[(o,a)I(A_{od} \ O_a)]$, which reads that the entropy of the crisis theory C^* at time t is the negation of the elements o and a as they are included in A and O during this time. Those elements not included in this summation are not entropic, for the equation pertains only to the defective area statements affected by or with the operational language. Thus, the minus sign indicated the statements that are negated with respect to the theory. The "I" signifies the theory's information content with respect to the defective statements, and the number of statements affected shows the extent of the entropic condition and hence the theory's viability.

3. See A. d'Abro's discussion on thermodynamics and entropy in *The Rise of the New Physics* (New York: Dover, 1951), Vol. 1, pp. 323-373, especially 344-373.

CHAPTER 7

Crisis Theory— Dynamics and Discontinuity

For if that distinguished line of inspired mathematicians has taught us anything in the last 2000 years, it is that dimension is in the eye, and in the imagination, of the beholder.

Michael Guillen,
"A Realm of Manifold Possibilities"[1]

INTRODUCTORY COMMENTS

Michael Guillen's comment is correct, but it applies not only to mathematicians, but also to physicists, chemists, philosophers, and of course artists. Dimension in the sense that Guillen uses it in his essay is a convention that holds great sway over people. He states that the British philosopher in the mid-seventeenth century, Henry More (1614-1687), held that the fourth dimension is where ghosts dwell and that Descartes rejected the concept of a fourth dimension as unrealistic. In modern science, the concept of the fourth dimension is taken as given. The convention of rejecting the reality of a fourth dimension, like most other conventions, gave way only after much work was done in the development of ideas. The discussion of such a dimension by learned people meant that the possibility that such a dimension existed with significance could not be ruled out. This may have been due to an intellectual exercise, placing 4 after 3, and then seeking to imagine the fourth dimension, but it was only when relativity captured the imaginations of physicists and philosophers that this dimension achieved importance in the intellectual world. The convention of the fourth dimension, being a region for speculation and a domain for ghosts, could no longer hold, given the advancements of relativity theory.

Conventions may be due to certainty or to uncertainty. Although our knowledge of astronomy has advanced greatly since the time of the ancients, we still speak of the sunrise and sunset. This convention is useful and far from standing in rigorous contradiction with the findings of science. Conventions such as trying to understand the fourth dimension, and perhaps considering its existence owing to a numerical precession, is an example of uncertainty and cannot be scientific, although it provides impetus to search further into nature to find it and understand it when we are convinced of its reality.

Because of convention, dimension is in the eye of the beholder. Imagination is also in the eye of the beholder, but unlike dimension, it is strictly personal, free flowing, and often related to nothing of significance in one's past. Only when imagination is applied to reality either in a conventional framework or in a challenge to a conventional framework do great contributions come about. This requires either the repairing of a theory damaged with entropy or the formulating of a new theory itself. It took great imagination for Einstein to visualize the world of macro and micro relativity and the inclusion of the fourth dimension of time, forging it into a working theory. But even on a smaller scale, working with theories requires imagination as the theory becomes the convention for those involved and imagination is required to bring it into new domains as well as to resolve its difficulties with entropy.

The founders of chaos theory had such imagination to introduce a new approach to explain physical, social, and economic phenomena. Their contributions, which at first were outside mainstream thinking, began to break gound, and chaos has become a respectable approach to understanding phenomena. However, this theory, like all theories, is an imposition on problem areas by those who conceived it. This is the way of all science, but as a theory, it too must stand and confront critique. For the reasons stated in Part I of this work, chaos theory is problematic, and as a result, crisis theory is being constructed instead. As crisis theory was presented in its static form, it must now be placed in its dynamic setting, with convention being the theory and imagination necessary for those who work with it.

CRISIS THEORY: DYNAMICS

Crisis theory in its formal status provides the basis for those who want to work with the theory so that they can learn it. For example, while studying Newtonian theory, one learns the three laws of motion and the calculus, and with sufficient background, one can compare and contrast Newton's theory with the formal status of the theories of Kepler and Galileo. However, the formal status is insufficient for using the theory, and its applications must also be studied. If one learns the history of science, one will also understand how modern quantum physics and relativity came from problems found within Newtonian theory and were brought to light, reluctantly, by Max Planck. To understand Einsteinian relativity, we must also first learn its formal status and then seek to understand its applications and ramifications. Similarly, with quantum theory, first its formal status must be learned, and then its developments and changes, as it has been altered over the years, have to be studied.

This point raises two questions. One question is, which theory in its formal status should be learned, when in the history of a theory it has undergone so many changes? The answer is that the current accepted version of the theory should be studied, for this, too, contains some of the information of the earlier versions. If not, the theory would not exist as a working format for the expansion of concepts. Newton's theory and Newtonian theory are different, even though the latter is based on the former. The particle approach that Newton advocated resulted in Planck finding packages or in quanta of radiation being ejected in his black box experiments.

The second question is, to what extent should the theory be considered to be representative of the original theory? The answer is that as long as the foundations of the original theory are intact, that is, as long as the original utility of the theory's languages remains and entropy has made no serious inroads, then the theory should be considered representative of the original theory.

The significance of this second question is that from grand theories come other theories, such as Brownian gas theory based on Newtonian theory, with gas particles in motion due to collision with other particles–this, based on Newton's laws of motion. It can be argued rightly that British biologist Robert Brown's (1773-1858) theory of motion would not have been formulated–nor would any comparable theory–without Newton's groundwork. Galileo's and Kepler's theories, while dealing with laws of motion for earth physics and planetary physics, respectively, lacked the wisdom that Newton was able to gain because of their works and the works of others before him. The final condition of a theory, even of one with long duration, is entropy. While Newtonian theory has not been discarded completely, its status has been diminished, having been relegated to a limit-case of relativity and quantum theory. But, even in this diminished–indeed entropic–position, Newtonian theory remains the grand theory for neoclassical physics.

The point is that with such theories as Newtonian physics, even though they are entropic because of their restricted uses, they remain important for their defined and delineated domains as they were when formulated and developed. The same holds for Einsteinian relativity and quantum physics, even though both theories have undergone significant changes since their formulation. For example, the finding of both black and white holes in outer space, though not considered by Einstein in his formulation of the special and general theories of relativity, can be explained by general theory, with the laws of relativity holding for black holes and the time sequence and different dimension holding for white holes. As for quantum physics, the weak and strong forces of gravity holding the atom together, and the finding of new subatomic particles are extensions of quantum physics. Earlier contributions, such as that of Lord Kelvin, who maintained that the atom is a vortex in the ether, or J. J. Thomson's conception of the positive electricity in the atom as a continuous fluid, have been rejected and because they are entropic, they are now of historical interest only.

Hence, grand theories may have utility, even though they have been replaced by other theories, with some grand theories retaining only historical interest. Aristotle's physics is one such theory. As it was rendered entropic by Galileo's and Kepler's contributions, it is of historical interest for the development of physics and for the philosophy of science.

Those theories that do survive in a working capacity after they have become restricted are theories that are continuous. Their utility remains in the domain for which they were developed, but because that domain remains limited by problem shifts, they are entropic in the sense that they are not being used for the new developments in the general field. Research in physics, for example, is not being conducted in the area of Newtonian theory, but rather in relativity and in quantum physics, although Newtonian theory is still used–in space exploration, for example. These theories remain dynamic through use, because until rendered entropic not in the physical sense but in the historical sense (such as Aristotle's contribution and those of Kelvin and J. J. Thomson) their dynamics will be maintained.

Theories that are rendered entropic not because of problem shifts but because of contradictions within their languages that cannot be corrected, or because of discrepancies between their theoretical predictions and the events in the real world, or because they are replaced by theories of consistently higher utility, are discontinuous. Nevertheless, they are dynamic in the sense that contributions are being made to enhance them.

Although the continuous theories are important, the theories that are brought into entropy and are revived through alteration are those theories that are of discontinuity and are of interest here with respect to chaos theory. Posited by its founders as a grand theory, chaos theory is entropic for the reasons stated in the first part of this work. Chaos theory is important for its emphasis on nonlinear mathematics and for the time-series computations that result from it. Where cyclical behavior exists, the theory shows the strange attractors that result in cyclical behavior. Where the cessation of development is built into the system, chaos theory shows where the decline begins and where the system–be it life form or mechanical–ends. Chaos theory is limited in its uses, however, and perhaps finds its fullest expression in analogical computer models of events or systems such as weather conditions or biological functions–where the terms are programmed into the process and the developments are expected, as with snowflakes, weather mapping, and other conditions whose specific dynamics are placed within their constructs.

Chaos and catastrophe theories have provided us with a unique approach to the natural and social sciences, but they have done so by establishing a conception of continuity in these disciplines. When using these theories, for example, economic analysis shows that long-term business cycles exist, that these cycles perform over the years considered by chaos economists, manifested in certain constant cyclical patterns, and that as economies become prosperous, the democratic processes that affect the economics politically will also bring them into a form of entropy.[2] Also, in biology, the concept that evolution with its tendency toward randomness can be directed by the ordering agent of dissipation has gained followers. The time-delay equations in models of feedback control in physiology are of great importance, however, for biological research. The research into time delays in physics can also yield valuable information.

The point is that chaos and catastrophe theories, for all their enlightenment and contributions, are limited.[3] With catastrophe theory incorporated into chaos theory and posited as a grand unified theory, its limitations have already been stated, and another theory, one relevant to our contemporary era, has to be constructed. Crisis theory lacks the difficulties that plague chaos theory and also has none of the complications of catastrophe theory. For this to be understood, crisis theory and its participants will be explained, after which a concept for testing contributions will be developed. Grand theories are formulated to be continuous, because they are presented as representing the truth in their respective fields. The theory posited here is also a grand theory but emphasizes discontinuity, with the dynamic of change in languages or areas bringing them down or strengthening them in competition.

CRISIS THEORY: IMITATION AND INITIATION

Given the formal status of a theory, it is only when worked upon that its dynamics are established. Only by working with theories, whether unique theories for a specific field or theories in competition, do shifts in areas occur. This holds for theories that are in the process of dynamics through imitation, or for grand theories such as relativity that develop slowly.

Here working with a theory as it is stated is termed "strict imitation." A theory is first formulated, and after being critically tested it may be rejected outright or win acceptance by those in the field or in other fields who become interested. At first, the theory is worked upon according to its languages and its defined and delineated problem area. Those who work with the theory as such are termed strict imitators; through strict imitation, the theory is worked out and developed as it was initially stated. Those who worked with Newton's theory–as contrasted with Newtonian theory–were strict imitators, just as those who work with chaos theory as it is stated are strict imitators.

Strict imitation is necessary for the development of a theory. It permits the languages to be used and experimented with according to the theory's terms, thereby drawing out consequences that could not have been realized with just the languages considered and without application. Hence, strict imitation is the application of the theory in reality as it has been formulated and accepted. The purpose of strict imitation, however, is not to bring out inconsistencies within the theory. When stated in its final formulation, all contradictions, all internal paradoxes that can exist linguistically, are considered to have been eliminated, if ever having existed at all. For this reason, the theory was accepted after passing the critical test determining its linguistic viability.[4] Strict imitation is also necessary for teaching the theory to others. This allows the theory to be explained and demonstrated as it is formulated, so that others can learn the theory and see it in operation. We learn of Galileo's theory when considering the pendulum, or when sitting on a train and watching the train beside us move–or are we moving?–demonstrating the relativity that Galileo expressed. We can learn Einstein's theory only by imaginary experiments, a situation that evolved from Galileo's and Newton's ideal experiments, such as discussing motion without friction. Quantum theory can be learned from observation as atoms are smashed and subatomic particles are produced as consequences. This is also strict imitation, demonstrating theories according to their formulation. Hence, strict imitation has the dual role of working with a theory as it is stated and of explaining the theory, again as stated.

Imitation takes yet another form: that of explorative imitation. This imitative process consists of the searching for difficulties within the theory. Although the theory contains the languages to be used, it cannot prevent the introduction of ambiguities within the languages once formulated and accepted as a viable theory. Explorative imitation is thus the intentional introduction of such ambiguities so that the operational and area languages take on nuances that are not strictly allowed within the theory's requirements. These ambiguities may result from the introduction of slight changes in the meanings of terms in general use throughout other theories, or in specific theories only, even though for the theories in question these terms in their contexts are already defined and delineated. The explorative imitator may transfer some of thse nuances into the theory to analyze the influences they may have. As a result, the nuances may be of greater utility when incorporated into the languages that the theory had previously. The explorative imitator may not at the time comprehend fully the dynamics of these nuances, or perhaps how they are best incorporated into the theory. Their being within the theory may also increase the utility of the theory, for the reason, being their incorporation may be the realization that the theory's utility has declined through a degree of stagnation and competition from other theories.

Once these nuances are incorporated, the theory first becomes entropic with respect to its former position. Thus, to regain its utility, the theory has to be repaired, because the statements in which the nuances have been incorporated are no longer adequate in light of the general theoretical utility, the explorative imitator leaves the job of repair to the initiator (who may be the same person).

Another form of explorative imitation is awareness imitation. This imitation occurs owing to the awareness and understanding of other, not necessarily competing theories, whose problem areas include segments of the imitator's problem area. As a result of the influences and impacts of different theories on a single area, the area undergoes changes that make the theory's area statements entropic to the degree of change within that segment of the theory. Although other imitators (strict or explorative) may not be aware of the alterations within the area, owing perhaps to the unfamiliarity with other theories in which that part of the area is incorporated, this imitator analyzes the differences betwen the area statements and the area as it has been affected. The imitator brings this to the attention of others, who when comprehending the issue engage in initiation to find the solution.

Awareness imitation is also manifested within the nuances of the languages being altered by other meanings that have entered into the operational or area languages. As a result, de facto shifts occur in the meanings of these languages, while the problem area itself remains stable. The language deviations have to be corrected through their reconstruction. This is the initiator's task: to find the terminology that preserves the theory's utility in light of these nuances and thereby maintain the effectiveness of the corrected statements.

However explorative, the imitator's role does not end with the introduction of entropy into the theory. Having done so, the explorative imitator assumes the role of strict imitator or initiator. In the former role, the strict imitator evaluates the initiative contribution; as initiator, competition is entered into in order to provide a contribution of the highest utility, according to the theory's probability. The initiator alters the entropic statement $o_d a$ to $o_d a$ ' and presents it for evaluation by the theory's imitators. It is not enough to reconstruct an entropic statement with the intention of restoring the utility of both the statement and the theory. The statement must indeed fit and meet the rigors of competition, being without dynamic entropic effects on other theoretical statements. This can be determined over time, for such influences may not be readily present.

While this topic is discussed further in the context of the critical test, some comments are now in order. Consider, for example, an initiative contribution in response to linguistic entropy. One of a statement's components, say the **a** statement, has become entropic because of nuances imputed into the term but not considered within the theory's construction. The initially corrected **a** leads to a corrected **o**; since the statement is part of the theory, these alterations may generate negative dynamics throughout the theory. The **o** portion of the statement may be used in part or completely with other operational terms, and its correction for the specific statement may lead to incorporation of the corrected statement's nuances into other theoretical statements. In our era, theories are weakened because of the incorporation of increasing knowledge that they generate.

With respect to knowledge, it is not increased in isolation, but its very structure and content depend on the theory in which it is formulated. Knowledge is not fact, isolated and stated independently of theory, for such statements, through informative, may reflect the homespun wisdom acquired through living. This is not knowledge but grass-roots philosophy, without a theoretical context. This information is private and not theoretical. It is therefore not at the disposal of others to be worked upon so that further knowledge can be derived through strict and explorative imitation and through initiation.

Although knowledge is increased through theories, it is also decreased within theories as theoretical statements become entropic and are replaced by corrected statements. The processes by which knowledge is generated in theories–through imitation and initiation–make knowledge public, available to all who want to work with it. As theories develop and through use are brought into partial or near-total entropy, the knowledge incorporated within these theories also changes. These changes are manifested in the entropy in the theory, and become the domain of the public working with the theory or interested in it.

With our theories as public domain, in our era of knowledge we are engaged in the search for truth, only to find that our theories are problematic. What we accept as valid, possessing utility within a theory at one time, may become entropic and questionable at another time. Through explorative imitation, the difficulties of our theories are brought forth for which solutions, untouched by entropy, are sought.

Theories are developed and expanded, and are altered by their imitators' offsetting difficulties encountered through their usage. Changes in languages are brought about by the influences of other theories' languages. Moreover, interacting theories and the uses of knowledge to innovate other theories can be considered hallmarks of our era of knowledge. This interaction in the form of languages adapting and incorporating terminology from other theories provides information and knowledge to an extent never generated in previous historical eras. In previous historical eras, fairly long periods of gestation were required to bring difficulties to the fore; paradigmatic theories were accepted as being true in the sense of being at least operable. In the seventeenth century, after the establishment of Newton's physics, it was inconceivable that this theory was correct for a limited realm of the universe. Not only was Newtonian theory accepted as the true paradigm of the physical sciences, but also mathematics (which Newton helped strengthen with his contribution of the calculus) was considered to be the queen of the sciences, only to be ruled over by the king of Newtonian physics. The gestation period was long, some 250 years, before the cracks in the strong edifice became noticeable, especially because of Planck's work. Even the queen, mathematics, began to lose her power of certainty with the attempt to base her foundations on the rigors of logic.

Einstein's theory, despite its great significance for complementary problems of space exploration and atomic physics, has also begun to show possible cracks in its impressive edifice. Black holes in space, considered to be the supergravitational fields that are supposed to be of imploded stars, may obey physical laws inconsistent with our Einsteinian space-time conception. Moreover, white holes, considered to be inverted black holes, are also though to be time-tunnels, leading to other parts of the universe, and these parts may have physical laws unique to their regions. Attempts to understand gravity in terms of a unified field theory have thus far been fruitless, and Heisenberg's uncertainty principle throws this important search into question.[5]

With respect to initiation, the corrected statement $o_d a$ ' the initiator must consider the presented correction within the theory's total dynamics, because this concerns the theory's probability. Should the initiation be only a matter of removing unwanted nuances, thereby restoring the statement to its original meaning, the probability assessment should pose no difficulty, for this tends to restore the theory to its original stable utility position. In a static equilibrium position, the dynamics of change due to infiltration have been removed, leaving the theory as it was initially. In this stable and static situation of equilibrium, when entropy of this kind is removed the theory remains intact.

Static equilibrium in theories exists when there is no competition to challenge their status. The correction of entropy leaves the theory as it was, with new information accepted only if it conforms to the theory's requirements. This lack of competition allows the theory to possess the necessary authority for its users to justify its unique position. While explorative imitation may bring the theory's languages into new domains, the initiator and strict imitators are under no obligation to deal with these situations, other than to remove them from the theory should they be troublesome, or to accept them as just being there and burdensome. In the development of science, the Ptolemaic theory of astronomy, and Aristotelian stellar physics on which the Ptolemaic theory is based, held sway for many centuries because of the influence of religion and the absence of viably challenging theories. The imitation undertaken during these centuries was mostly strict, with initiation correcting deviations in calculations. Thus, no new contributions were acceptable. It was only Copernicus's work, and later the works of Galileo and Kepler, that brought about real changes in the theoretical and practical situations. Their contributions were innovative. In the arena of challenge and debate backed by whatever experimentation they and their followers could offer, they won over their ancient and glorious predecessors.

Given the dynamics of our era of knowledge, theories cannot enjoy the luxury of equilibrium. Entropy cannot therefore be removed or ignored and the theory restored to its original paradigmatical status. This entropy is in the form of information either from competing theories occupying some common ground or, when no competition exists, from other sources that affect the theory's utility. It may be caused by shifts in the problem area which the theory as it stands is unable to handle. Since the initiator's role is to remove entropy and restore the theory to utility, if the contribution is accepted the theory's integrity is thus preserved. It will remain so until a major shift renders the theory no longer viable; until too many corrections are made, thereby obscuring the theory's original identity; or until competing theories are proven through competition to be superior, thereby bringing the theory into disuse and to irreparable entropy.

Initiators seek to avoid the last case in their attempts to strengthen their theories through understanding of the difficulties of the problem areas for which their theories have been constructed. Again, consider the entropic statement $o_d a_t$. First, the initiator has to analyze the statement in order to determine which of its component languages is entropic, and to assess the effects of the language that is not affected, providing that only one of the languages remains unaffected, perhaps owing to the influences of one on the other. In all cases, languages may be inundated with nuances that do not affect the statement's utility. Only when statements are brought into entropy is restructuring necessary.

If such entropic nuances have infiltrated **a**, to the extent that **a**'s meaning has been altered, then $\mathbf{a} \rightarrow 0$, reducing its utility in $\mathbf{C^*_t}$, then $\mathbf{o} \rightarrow 0$. Similarly, if **o** tends to the lower boundary, then so does **a**. Initiators attempt to restructure the statement, but the difficulty lies in providing a formulation that meets the theory's probability requirements. Assume that a limited number of possible formulations exists, and given that the language in which the difficulty lies is known–say, the **a**. Because languages have their modalities, restructuring takes a possible solution of the reformed statement $\mathbf{a} \blacklozenge_d \blacklozenge \mathbf{o}$. The diamond-shaped sign stands for "possible," meaning that the restructured statement signifies that **o** is a possible solution for **a**, regardless of which language was affected originally. Given the assumption that the possible solutions are finite in number, the decision has to be taken as to which of the proposed possible solutions are to be chosen for competition. The structuring of a solution and the decision as to the best solution among the chosen are the work of the initiator.

Given a limited number of solutions, it is apparent that each is potentially viable. Therefore, the status of each solution must be decided by measuring the proposed solution according to the theory's probability requirements. For both static and dynamic theories, $[P(\mathbf{UC^*_t}) + P(\Sigma\mathbf{o}_d\mathbf{a})] \equiv \mathbf{I} \, [(\Sigma\mathbf{o}_d\mathbf{a})]_t$, meaning that the probability of the theory's utility is identical to the theory's total information of its operational and area languages and provides its utility. Given this assessment in a moment of time, when time changes and information flows so that one or more statements deviate from their original utility, the solutions to the entropy being considered must be placed in the probability equation for their evaluation.

Since each of these solutions is possible, the selection process to determine the best possible solution has to be undertaken. This process, the critical test, is discussed in the next chapter. However, it can be stated here that as each of the proposed solutions appears to fit, the issue of solution dominance has to be considered. One proposed solution may be conclusive, thereby providing the best fit; it may be in error, with the apparently dominant solution providing the least de facto viability for the theory. Nevertheless, solution dominance comes from the ordering of solutions established by initiators on the basis of understanding and working with the theory, as well as the awareness of languages of other theories, together with the ability to restructure languages to place their nuances in well-ordered patterns in context. Before this subject can be discussed further, however, we will comment on innovation.

CRISIS THEORY AND INNOVATION

While initiation increases knowledge through the restructuring of theories, there is another form of generating knowledge: knowledge gained from innovation. This form entails the construction of a unique theory for a set of problems conceived by the innovator (and perhaps independently by a few others) for which no previous theory existed. This, however, is strict innovation and must be distinguished from competitive innovation.

Strict innovation is the process that brings the elements of knowledge from other theories into a new and working theory for a set of problems that the innovator comprehends but were not acknowledged generally as problems. The construction of such an innovative theory requires that the problem area be well-defined so that the area language is clear and has an operational language capable of working effectively with the area language. After formulating the theory's languages, the innovator has to establish the utility criterion and must therefore assess each operational and area statement within the context of this criterion. As the innovation is unique, the case has to be put convincingly for its consideration by those for whom the innovator wants to work with the theory. Journals and conferences are available for providing exposure, and, of course, proper evaluation.

Competitive innovation is the construction of a unique theory that is intended to replace the existing one. In this case, the innovation may be one or several, as competitors may have entered the field. For competitive innovation, the problem area is already defined and the innovative aspects undertaken must be in the development of a better formulation or approach to the problem area that reduces or eliminates the utilities of the competing theories. In addition, the problem area itself can be the focus of the new theory that redefines it, thereby making it more functional than its competitors, especially with regard to the corresponding operational languages incorporated into the theory. Hence, while strict innovation defines problems and formulates the languages to work with problem areas, competitive innovation already has the problem stated and seeks to do a better job of handling the problem area. In this way, competitive innovation attempts to reduce the utilities of the other theories and to establish its predominance as the viable theory. For competitive innovation, the audience for the theory already exists, and journals and conferences provide exposure for proper evaluation.

Innovation, imitation, and initiation are thus necessary for the development of crisis theory. The term "crisis theory" is used for two purposes. The first to contrast the concept with chaos and catastrophe theories, for the treatment of those theories relates only to their theoretical aspects, whereas crisis theory relates to both the theoretical aspects and the participants involved in its development. Imitation requires understanding and using the theory's languages, and in the case of explorative imitation, to bring the languages into new domains, allowing initiators and innovators as they perform in their roles to work with and evaluate their theories and the problem areas for which they are constructed. Crisis theory also permits testing procedures for initiation and strict and competitive innovation. Chaos and catastrophe theories provide general statements only, without the possibilities for critical debate and testing.

The second purpose is to demonstrate that these theories are dynamic and as such are in equilibrium only for the period after their initial acceptance. By the very nature of equilibrium, theories are in states of crisis owing to their entropy, and this entropy allows for the development of knowledge within theories. By removing entropy through successful initiation, new knowledge as information is incorporated into the theory, with the alterations strengthening it.

Another important point needs mentioning here. Chaos and catastrophe theories are about events, such as the development of snowflakes, the expansion of gases, the oscillation of cells under laboratory conditions, and movements of business cycles around strange attractors. Crisis theory is about the domains of problem areas and about the development of theories that deal with the world. The world is a given fact and is objective; our interpretation of this world is subjective, and our imposition of our understanding of it on the ways we conduct our daily lives and with respect to our theories is the basis of crisis theory. When we use theories, we perform according to our roles, either as imitators, initiators, or innovators. We find grounds for contesting; we challenge and explore, entering into new realms, using our theoretical languages as vehicles for our exploration. When we innovate, we do so on the basis of our own personal comprehension, understanding, and even daring as we seek to formulate new theories. We thus impose ourselves on our objective and impersonal world, and our interpretations respond accordingly to the changes in the theories we impose on it.

Crisis theory can be contrasted to chaos and catastrophe theories on several points. First, they are evolutionary in orientation, yet ceasing in evolution when equilibrum is reached. Crisis theory is evolutionary, as theories decline into entropy, while others are innovated and operate with utility. They require fractals and bifurcation; crisis theory deals with the way linguistic nuances influence problem areas. They treat strange attractors that bring chaos systems into equilibium; crisis theory denies the existence of long-term equilibrium, as equilibrium exists only when the theory is first accepted. Thus, when in use, the theory becomes dynamic, subject to utility and entropy.

The chaos that exists in analyzed systems is due to our own interpretations of the systems, such as in programming the development of a snowflake or feeding into the computer econometric data that show cyclical fluctuations in a "strange attractor" pattern. When we observe a domain and formulate theories to work with it, we are necessarily imposing our interpretation on the domain and we do so because we have a world to which we have to relate. As our theories are our own impositions, we have to adjust them as the domains are altered through use and through changing information. Because chaos and catastrophe theory are equilibrium oriented and cease developing when equilibrium is reached, they cannot handle these changes. Crisis theory, evolutionary to the extent that theories continue until brought down by entropy, does relate and deals effectively with these changes.

Nonlinear analysis as the basis for chaos and catastrophe theory is also useful in the construction of crisis theories. For example, economics with its time-series equations permits the consideration of events over time that cannot be considered in static evaluation. As a result, understood, events can be controlled more effectively. Since time-series equations for equilibrium models result in the "strange attactor" effect, no such attractor exists for models in disequilibrium because there is no theoretical-model position in that the real world and its domains of problem areas are themselves dynamic and in disequilibrium.

In biology, isolated cells may oscillate according to biological dictates, but this is neither an example of nor an explanation for chaos theory. These cells take on significance only while they function in organs in which their tasks are interrelated. The study of cells in isolation is important, but for the organ in its entirety the cells assume their tasks according to the laws governing the specific organ.

Chaos theory is therefore accepted as a valuable intellectual exercise in which models are supposed to act according to specified laws, with these actions tested and analyzed to determine whether they correspond to the conditions of the theory. In spite of the importance of chaos theory, for the reasons argued in this work crisis theory has been formulated and developed. The critical test is an integral part of the method of crisis theory, and is discussed in the next chapter.

FURTHER COMMENTS ON OUR ERA

Historical eras possess a momentum that carries ideas and theories over into different domains. Eras come to their end when their representative features are no longer dominant and are replaced by other characteristics. The outstanding features of the previous eras remain, albeit considered in their previous contexts and in the context of the current era and its social time. Our contemporary era of knowledge has moved us from the difficulties of the Industrial Revolution and the Great Depression and World War II that signified the finality of that era to the difficulties of the postwar period and the Cold War that ensued and, in our social time, to a period of the paradoxical situation of both the search for peace and the waging of ethnic war, of great prosperity and poverty, of political leaders seeking the luxuries of our social time while behaving like the dictatorial rulers of earlier historical eras.

Our era has developed to the extent that our social time is more than ever represented by the interactions among theories and the uses of information from initiation. This process has produced information and knowledge unprecedented in human history. Previously, as noted earlier, fairly long periods of gestation were required to tackle theoretical difficulties, with exceptions being those theories that were rejected out of hand. Paradigmatic theories were accepted as being true in the sense that they were operable. Newton's theory held sway for some 250 years, but this is just one example. Another example is Einstein's theory, with the duration of this reign not yet determined. With the problems of black and white holes, and with no adequate formulation as yet for a theory of universal gravitation within the accepted concept of space-time, this theory will no doubt also be replaced by a theory of greater explanatory power.

The point is that since the beginning of our era, the rate of knowledge turnover has been greater than ever before. Theories exist in greater number, and entropy sets in at a faster pace, bringing problems to the fore through explorative imitation. Knowledge, as determined by theory, soon becomes entropic and is subject to the repairs of the initiator. Information is gathered and adjusted to fit into innovative theories; this stimulates explorative imitation in competing theories, which, in turn, become entropic and require repairs.

Although there is a great turnover of knowledge and manifold theories exist in our era, each theory has a period of gestation, a span of time during which imitators work out the dynamics of the theories and society accepts the results. It is not as if every explorative imitator finds fault with the theories and as if these theories are in constant flux between entropy and utility. Nor is it a psychological condition in which people seek a rest from change and search for a degree of stability. Theories must settle after they are established and after their difficulties are resolved to a fairly reasonable extent. They must be worked upon through strict imitation in order to determine what they can accomplish within their defined and delineated problem areas.

Thus, for any period of time, the situation in contemporary society that has entered our era of knowledge takes the form: $C^{**}_t = \sum^n C^*[C^*_e \, UC^*_u]_t$, where C^{**} is the society in which the dynamics of knowledge occurs, and C^*_e and C^*_u represent the total number of crisis theories, both entropic and of utility during time t under consideration.[6] The total number of working theories in C^{**} is altered over time owing to the phasing out of some theories and the introduction of others.

There is an exception to this situation in which some theories are entropic while others are not. The exception is when C^{**} is in a condition of (near) total gestation, and this usually follows a period of intensive innovation and initiation. Society becomes saturated with theories during these periods of activity, and there is great reluctance to consider further innovation or to undertake explorative imitation. The point is that new theories making their debut when established theories are being worked out through strict imitation are not very likely to find audiences that will shift their loyalties and work with them. The gestation period, when theory saturation is setting into the social knowledge structure, requires that imitators work out most of the theories' ramifications before explorative imitation can seriously get underway. Until this is achieved, innovation is likely to be slow, for problems are seen to be handled by the prevailing theories, and individual conceptualization of new problem areas will not readily find interested audiences or even those who will offer critiques. The exception to this situation is if the innovation is so profound and the problems with which it deals are so elusive for other theories that its impact, for both followers and critics, is in fairly equal response to its profundity and contribution. This type of innovation stimulates explorative imitation in many theories, at a time of gestation when strict imitation prevails.

A common situation determining the shifts in dynamics is that of the various theories being in different stages of utility and entropy. There is the situation in which C^{**} is in gestation, so that the totality of theoretical activity is of strict imitation. As mentioned before, this situation occurs following burgeoning activity in innovation and initiation, in which many changes in existing theories were brought about, and innovation resulted in competition for followers. The public is therefore not prepared for further changes, and the emphasis on imitative activity is the working out of the theories' ramifications. In this situation, should explorative imitation occur, it will most usually take place because genuine problems have been found, and not because of a new drive for explorative imitation or because of general public restlessness with the status quo of theoretical knowledge.

Gestation on this level is a somewhat rare situation, and it places the theories in a state of dynamic equilibrium in which the activity within the theories is related primarily to strict imitation. These theories are in equilibrium because they are not undergoing alterations owing to the difficulties of resolving entropy, as the theories' integrities remain intact. They are dynamic because they are being worked upon, having their nuances and ramifications drawn out in which the consequences of the operational and area languages are being derived. The utility positions of these theories are maintained, leaving entropy without any inroads, except for those cases where genuine difficulties have been exposed.

The usual situation, however, is one of dynamic disequilibrium. On this basis, theory shifts are due to the correction of entropy and the significant innovative theories that are formulated. In this state of dynamic disequilibrium, theories are fluctuating between those in utility and those in entropic conditions. As time moves, so do the positions of the theories, so that where entropy prevailed, bringing theories into tenuous positions, the entropy has been removed and the theories, albeit somewhat different, have been restored to utility. At the same time, theories that were in positions of utility may be entropic and are being worked upon through initiation to remove the sources of entropy.

The general condition of dynamic disequilibrium does not rule out gestation for theories. Some theories, especially newly formed ones, are being worked on by strict imitators operating according to the utility requirements established for each theory. These theories are functioning, and the results of their operations conform to those allowed by their utility requirements. No explorative imitation to any serious extent is being undertaken, nor is there yet any need for this activity. The fact that some theories are in periods of gestation, while others are entropic and still others are in limited stages of explorative imitation but are still of high utility, demonstrates the equilibrium prevailing in societies' theoretical systems and indicates their states of knowledge.

Thus, for societies having entered the era of knowledge, the C^{**} of each society is placed between the boundaries of utility and entropy, so that $0 < C^{**} < 1$ for time t. Can there be a situation where $C^{**} \rightarrow 0$ in our contemporary era of knowledge? This situation can exist only if a society, once having entered our era, can no longer perform because of political paralysis or because of a war that requires the diversion of innovation and general human intelligence into military matters. (This is discussed in Part III of this work.) In the scope of history, these are short-term situations, because in the first instance a society operating in our era of knowledge will already have sufficient internal dynamics to overcome political paralysis, and in the second instance wars are of shorter duration now, and once settled, internal matters and the dynamics of knowledge can again be undertaken.[7]

In our era of knowledge, the issues of acceptance and rejection are of great significance. The critical test, which is an integral part of crisis theory, contributes to acceptance or rejection. Determining the validity and utility of contributions, especially when competition exists, is of great importance given the rapid development of theories and the turnover of knowledge. Also of great importance are the psychological aspects of acceptance and rejection, regarding, and regardless of, the outcome the critical test.

NOTES

1. Michael Guillen, "A Realm of Manifold Possibilities," in *Bridges to Infinity* (Los Angeles: Jeremy P. Tarcher, 1983), p. 92.

2. This point is treated in Part III of this work.

3. See example, Joseph Ford's preprint, "What Is Chaos, That We Should Be Mindful of It?" in the Georgia Institute of Technology Archives.

4. The critical test applies to both the testing of the theory after its formulation and in competition with other theories when this occurs. The critical test is described in detail in Chapter 8.

5. A force-field of gravity must be analyzed, but according to Heisenberg, this asserts an unavoidable influence on the field because of the interaction of observation on the field. This is a difficulty to be surmounted by innovative activity.

6. Time period **t** is the social time as determined by the number and quality of theories in their various stages of development and dynamics.

7. The underdeveloped societies and many of those in the various stages of development cannot cope effectively with the contributions made by the postindustrial societies in the era of knowledge, because they have not yet fully entered our era.

CHAPTER 8

The Critical Test

A philosophy of science committed to the view that it is possible to succeed in our quest for truth about the physical world is required to provide some acceptable account of how knowledge of this truth can be achieved. It was the distinctive way in which, according to empiricist philosophy, this was accomplished–in particular, the way in which a coordination between our thoughts and their objects is achieved by an "unclouded and attentive mind"–that was increasingly discredited by increasing emphasis upon social determinants of our language, our ways of thinking, our "conceptual schemes."

Frederick L. Will,
"Reason, Social Practice, and Scientific Realism"[1]

INTRODUCTORY COMMENTS

A philosophy of science must be committed to the truth and the possibility of obtaining truth. It differs from science itself in that science is the pursuit of knowledge in order to obtain the ultimate truth. All of its activities are directed toward this objective. The philosopher of science, however, while also being engaged in the pursuit of truth with the intensity of the scientist, has the further obligation of providing an acceptable account of how this knowledge and truth are to be achieved. However, the philosophers of science, in working with their own theories, tend to be exclusive in the domain and range of science.

Two schools of the philosophy of science demonstrate this exclusiveness. Consider logical positivism. This school of scientific method is based on the requirements of consistency and corroboration. In this point of view, a theory is valid if experimental consequences corroborate the theoretical expectations. Moreover, to be valid, a theory must be consistent, because inconsistencies can produce unwanted experimental results, even though they may conform to theoretical expectations. Popperianism, unlike logical positivism, requires that a theory—or a theoretical statement—be constructed so that it can be refuted by experience. It must be clear that reputability does not mean that the theory or statement is indeed refuted, but that it can be so by experience, meaning, in scientific terms, experiments. Hence, one school emphasizes conformation, whereas the other emphasizes refutability.

Neither school operates with the consideration of the other. The emphasis on corroboration and consistency on which positivism relies is in sharp contrast to refutability, which is the basis of Popperianism. Each school shares with the other the emphasis on consistency, for the proponents of each school understand that from inconsistencies can come statements that may be true or false, but that would nevertheless conform to the rules of logic as being true.[2] But they differ on the approach to science. Corroboration and refutability aside, theoretical construction must be such that it relates as closely as possible to its problem area domain. Thus, the consequences of experimentation should conform to both the theoretical construction as it relates to the problem area and to the problem area itself. For an accepted theory, when this relationship does not hold as expected, and as determined by its probability and utility requirements, it is because of the presence of entropy, which may or may not be correctable.

The theories of logical positivism and Popperianism were perhaps necessary because of the revolutionary movements in science that were occurring at that time. Einsteinian relativity and quantum physics were not only new, representing a major break from Newtonian certainty, but they were also far from fully comprehended at that time by the scientists who worked with them and explored them.

Consider certainty, for example. Certainty in science is necessary in the development and testing of theories; certainty is also necessary in judging theories that are competitive, with critical testing undertaken to resolve the competition. For the Newtonian theorists, certainty is important because of the determinism Newton's laws imposed on nature, which posited that the universe is being governed by well-defined causal relations. Both Galilean and Newtonian relativity are based on determinism, and determinism implies certainty. With the works of Planck, Einstein, and the quantum theorists—perhaps foremost among them being Heisenberg—certainty in physics not only underwent revaluation, but in both the micro and macro spheres, it was also discarded.

All philosophies of science, whatever their persuasion, require a degree of empiricism, because observation is necessary for theorizing, testing, and ultimately applying the results of the theory. In this respect, empiricism as incorporated into method—and not as a method itself—is not affected by social determinants, languages, ways of thought, and conceptualization. With respect to language—which is so important in the positivist and Popperian schools—this is so because each discipline has its own language, with its terms and syntax. While among the disciplines there are common terms, the nuances of these terms differ significantly according to the theory, thereby containing different meanings and dimensions.

Throughout the development of the philosophy of science, its purpose has been to allow scientists to step back, as it were, to view their disciplines and their specific roles in the unfolding of science. Descartes sought to establish his method of investigation on certainty, stemming from the comprehension of his own existence and formulating scientific theories with the assuredness that his approach was correct based on epistemological-cum-metaphysical certainty. Francis Bacon, on the other hand, sought certainty through an established method of investigation, in which guidelines served practicing scientists in their theoretical formulations and their testing.

It was Newton, however, who bridged the gap that was being formed by Copernicus, Galileo, and Kepler. These earlier thinkers did not study science from the traditional position of philosophy but sought knowledge and not wisdom in scientific inquiry. In their investigations, they sought total objectivity, each from his own perspective. Copernicus's work was an exercise in astronomy from a purely speculative point of view–a "what-if" argument to explain astronomical events that the Ptolemaic system could not handle simply and adequately. Galileo's work challenged the Aristotelian approach with its metaphysical foundations, employing the rationality of mathematics within real and ideal experiments, thereby ridding the subjective aspect of conjecture and theoretical formulation and experiment. Kepler, through influenced by metaphysical argument, nevertheless sought to place his reasoning on the same mathematical asuredness that his contemporary Galileo had used. Neither of these thinkers established a direct approach to method, however, as did Descartes and Bacon.

Newton was both a respected philosopher and scientist, having analyzed the physical properties of optics, using rational mathematics. Yet, in his great opus, he argued for philosophy while developing the calculus and formulating his laws of motion that relate earth physics to astronomy. Unlike Descartes who also worked with optics but whose general physics yielded nothing, new, Newton established his physics on the basis of philosophical inquiry, using rational mathematics and making his great contribution. Bacon's method would serve as a guide for the Newtonians in their application of the theory in their inquiry.

Throughout the development of the philosophy of science, in the tradition of Bacon, Descartes, and Newton, philosophers of science have sought to clarify the workings of science to rid theories of their ambiguities, to maintain consistency in reasoning and in theoretical construction, and to assess whether a theory relates to its domain as it claims. With logical positivism and Popperianism, however, the emphasis of the philosophy of science had changed somewhat owing to the new uncertainty in both science and mathematics that prevailed.[3] Each school sought to establish criteria for determining whether or not a theory was scientific, and while these schools shared the concern for consistency, they parted ways over corroboration. The positivist concern for corroboration differed from the Popperian refutability, and a scientific theory not only had to be checked for its consistency and validity in its application, but also had to be considered with respect to its scientific credentials, according to one or the other school.

Both the positivist and Popperian schools were founded before World War II, in the aftermath of the new relativity and quantum physics. The further expounding of these scientific methods was forced to pause during the war, as the depletion of resources, the loss of life, the movement of peoples, and the deaths in the concentration camps brought the development of the philosophy of science to a halt. After the war and into our era, these opposing sides met one another in intellectual battle, but the arguments were being waged for an approach to scientific method that was no longer relevant owing to the conditions of our era.

With the development of theories due to the emphasis on knowledge in the early post-World War II reconstruction and industrialization, a de facto shift had been made from the positivist and Popperian methods which themselves were advances in the methods inherited from Bacon and Descartes and those in their traditions to the contemporary approach that all knowledge systems are to be treated similar to strict scientific theories. The development of computer science is an example in which a discipline is expanded and used in the research and development of other sciences, so that it is both a discipline in its own right and one whose applications are employed by other branches of inquiry.

Because so many disciplines are included within the expanded conceptual term "science," this term has been altered in our era with respect to its historical origins. Traditionally, science, as knowledge, was used to refer to the knowledge of the physical world. However, as the term has become so important and so broadly based in our era, the philosophy of science and the dynamics of inquiry it entails should be concerned with both the consideration of knowledge and the construction of theories by which knowledge is developed and expanded. This also includes the methods by which theories are critiqued.

The orthodox physics of the early twentieth century has been infiltrated by conventional methods and concepts such as superstrings and theories of everything and the merging of physics with Eastern philosophy.[4] In our era, workers in scientific fields have tried to control their disciplines, while these disciplines tend to overlap nevertheless because of the uses of similar terms with different nuances, resulting in the entropy of these theories. Nonrigorous languages have little or no influence on theories, since our theories are not socially oriented but problem oriented. As theoretical operational and area language exist and are worked with in their theoretically definitive relationships, even though languages in our era are often intermingled, the difficulty lies not with the socially oriented languages but with knowledge-oriented languages, whose terms may be used effectively in one language and then taken over–such as the uncertainty principle in physics and its adaptation in sociological theory.[5]

Hence, in a sense we live as dual personalities. In our personal and social lives we live according to our conceptualizations, and our ways of thinking are socially oriented. They are dictated to a large extent by our socioeconomic circumstances and, to sharpen the distinctions, by our social status. In our social lives, rigorous thought is often unnecessary; but for the other aspect of our lives, we deal with theories and their ramifications. Methods of work, for example, are theory-oriented, and time-and-motion studies are based on mathematical programming, with these approaches applied in industry and even in small businesses.

With respect to theories and their applications, rigor is indeed required. As our ways of thinking and conceptualizations when working with theories and their applications are so oriented, in this sense their scope tends to be limited. The theories' problem areas, and their area and operational languages, require focusing on the theories' unique situations, with our thinking and conceptualizing being limited to the determinants of our respective theories. This is strict imitation, and the exception to this occurs when explorative imitation is conducted, bringing the theory into entropy, to be corrected by initiation.

COMMENTS ON THE CRITICAL TEST

The critical test as a means of evaluating contributions has to be approached from three different aspects: (1) The psychological aspect which pertains to the proclivities and personal dynamics of the evaluator; (2) the social aspect pertaining to both initiation and innovation and depending on the state of gestation with respect to the amount of contributions existing and those being presented; and (3) the critical aspect in which the results may not be decisive over time.

Before developing these aspects, some further background comments are required. Throughout history, whenever people worked, they performed their tasks according to the procedural patterns of their occupations. They deviated from these patterns when circumstances were unsuitable for these procedures, thereby requiring different methods for dealing with these situations. These deviations in working procedures were, seldom radical, however, occurring mostly within the work format.[6] Great changes arose mostly when challenges from nature or in the form of war posed problems for which conventional methods could not provide effective solutions. Throughout history, in these situations individual initiative came to the fore, providing the leadership to mobilize forces for changing and repairing.

The exceptions to this have always been the great historical changes that brought historical eras to an end and in their wake brought forth new eras. With these eras come new social, economic, and political situations and problems unique to these situations. New theories in science are developed using the conceptual tools of the era and the dynamics of knowledge that result. New schools in the arts are also developed to clarify and contribute to the new era, with the different artistic forms of expression interpreting the era and its changes over its various social times.

Over the span of human history, the methods of work developed according to the requirements of social groups, such as clans, cities, states, and countries. Moreover, the rapid changes in work procedures and policies that occurred during the Industrial Revolution demonstrated the continuity of history in the applications of the arts and sciences that developed during the Renaissance to the issues and problems of production. This allowed the work procedures to undergo changes, not in accordance with the demands of societies or to meet the challenges of natural or man-made disasters, but according to the introduction of science to the work process and the development of new products. This meant the refinement of marketing and hence advertising, not only to make these products known to the consuming public, but also to meet the competition that ensued.

An outstanding example of the application of science to production is the assembly line, which Henry Ford brought into use and which still serves as the best model for mass production and the introduction of new technologies into production. The assembly line that Ford developed utilizes technological contributions such as electronics, blueprinting techniques, advances in metallurgy, time-cost studies that rely on linear programming, and matrix algebra for determining efficient work procedures for assembly-line modification for different models and products. The use of robotics in production is still based on the assembly-line approach, serving as an example of Ford's vision. The assembly line is still effective in its adaptability for procedural changes, while keeping its basic concept intact.

In the aftermath of World War II and in light of the end of the Industrial Revolution, a certain ambiguity to change developed. In the post World War II period, when production reverted to the peacetime manufacture of goods and services with demand rising because of the demobilization of the military, there was an initial return to prewar conceptualizations of the methods of production. Military regimentation prevailed to some extent so that conformity in both industry and society was expected. The organizations that had provided the techniques for wartime production had both the means and the resources to mobilize productive forces for peacetime production. These organizations therefore provided employment for the newly released soldiers that was required to move the economy upward again. It was necessary for these organizations to impose a different civilian-oriented discipline on their employees, and by so doing they established policies for upper echelons and sought to reduce significantly disruptions in production within their workforce in light of the development of the labor movement. This rigidity was both necessary and justified, given the transition to peacetime production, and only by these policies could the objectives of industry be achieved.

To a certain extent, this approach was also untenable, because the organizational structure inherited from wartime production clashed with the dynamics of the era that was being formed. What was required and what eventually developed as the era got under way was a different approach to production from that of the Industrial Revolution. This required critical thinking as well as organizational discipline, which was eventually introduced in the upper and lower echelons as workers were allowed some freedom of expression about their work ideas based on their experience. This complemented the explorative imitation that was opening up existing markets for further competition, as well as leading to the conceptualization of new products and the market research required for testing the products' potential as commercial successes. As a consequence, the conformity was eventually relaxed as these organizations confronted and dealt with the problems of domestic and foreign competition from both allies and previous enemies, both untouched and recovering from the ravages of the war. The struggle for both economic and intellectual supremacy had become intense, and the era of knowledge provided the condititions conducive to the struggle.

Soon a conflict developed between the dynamics of knowledge by which existing theories were subjected to intellectual scrutiny and brought into entropy, and the psychological attitudes of many who innovated theories and imitators who worked loyally with them. In theories, knowledge is the objective as it conforms to the theories' probability requirements and can be worked with by strict and explorative imitation. The development of theories is the result of individuals' efforts, of their energies and imagination, in solving problems raised by others or by themselves. Because of the development of knowledge through the rise and fall of theories, and because people are sometimes reluctant to have others question their contributions, theories are developed and initiative solutions to difficulties within the theories are formulated. There is also the defense of theories and initiative contributions by way of the rules established for the critical test.

Some resistance to accepting new and viable theories is always exhibited, partly out of jealousy due to the need to guard existing theories in competition and partly out of the need to allow theories to be proved on merit through their use and the utilities and contributions derived from them through explorative imitation and initiation. Theories are brought into question and either maintain their strength or fall, due to the critical test. Throughout history it has been the nature of the development of knowledge through the dynamics of inquiry that great contributions to knowledge have become outmoded and superseded by other and competing contributions. For example, Aristotelian physics is relevant today only for its historical value; when Galileo argued against it, however, it was an important scientific theory. Modern physics is based partly on Galileo's earth physics and Kepler's astronomy, which Newton merged into his physics and with the calculus developed a new theory, which in turn proved to be a limit-case on micro quantum physics and macro relativity.

Great contributions eventually decline, to be replaced by new ones. Galileo's and Kepler's contributions were outside the scope of Aristotelian physics, and quantum physics and relativity in the contemporary context have greater explanatory power than does Newtonian theory. In this sense, the Newtonians who held fast to their theory in light of the developments in quantum theory and Einsteinian relativity have, reluctantly, had to release their hold and adapt the current theories. Planck was still a Newtonian, although he worked with radiation and founded quantum theory.

Gerald Feinberg wrote that "Progress has come from finding novel ways to test the theory, and by deriving unexpected consequences from it."[7] Einstein's theory was put to the test by Eddington's ellipse experiment, by which it was demonstrated that in accordance with Einstein's theory, light bends under the influence of gravity. However, Eddington's geometry was superior to Einstein's because in the novel form of the critical test, the geometry posited by Eddington demonstrated the relationship between gravity and light, while Einstein atempted to unite gravitation with electromagnetism only in 1950, as a result of the problem of bending light raised by Eddington's eclipse experiment.[8]

The point of testing is that it not only focuses on the issues being challenged, but it may also generate concern for other issues that may be important for the contribution's development. As new theories stimulate interest, ideally critics of these theories examine them on the basis of their stated objectives and claims. In cases of initiation, critics examine the contributions' abilities to replace the entropic statements so that their utilities are maintained. For innovations, each theory in its entirety is under critical scrutiny. Critique is necessary and serves as a social filter, removing from the general body of knowledge ideas and theories that have no real merit and provide little or no viable information. In this situation, a conflict exists between contributor and society, as theories posited with the best intentions are shown to be completely inadequate. However, this conflict may be advantageous to the contributor, for it permits the reconsideration of the contribution, perhaps leading to its revelation in light of the critique that may bring forth another contribution. One such contribution was Galileo's rejection of Kepler's astronomy and his mystical search for the harmony of the planetary spheres, resulting in the concept of elliptical orbits around the sun.

Critique does not necessarily eliminate misunderstanding, for those who devise critical tests may not fully comprehend the contribution or may provide a critique that is not quite accurate, albeit not intentionally, but because of a misunderstanding of the rigor and nuances of the contribution. These are honest errors in judgment and are not made because of personal involvement or dogma. Without a personal clash of professional dogmatic rejection, and stated in good faith, errors in critique stand to be investigated by others concerned with the problem area and the contribution formulated to deal with it.

Critique conducted in good faith is objective, regardless of its potential for error. Though not ideal, works rejected by some critiques may be accepted by others. Copernicus's work is an example; it was critiqued on the grounds that if the earth did indeed move around the sun, its inhabitants would fall off. Often, a certain historical period of social time—perhaps an era itself—has to pass before a theory can be worked out sufficiently for its utility to be realized. The Darwinian theory of evolution and natural selection is still being studied, and it continues to provoke religious arguments, with the seven days of creation being considered as seven historical eras.[9]

THE CRITICAL TEST AND THE FIRST APPROACH: ANXIETY

Critique is made on the basis of education and experience, and the lessons derived therefrom. But as humans are complicated creatures with tastes, opinions, likes and dislikes often varying over time and determined by irrational emotions, total objectivity has never been part of the human condition. Even people evaluating a contribution have to deal with this aspect of behavior, no matter the extent to which critics attempt to suppress their own personal considerations when evaluating a contribution, while seeking to understand the contribution's importance and utility for the problem area. The total negation of personal propensities is impossible; even a seemingly unimportant factor such as personal feeling at the time of a critique can be relevant in the evaluation.

Critique, however, can be made on the basis of professional objectivity, as contrasted with personal objectivity. This is accomplished when the critic takes into account his or her personal feelings and tastes, and either suppresses them as far as humanly possible, or states at the outset the influences of personal bias in the critical process, and evaluates the contriubtion, given the personal constraints.

Critique also has objective complications. Where one critic honestly and openly rejects a contribution and another recommends its acceptance, it is incumbent on the imitators using the theory and to which the contribution is directed to assume the role of critics, devising a critical test to determine the contribution's value and utility with respect to the problem area. Hence, the work must be evaluated according to its probabilistic structure and assessment, as well as its workability within the area. These criteria may, over a period of social time, be valid; an example is the movement of light waves through (Frenzel's elastic or Lorentzian) ether. However, in some situations contributions are vindicated after being rejected. One such example is Lamarck's theory of evolution, which has been revived in a Darwinian context, as natural conditions impose themselves on life forms, resulting in natural adaptation and selection, with the changes being imprinted on the genetic code.

Neither acceptance nor rejection is always permanent, unless the work is either so insufficient that in the case of rejection critics demonstrate that the work bears little or no relationship to the stated problem area, or the problem area is so defined and delineated by the theory that no competition exists. The social inertia toward reviving respectable yet rejected contributions is far greater than discrediting accepted contributions, unless these theories become entropic and remain untreated. Usually, theories are rejected with general consent, yet those theories that retain some viability after their rejection may be revived. In this case, adjustment is necessary for this contribution to regain its utility, and this often requires the contribution to be incorporated with the adjustments into a greater theory–such as the example of Lamarckian into the latter Darwinian theory. This is the task of the initiator, for the contribution must be reconstructed before its utility can be reestablished.

Given the dynamics of inquiry and the development of knowledge, the longevity of accepted and enduring contributions can be promoted only in the historical sense. For example, the long duration of Ptolemaic astronomy was due to its utility and to the religious authorities' acceptance of the theory because it suited religious dogma. Thus, Ptolemaic theory in the history of ideas is secure, but no astronomer would act on its validity. This theory is taught only from the viewpoint of the history of the development of knowledge, as an example of the ideas of the time and their duration.

With respect to acceptance, theory construction, the establishment of the criteria of utility and the probability assessment, must be of such significance as to stimulate interest in the theory. While this requires a degree of publicity in journals and lectures, general acceptance relies on the positive outcome of the critical test. Should the outcome be negative, the contribution will be rejected. While the theory may still attract supporters, in this case they will be of only marginal influence.

In the case of initiation, there are usually several competitors, each which with its own supporters. These supporters are explorative imitators, who prior to having committed themselves to a contribution, have analyzed the competing contributions and then decided on which contribution to support. There are different supporters because of their different perspectives and requirements for the contributions. The results of the critical test determine not only the outcome, but also the contribution that is to be accepted. This assumes that only professional considerations are involved.

Let us now consider acceptance and rejection from another perspective. The turnover of knowledge and the formulation of theories to provide solutions to difficulties within problem areas through initiation and innovation occur at a rate and intensity unique to our era. Nevertheless, while people are receptive to change and newness, they often require a period of gestation under certain circumstances to absorb changes and the newness that have already occurred. This often sets up a psychological resistance to new contributions in light of the many problem areas and theories working with them. This situation tends to build up a bias among critically thinking people which, in evaluation, is suppressed as much as possible. Nevertheless, the tendency toward bias is part of the contemporary human condition, and during periods of social gestation it poses difficulties, manifested in the critical processes of evaluation. These difficulties are associated with anxiety, as when a contribution is rejected not on its merit, but because the society is unable to absorb the contribution. Before this point can be discussed further, clarification of the anxiety approach is needed.

For critique and the critical test, regardless of the extent of gestation, another difficulty exists: those giving the critique are, at one time or another, most likely to have been engaged in innovation or initiation, and the contributions they are reviewing are usually those within the same problem area as their own contributions. Initiations may be viewed critically, yet with a bias that the critic does not recognize owing to his or her capacity as initiator. Innovations may be viewed critically from the same approach, especially if the contribution competes with that of the critic. However, should a contribution be reviewed from a genuinely biased position, people considering the critique will soon be aware of this bias and view it as such, and its influence will be minimized.

In some instances, however, an unintentional bias exists, resulting in erroneous evaluations and thereby posing a difficulty of another dimension. In this situation, because of the rapid turnover of knowledge in our era, many critics are having to subject their own contributions for testing. Their objectivity may be distorted when evaluating others' works because works they support may be in competition with those works they are evaluating. In extreme situations, this may pose a threat to them in as much as the works they are evaluating may be superior in depth and function to those works with which they identify.

With respect to the anxiety aspect of the critical test, further comments on truth and knowledge are in order. The argument in this work is that theories pertain not to truth as such, but to knowledge as a way of reaching the ultimate truth. In this context, knowledge statements as facts are relevant within theoretical frameworks, where they have the dynamics with which to work, and knowledge changes as a way of approaching the ultimate truth. It was a fact that the sun rose in the East and set in the West, until the Judeo-Aristotlerian-cum-Ptolemaic theory was replaced by the Keplerian-Newtonian theory with the earth rotating around the sun. We accept the truth that, within the context of the greater astronomical universal construction, the earth is maintained in its solar system, which is kept in balance as the planets relate to one another's and to the sun's gravity in their orbits around the sun. We also accept that this system is held in balance by the influence of other such systems in their constellations. It was a fact that what goes up must come down; now, it is apparently true that "up" is relative and that not all objects that break away from the earth's gravitational pull will return as the properly functioning satellites and exploring spaceships aptly demonstrate.

Hence, knowledge and fact are intimately related in the goal of reaching the ultimate wisdom, understanding, and truth. In this context, truth is philosophical in the sense that it pertains to comprehending the human condition within the comprehension of the dynamics of the universe. After science and philosophy parted, the method of philosophy became the inquiry into the metaphysical dynamics of nature and existence, employing the sophisticated tools of logical reasoning. For the sciences, truth shares with philosophy fact and the greater understanding of humanity and the universe with each valid theory. For example, while fact, as such, indicates that the universe was created by forces resulting from the Big Bang, it seeks to explain these forces and the very cosmological explosion through theory. Philosophy as such seeks to understand these forces and events that brought the conditions into place for the Big Bang to occur.

Facts, in this context, are theory-based and hence are so derived as the theory is worked upon. Within the theoretical context, facts can be neither true nor false but valid or invalid, that is, of utility or entropy. Facts are, therefore, as relevant as their theories.

Herein, however, lies the problem of evaluation. Critics who evaluate new contributions, be they innovative or initiative, must consider new facts as they are presented within the contributions. These may conflict with the critics' own theory or contribution. In the case on initiation, the critic may not consider the competing contribution credible, and for innovation, the critic may consider the new contribution as a threat to his or her own innovation. The problem for evaluation–and this is also expressed in the critical test–is that the irrational aspect of human behavior takes over judgment. As a result, the contributions are rejected, not because of their objective quality, but because they pose a threat to the previous and competing contributions and to those who are interested in supporting them. Galileo's condemnation by the Inquisition was based not on the study of his works and their rejection of the theory he constructed, but on the threat they posed to established teachings.

The adherence to a theory is also manifested when a theory becomes heavily entropic, but several of the theory's supporters do not recognize this entropic condition, and continue to work seriously with the theory. In this situation, when competitors challenge the theory, or when initiation is undertaken to remove the entropy, these people will still hold to the theory as it is.

Rationally, holding onto a theory depends on the theory's viability, with its utility at its highest level when it deals with an unchanged problem area with unchanged operational and area languages. Objectively, a theory is as valid as its utility, and when its utility declines and cannot be repaired without altering the theory beyond its original general purpose, but is still maintained as a working theory by some people, these people are acting irrationally and according to their personal commitment to the theory.

This attitude is held as a means of coping with anxiety, perhaps with the intention of abolishing it, thereby achieving a sense of belonging to a worthy endeavor such as being acknowledged as a strict imitator with a theory. This does not mean, of course, that people working with a theory should not hold a degree of loyalty to the theory. Indeed, loyalty exists as people seek to exploit the theory to its fullest as strict and explorative imitators, drawing out the theory's advantages and difficulties and, as initiators, correcting these difficulties. Working with a theory requires a commitment, but this commitment should be professional, with the theory defended in terms of professionalism, and not from emotional attachment. When the theory's utility has declined sufficiently that corrections can no longer retain the theory's utility as originally intended, it should be abandoned because entropy has become too intensive and the theory cannot be preserved. While there are no Aristotelian physicists today,

Aristotelian physics is taught in courses on the history of philosophy.

With the theory no longer being one of utility, the tenacious person's emotional identity with it is irrational; this person has found psychological comfort in belonging to a group that identifies with the theory and that refuses to relinguish their hold on it, even after it has been demonstrated to be entropic beyond repair. The person makes an enormous psychological commitment because of his or her strong emotional attachment, resulting in mental confusion between theoretical fact and absolute truth. This person believes that because the theory at one time had the ability to achieve its objectives, it is therefore true in its content. It is all-enduring, with all changes made to correct entropy not affecting the theory's original purpose or reducing its utility. The erroneous association of fact as expressed by the theory's utility with truth as seen in the theory's durability has become fixed in this person's mental awareness. This situation is clearly different from the pre-Planckians who considered Newton's theory during its development as the true and enduring representation of nature. Thus situation was altered by Planck's findings and the subsequent contributions made by Einstein and the quantum theorists. They were not "true believers"; they recognized the limits of Newtonian theory and abandoned their belief in its endurance and total applicability for all the dimensions of physics. There was no judgmental error here, but just the natural decline in the utility of a theory as a result of the dynamics of inquiry based on Newtonian theory. Planck brought the theory into new domains, resulting in innovation to resolve the difficulties. In this context, the confusion between fact and enduring truth results from the commitment to a theory, no matter the extent of entropy and the decline of theoretical value stemming from its reduction in utility.

How does a strong personal–as opposed to objective–commitment come about? The answer lies in the dynamics of existential anxiety expressed in the emotion aroused by not belonging, the lack of feeling of personal importance caused by not being recognized by a segment of society, and the dread of being intellectually impotent with the theory's decline. This is part of the social and psychological pathology in our contemporary era. It is prevalent among the true believers in theories as such, especially in those theories rendered outmoded by the developments in the various aspects of knowledge and the formation of competing theories. This anxiety influences critical judgment, often to the extent of its being negated, so that inaccurate or inadequate criticisms are raised against theories that are being scrutinized or critiqued.

Anxiety is a common existential awareness. In its greater intensity, it becomes manifested in feelings of intellectual impotency, rendering the person undergoing the anxiety unable to contribute to the development of knowledge through the dynamics of inquiry by way of explorative imitation, initiation, or innovation. To overcome the feeling of anxiety, the person clings to the theory as a strict imitator, regardless of the theory's status with respect to utility and entropy.

The role of anxiety has been recognized for some time. Although in our era it serves as a drive for personal recognition and the removal of uncertainty regarding personal worth, it is an ontological condition termed by Søren Kierkegaard as the sickness unto death. It is paradoxical in the sense that the only way to rid one's self of this sickness is to cease living.[10] Because it is an ontological condition, it is within each of us, waiting to catch us unawares and come to the fore as an anxiety attack. It is, perhaps, triggered by events outside of us personally, but nevertheless it is devastatingly emotionally in its consequences.[11]

The inability to make significant contributions, either as an explorative imitator, initiator, or innovator, produces feelings of inadequacy that trigger the emotion of stark and dreaded anxiety. This is the awareness of noncontribution, the horror of nonexistence as an inactive participant in the development of knowledge as expressed through society's theories, in the struggle among competing theories, and the importance of those people active in generating and perpetuating knowledge.

Anxiety is thus important when the respected critic in a field rejects contributions that are closely related to those contributions with which he or she works. This anxiety, through manifested in bias, differs from generally accepted bias because while critiquing from a biased position the critic emphasizes his or her own theory, bias as such does not usually enter the critic's judgment; for if so, the critique will be rejected as invalid. Professional biases in judgment are usually made known, either through the opening statements or from the actual evaluation of the work under consideration.

In cases of anxiety, it is not the contribution as such that is evaluated, but the audacity to propose a contribution that goes against the critic's position. The work is dismissed as being either uninteresting, irrelevant to the growth of knowledge, or unimportant and a misuse of time for someone to make the effort to construct the contribution. Hence, while the critic may be respected in the field, in this instance he or she employs irrational and dogmatic rejection, dismissing the work outright because of the threat to the critic's self-contained ambience as a protection against anxiety. Cushioned by the prestige gained in his or her field, as critic, he or she is wary lest the contribution poses a real challenge to his or her position. The critic then rejects the contribution outright, as well as the problem area in question if it, too, deviates from the position from which the critic's reputation was gained.

Critics are aware objectively that their own evaluations are not generally accepted in all instances. The work must stand on its own merit with respect to its purpose, and if over time it is accepted, it will nevertheless become entropic beyond repair. Where the ontological condition overrides the critic's attempt at objectivity, the critical edge in the reasoning processes is blunted to the extent that the tendency toward unfairness–even hostility toward the work–is often exaggerated, and, being complimentary and often too full of praise when critiquing a supporting work. Of course, this critique must be viewed in the light in which it is presented. For while the works of this ontologically oriented critic are important, their importance is irrelevant when considering the critic's opinions on others' works, and these works should be isolated from the critic's own works.

Our era of knowledge is restive, with theories infiltrated by entropy and corrected at rates unique to our era. As a result, critics seek to maintain objectivity at one time and become ontologically biased at another time. Thus, in the spirit of fairness and because works may influence people differently from the critic's response, people who serve as critics should take into account the ontological condition of anxiety when presenting a critique, especially when a critical test is involved to evaluate a contribution.

If ontological anxiety has a role in the dynamics of inquiry, it should be to spur on explorative imitation after a period of time. Strict imitation is necessary for fulfilling the theory's initial objectives, such as demonstrating that the theory performs with utility according to its operational and area statements. But while strict imitators contribute to the theory's status quo, they bring nothing new to the theory. This is not to belittle strict imitation, for it establishes the theory as a viable performer in the problem area, which is extremely important in competitive circumstances. Strict imitation provides the foundations for explorative imitation, and the constructive activity of explorative imitation tends to neutralize anxiety. For initiation, the support provided by the theory is weakened as the initiator has to make the effort to formulate a new construction and take his or her chances that the contribution will be accepted. In this circumstance the potential is much greater for ontological anxiety than for imitation. For innovation, however, the potential for anxiety is the highest, for the innovator has to formulate a viable theory, not only in his or her opinion, but also in the opinions of critics and critical testers.

Because of the personal and public aspects of innovation and initiation, there is uncertainty over the merit of the contribution and the possibility that rejection will mean more than just a personal obstacle to be confronted. It may also mean that rejection will be taken personally as both a measure of the contribution's and the person's merit. This can be a cause of anxiety, with all its impact during self-doubt. For this reason, persons who cling to outmoded theories and either condemn or ignore those who challenge their position have neither the fortitude to engage in the dynamics of inquiry offered by other theories, nor the willingness or emotional strength to become initiators or innovators and take their chances with critical evaluation.

The ontological condition of anxiety is debilitating, and when it attacks, it renders the person temporarily inactive, with the person closing in on himself or herself. Anxiety attacks mostly when people are feeling fragile and sensitive to their situations. When anxiety or the fear of it results in dogmatism, it becomes a condition for mental instability with improper personal functioning in our contemporary era when relating to their own theories and to others in our contemporary era. Dogmatism results and, expressed in critical valuation, leads to a distorted impression and opinion of the work in question. This leads to inadequate evaluation, one that is not in accordance with what the contributor intended to portray. This is counterproductive and in previous historical eras may have prevented the contributor from receiving a fair test and evaluation. In our contemporary era of knowledge, however, there are many sources of information and publication, to the point that there is competition for evaluating and testing works. Thus, whereas one critic condemns a work because of anxiety, others will be ready to provide as unbiased an opinion as in professionally possible.

Anxiety is part of the human condition. When it debilitates reason and distorts judgment, it damages the critical processes required for making contributions and for evaluation; when it motivates, it may close off one's self from the dynamic real world, or it may inspire many significant contributions, including the innovation of new theories. The frequency of its attacks and their impact depend on the person's inner strength to act productively both as contributor and as critic regardless of anxiety's effects.

THE CRITICAL TEST AND THE SECOND APPROACH: SOCIAL GESTATION

Social gestation is the result of one of two conditions. In one condition, the current quantity of theories reaches the social restraints that do not permit new theories to receive the attention they deserve in light of their problem areas. The other condition is more specific: it prevails when theories relating to a problem area are no longer relevant for the social time in which they are active. Use of the term "relevance" in this context does not refer to the history of theories and their development; rather, it refers to the present utility of the theories for the conditions of the social time. We may refer to different social times in a historical era when discussing comparisons in the development of knowledge among these periods, but the utility of our current theories is relevant for us now. Historical comparisons are useful for our understanding of the past and indeed the present. But while theories in physics, biology, and the social and computer sciences expressed in the contexts of earlier social times may be interesting, especially for purposes of clarifiying the progress we have made, other than this and the interest in history, these theories have little practical utility now.

Social gestation is manifested in two forms: the *specific* or *special form* that refers to a problem area and its theories; and the *time form* that expresses the termination of either a social time or a historical era. The dynamics of both forms is the same; the difference between them lies in the scope and social significance of the gestation periods. For these forms with respect to the critic and the critical test, an awareness of the changing circumstances for which a work is presented, and the period of gestation, should the work be critiqued during such a period, influence the critic's objectivity in the sense of his or her position with respect to anxiety as discussed earlier.

Periods of specific gestation occur when the problem area is saturated with contributions. As a result, a new contribution receives little or no enthusiasm, the critical test is most likely not applied, and critique, such as it may be, is excessively harsh. This is the case not only with scientific theories, but also with all other forms of intellectual endeavor in which inquiry takes place and results in an abundance of theories in competition in a single general problem area, taking into account the overlapping of theories and their unique differences. In this situation, an innovator taking a slightly different approach to a problem than any approach that is already in operation–even though the difference may be of great utility but still without an immediately strong impact–will attract little attention. It is only for theories that do attract great attention in a saturated problem area that the critics will be sufficiently enthusiastic and will critique and provide for testing.

Periodic gestation is necessary for theories and their areas, as saturation sets in because of the exploitation of these areas. During these periods imitators find limits to their theories, and innovation slows down considerably. An example is the current situation in physics, with the final particle considered found, thereby completing the range of possible particles from reactor-induced collision. The area is saturated with theoretical information, leaving, however, the two views of wave and particle dynamics still to be reconciled. [12]

Each specific gestation period is era-oriented, as only certain and specific conditions and contributions during eras give rise to new knowledge, thereby enhancing the eras' development. While conditions for the computer were present in the latter part of the Industrial Revolution, this device did not come into its own until after World War II, during the early social times of our era of knowledge.[13] While scientists experimented with rocketry during the last part of the Industrial Revolution, only in our era did we develop technology for using ballistic and cruise missiles for strategic military uses,[14] and for the exploration of space. This is not a tautological concept in the sense that these and other outstanding contributions were made in our era because they occurred within the circumstances available in our era. The position is both more sophisticated and realistic than that.

Each historical era is defined according to its unique conditions. While the Renaissance era was unable to produce spaceships, its artists contributed outstanding works and its thinkers ushered in the concepts of modern philosophy and science. The Renaissance was also an era during which the previous historical era of the Dark Ages reasserted its fight against worldly knowledge by way of inquisitions. Nevertheless, the dynamics of knowledge had taken hold, and its rebirth was initiated by Aquinas's neo-Aristotelianism and those who followed in the pursuit of knowledge. The Renaissance was also an era of great shifts in territorial possessions among the monarchies and the development of modern political philosophy, with the works of Dante and Machiavelli most prominent. It was an era of mathematical advancements such as the calculus, but it did not contribute much to space exploration. Newton's three laws of motion worked for the space of our solar system, but that was as far as our space observation took us then. Nor was the exploration of the micro universe undertaken except by Anton van Leeuwenhoek (1623-1732) and his followers. This was an era of the great revival of ancient Greece, its architecture, its philosophy, its literature. This led to advances in the arts and sciences, thereby developing fertile ground for growing strong roots for the Industrial Revolution that was to follow. The Renaissance ceased when its arts and sciences were in gestation, resulting in artists seeking new vistas and approaches and scientists seeking fields other than strict abstract thinking and striving to apply their knowledge in the processes of production.

An era is thus defined and delineated by its main properties. The Dark Ages, as we have suggested, was an era in which intellectual and artistic pursuits were overshadowed by religion and superstition. This era gave way to the Renaissance after Aristotle's writings were discovered and incorporated into the writings of Aquinas and his followers. The Renaissance gave way to the Industrial Revolution once scientific theory was applied to the processes of production. With the Great Depression, the Industrial Revolution came to an end, and in its wake, with the strong industrial base and the development of knowledge, came our contemporary era.

Even though theories become entropic over time, special gestation exists when theories have saturated an area. All further contributions, unless monumental to the extent of regenerating renewed interest, will most likely be either passively accepted or ignored, regardless of their merits. In situations with competing theories that are very similar, and with little interest in new theories, the area itself as defined and delineated by the theories also stagnates and declines in utility because of the lack of new dynamics. Given regular circumstances, established theories decline as new theories rise; the problem area is altered as new and different theories are formulated and exert their influences. During special gestation, initiation is slowed as explorative imitation has been reduced by the lack of incentive because of saturation. This condition prevails much more strongly for innovation as the interest in new theories has declined accordingly.

The role of critique during periods of special (or specific) gestation lies in the ability to assess the conditions of the problem area and theory saturation. If the specific gestation period is one in which, during saturation, strict imitators are working out the dynamics of their theories, then critique must take this into consideration when a theory is being (re)evaluated. The gestation period may be brief enough for some theories to maintain their utilities, whereas others are being eliminated through competition by attracting their supporters and through the decisions of the critical tests.

For the process of evaluation, since it is the domains of theoretical difference that tell in competitive situations, these differences must be considered when discussing problem areas and testing their theories. Consider N theories, each containing operational and area statements a, b, ..., n with linguistic differences that exist only for clarification and embellishment, and that are critically unimportant. Each of these theories will also have statements that distinguish them, so that theory A^*_t has **g, r, s** and theory B^*_t has **as, pc,** and **dx,** and so forth. The similar statements in isolation will have no effect on the theories' utilities for competition and testing. Only changes in the nuances of a theory's languages will place it in a different competitive situation, perhaps improving its position as the alterations may strengthen its utility. Each theory is affected when area changes are brought about, but the domains of difference among the theories may well compensate for these changes.

Since theories are dynamic, statements of similarity among the theories are influenced by statements of difference within each theory. This is because they generate dynamics within the theory owing to alterations in their linguistic structures and within their specific aspects of the problem areas to which they relate. Should any of these statements become entropic, the entropy will affect the entire theory as a unit for generating knowledge. Alterations made in the entropic statements, correcting them and thereby removing the entropy from the theory, nevertheless affect the theory's utility. Consider statements **a** and **r** in theory A^*_t. These statements have become entropic because of the linguistic infiltration that has brought about changes in their nuancnes. As these statements are isomorphic onto their respective parts in the area, they have become inappropriate and entropic, and so have to be altered.

Two questions must then be considered. First, prior to their alteration, in what ways do they affect the theory's other statements? Second, once these statements are altered and the theory's utility is restored, how will they influence the theory? These points must be considered, not only with respect to the theory in isolation, but also with respect to its status as a competitor in a dynamic setting.

These two questions have to be approached from the standpoint that the theory under consideration functions in an area in which there are influences of changes and, as competition is involved, influences of the dynamics of the competing theories. Nuances in one theory that are incorporated after they meet the requirements of the probability assessment may be incorporated into other competing theories, and these in turn have to be altered to preserve their utilities. The changes made in one theory may influence the area, thereby requiring changes to be made in the other theories working in the area. This situation usually results in a fairly rapid turnover of information within the theories and generates the conditions for theories of high utility to enter the area, even though saturation exists and the dynamics of the various theories are being worked out by strict imitation. This is why only a theory of very high utility and originality will stir up enthusiasm in these circumstances, and be considered for evaluation and critical testing.

Nevertheless, since specific gestation is a period in a well-defined problem area in which existing theories are worked on, it is also usually a period when explorative imitation is subdued. Because of the statements of difference generating dynamics within the area and among competing theories, explorative imitation is still being conducted to strengthen the theories' competitive profiles. Hence, special gestation does not mean a tendency to the cessation of all activity. Nor does it mean that the emphasis is still on strict imitation, working with the theories as they exsist within their own dynamics. Such specific gestation will remain until competition alters either the theories, the problem area, or both, for it is competition that generates the dynamics necessary for bringing about change. In this circumstance, innovation that is extremely unique while being relevant can be of significance, providing that the innovation performs according to its claims. It may attract people to the theory, resulting in the existing theories being strengthened by those still working with them, or decline with severe entropy as the innovative theory gains adherents who abandon the other theories.

Whatever tranquility may have been associated with specific gestation, in most situations it is usually of short duration. This is because of the statements of difference among the competing theories that make each theory unique. The entropy that invades these theories and is corrected strengthens them and improves their competitive positions. As these corrections may well generate changes within a theory's statements of similarity, these changes could possibly alter the theory to the extent that–if they are in accordance with the theory's probability assessments–thus could affect the theory's competitive position and might well generate dynamics in the problem area that require the other theories to be reevaluated.

Special gestation is, therefore, a period of tranquility and calm only as long the statements of difference are not altered, or an innovative theory of high quality is not brought into the area. It is a period during which competing theories have their dynamics worked out by strict imitators; it is a period of competition among the theories during which new theories entering the competition have to be of extremely high quality to generate new dynamics, bringing about area shifts that result in changes made in the competing theories' operational and area statements. It is also a period during which theories become entropic as a result of the dynamics of competition, bringing about area shifts because of the theories', influences on the area. This results in the information entering both the area and its theories, altering them through the changes in both, due to the incorporation of this information restructured to meet the probabilistic requirements of those theories using it, and the conditions of the area that has absorbed it.

The critical evaluation of theories in competition depends on the theories' strength and the situation in the problem area. If the area is changing and some theories do not respond accordingly, the evaluation will indicate this and those unresponsive theories will have low utility ratings until the appropriate alterations are made. If the theories do not respond because their strict imitators fail to recognize the need for changes or because having recognized this need, the initiators do not provide contributions of sufficiently high utility, then these theories will decline in competition.

Strict imitators may fail to recognize the need for changes for one of two reasons. Either they are concerned about working on the theory as it is and unconcerned about the effects of dynamics from other theories on it, or, for reasons of anxiety stated in the previous section, they prefer not to be concerned about these dynamics and the influences they exert on the theory's utility. In either case, the contributions may fit the probability requirements but may not be of sufficient utility to restore the theory to its previous status. Critical evaluation must take into consideration the contributions and their utility fit within the theory. This is especially important when the problem area is changing due to the influences of information from the competing theories and information that may have entered the area from other sources.

Two points significant in the broader context of the critical test must be made with respect to critical evaluation: the validity of the critique over time, which bears specifically on the critical test, and the relevance of the critique over time, which refers to the critical test and so specific critiques. These points are relevant for both single theories and for those in competition. Critiquing a theory that has no competitors requires that if a negative critique of the theory is given, the theory should be critically tested to determine the critique's validity. The critical evaluator proposing the test should devise testing guidelines if they are not included in the theory's format. Should the theory then fail, its reasons can be demonstrated by the test.

From here, the argument can be taken, if necessary, to the critical evaluator's guidelines if they are different from those of the theory and their relevance to the theory's utility. Given that these guidelines are sound, the theory can be tested again for a confirming or rejecting opinion. Whether the theory is static at the time of evaluation, or whether it is undergoing changes due to initiation or to changes in the problem area, the critique is made public so that no difficulty is encountered in assessing the critical evaluator's own position. This is important because critical evaluators may have differing opinions, and since these are made public and available to those who work with the theory or who are interested for other reasons, these critical evaluations can be examined and tested.

The same holds for competing theories, although here because more than one theory is involved, the critical evaluations will be numerous, resulting in debate among the various theories' supporters and the demand for more refined critical testing. This is important because, as the result of competition, some theories are abandoned, whereas others are strengthened. Such a situation at the time of specific gestation allows only the theories with the highest utility to enter the arena. A positive critique has little value if, over time, the critiqued theory declines rapidly into entropy. Similarly, a negative critique has little value over time if the theory that was so considered increases in utility while other competing theories fall.

The dynamics occurring in problem areas and their theories take place within the historical era. The sum total of these area–theory relationships, their beginnings and cessations, and the contributions made within them, lead to social gestation. In this period, the general dynamics within theories and their problem areas have stabilized to a large extent, and no theories of revolutionary significance are formulated. It is a period in which competition is well defined among the theories, and theories are entering and dropping out of the respective arenas. It is not a static period, as new theories and problem areas are being formulated. It is therefore a period during which activity is occurring among theories, but at a socially slower rate than previously. It is also a period that signals the demise of a historical era.

The Renaissance, for example, began with the developments in science from the perspective of neo-Aristotelian thought as advanced first by Aquinas and his theological and naturalist followers, then by Galileo in light of Copernicus's intellectual work, and next by Kepler, Newton, and other great scientists and mathematicians of the era. However, most of the physics was Newtonian (the problem of the nature of light remained puzzling, and the anti-Newtonian argument for light behaving as waves was very strong), and Newtonian theory reached a stage of gestation. The Renaissance declined when the value of science began to be recognized in the production processes, and when the arts that had developed throughout the era had become saturated in its themes and styles.[15] The applications of science to the production processes resulted in the specialization of labor and efficiency in the manufacturing procedures due to the ease of machinery. The different art styles and artistic conceptions that were inspired by the urbanization processes resulting from the centralization of industrial plants and the housing and communal services that were required for working in the manufacturing factories expressed these conditions. They also helped clarify them for the new city dwellers and industrialists who developed the new era. While Newtonian theory remained dominant in the physical sciences, developments in biological theory were taking place as industrialization continued and new urban centers were accommodating this expansion. Lamarckism and Darwinism were competing, and in light of industrialization and urbanization and the new economic theories that resulted, Social Darwinism and other attempts to explain events in terms of metahistorical forces were in vogue.[16]

In physics, it was only during the final years of the nineteenth century that Newtonian theory was brought into question with the work of Planck, a staunch Newtonian. Poincaré's work in nonlinear analysis contributed to economic theory and was used by macro-and microeconomists to explain business and production cycles. Poincaré contributed to the discipline of mathematics during a period when many theorists were searching for the foundations of the discipline.

In industry, production expanded as more people migrated to the countries that offered the greatest potential for personal advancement due to the industrializing era. Railroads were built and the airplane was developed, for both transportation and for purposes of war. Communications were also improved by the telephone and telegraph; with better transportation and communications, the applications of science lowered the costs of production, and made the goods and services available to a wider consuming public.

As the theories of relativity and quantum physics were being worked out, the Great Depression took place, bringing industrial output to a near standstill. The defining and delineating aspects of the Industrial Revolution ceased to hold, and so the era came to an end.

Our era of knowledge has its foundations in the Industrial Revolution. But the applications of industrialization in conducting World War II were also necessary in the early years of our era. For all the prewar theoretical developments in atomic energy, it was the need to beat the Axis powers in the weapons race that brought about the atomic revolution and the postwar applications of atomic energy to both military and peacetime uses. Moreover, the computer came into its own to provide rapid calculation and programming. Air travel became jet-oriented, another development arising from the war. The lessons that were learned from the war and their applications in peacetime rectified the social gestation that terminated the Industrial Revolution and established our era of knowledge.

Hence, the factors that bring about social gestation are those that terminate an era. The Dark Ages ceased with the rediscovery of Aristotle's works, which resulted in a renewed interest in nature; through the authority of Aquinas, the Scholastic thinkers examined this world as well as the other world, and the concepts of science offered by William of Occam, Jean Buridan, and John Duns Scotus began to take hold. The personal expression and the choice of subjects in the arts were acceptable, and the processes of scientific inquiry had begun. With these developments in the arts and sciences, social gestation in the old era and its approaches to thought and expression had set in, and the era declined, yielding to the era of the rebirth of knowledge.

The Renaissance declined with the applications of science to the problems of production. The tradition established during the Renaissance of expanding the arts and expression, as well as the development of the pure sciences, continued. But the new applications of science in the form of technology brought about a change in the emphasis of the arts and sciences for their own sakes. The artists had become interpreters and clarifiers of society, but the scientists who dealt with technology shaped the societies according to the requirements of industrialization.

The Industrial Revolution experienced social gestation when the old method for settling conflicts, that of war, brought the industrializing nations into a world conflict. The political judgments that led to the war were medieval in conception, and the settlement of the war proved no different. Issues were still to be resolved, and industry, while providing employment and output, became highly speculative, with the emphasis on paper–on stocks and bonds–as well as production. The uncertainty in the international arena also contributed to the search for financial security and hence to the overextended purchasing of commercial paper. As the uncertainty grew in Europe and Asia, the paper chase become more intense, until stocks and bonds became prime commodities obeying the pricing laws of supply and demand. The U.S. markets fell, bringing down all major markets, and as the amount of money in circulation shrank, industrial output declined, resulting in a fall in employment. The Great Depression had set in, bringing in its wake World War II as a means of settling the scores of World War I, and the era of industrialization came to its end. In the aftermath of that war, our era of knowledge began.

Social gestation therefore indicates the decline of an era. Even though theories are still being innovated and brought into entropy, the conditions that provide the era with its main definition cease to be dominant. Even though the Industrial Revolution has come to an end, the processes of industrialization are continuing, but the defining properties of our era are knowledge oriented. Hence, during social gestation those theories being formed are part of the transformation into the new era, just as mechanical computation in the 1930s was part of the computer transformation in our era, and just as the theories of the atom led to the development of atomic weaponry and changed the directions of research and its applications in peacetime energy uses and military strategy in our era.

At this point in the discussion, an intentional ambiguity must be clarified. Throughout this discussion, the terms "critique" and "critical testing" have been strongly related, to the extent that little difference seemed to exist between them. Of course, they are different, but their uses in this context have been intentional. This is because criticism of contributions, be they innovative or initiative, may itself be sufficient to influence the opinions of those who are interested in the contributions and are working in the designated or related areas of concern. However, it is the actual critical test, devised in agreement between the proponents and opponents of the contributions in question, that will come down on one side or the other in the argument, and this, not necessarily at the time that the test is undertaken. Even those contributions for which no experimental test has been devised in the traditional sense of controlled laboratory conditions can be subjected to ideal experimentation and testing, once the sides concerned agree on the conditions.

An example of theories that cannot be tested in the traditional sense of controlled laboratory conditions are two opposing approaches to cosmology: the Big Bang and the Steady State. The proponents of the Big Bang theory maintain that the universe came about because a tremendous explosion of immense proportions scattered cosmic debris throughout what would become space, after which cosmic matter formed into solar systems owing to the intense gravitational forces that were established after the explosion.

This position is substantiated by the spectrum shifts of the light generated by the heavenly bodies as they move away from our solar system, in the form of the red-shift indicating movement away from our planet. The Big Bang argument is also substantiated by the many solar systems and galaxies, indicating that the initial explosion spewed vast amounts of debris at tremendous speeds until the forces of gravity placed them into galactic and solar-oriented relationships.

Proponents of the Steady State approach argue that the Big Bang is only surmise, oriented to a large extent to the Bible story of the creation of the universe. But according to observations, galaxies exist, and while they are in celestial motion, with some moving away from us, others are approaching. What we observe using the finest telescopes and other sophisticated methods such as spaceships is a universe changing, dynamic, with solar systems collapsing into black holes and new systems being formed, with galaxies in motion, and with all changes occurring in accordance with physical laws that we have yet to understand. While the evidence supports the Big Bang theory, the creation of the universe is still subject to speculation, and perhaps there is no real conflict between the Big Bang theory and the teachings in the Bible. As scientists, this is something we may never know.

The Steady State argument is ancient, going back to Aristotle's writings on physics and teleology. The planets are said to move on spheres, each layered higher to the final cause, the Supreme Being. However, the Big Bang approach has won many more adherents, even though both approaches are now theory oriented and their arguments are accordingly theory-derived. The contemporary appeal of the Big Bang theory is that it provides greater intellectual stimulation, leading to such contributions as Alan Guth's "inflation" theory. According to Guth, the inflation of infinity generated tremendous forces causing the giant explosion.[17] The Steady State theory has provided no viable innovative explanations, for according to this theory there was no physical first cause for the creation of the universe. How these theories can be put to critical testing depends on the future contributions of the proponents, especially the evaluation of the logic and utilities of their arguments and the incorporation of these arguments, together with whatever new technologies may be used in the development of their arguments and in their testing.

It is, of course, ideal when competing theories are debated for a single problem area for which a critical test, one agreeable to all sides, can be devised in order to determine finally and permanently which theories are to be accepted and rejected. With respect to the theory of evolution and natural selection, Lysenko's corruption of Lamarck's theory and his applications of this corrupted theory to Soviet society were shown to be unfounded, for communism never worked. The argument in its favor was that given sufficient time, it would be shown to be applicable, but the duration of "sufficient time" was never established. Its importance in terms of the Lamarck–Darwin debate placed Lamarck's theory in a negative light, even though, in his later years, Darwin was influenced to some extent by Lamarck's argument. Survival of the fittest requires adaptation to circumstances. This is a major point in Lamarck's theory, expressed in the concept that external circumstances impose adaptive changes on life forms. The real issue now is not so much the debate between Lamarckians and Darwinians, but between evolutionists and Creationists who deny all forms of biological evolution. Critique can assist in this debate, and in this manner, through the development of the arguments, rigorous critique can serve as a substitute for critical tests that may be inapplicable in the circumstances of this debate.

   This does not mean, of course, that technical advances in the future will prevent us from coming down conclusively for one side or the other, even though critique is used as a substitute for, or in addition to, a critical test. Moreover, such technologies always permit a critical examination of tenets accepted by the proponents of an argument. For example, assume that experimental technology far more sophisticated than that employed by Michelson and Morely did detect a difference, no matter how slight, in the velocity of light when measured in different directions.[18] Assume that both the equipment and the finding had been examined by impartial observers (impartial, in terms of being objective as discussed earlier), and that the equipment was found to be without fault. How would this affect modern physics? Both Einsteinian relativity and quantum physics assume that the velocity of light in vacuo is constant and is the absolute limit-value of energy. Shifts in this limit brought about by changes in the direction of light would cause great disturbances in relativity and quantum physics—similar to the cracks in the Newtonian edifice brought about by Planck's findings. This would surely revive the argument of light traveling in waves through an ethereal medium—a "neoether"—and would place on physicists the obligation to resolve finally the nature of light.

   Such an explanation may well take the form of the argument that light, consisting of particles, is influenced in its motion by other and less energetic fields in close proximity, thereby exerting a wavelike effect when traveling through matter-filled space, moving from one field to another. Spectral measuring devices can be set up, once in a pattern, once at random, with their measurements taken. Moreover, the influences of gravity on light through its movement from one spectral measuring device to the next can also be assessed, thereby determining whether the wave or particle theory stands.

   Given that light does indeed consist of wavelike motions, its particle properties can be explained in terms of vortices of energy traveling through space, exerting particle-like properties due to its tremendous velocity, with the vortex acting like a particle. These vortices would be brought about by the motion of the light waves as they are influenced by the gravity of the spectral measuring devices and by the gravity of the surrounding matter. The wave-particle controversy can then be resolved by either of these arguments, and the position that is correct will be determined by the finding of a "neoether," or by the rejection of such an ethereal medium, depending on the readings of the tests. Whichever position is accepted, research will be geared toward the innovation of new theories to account for either the particle approach, the wave approach, or a novel theory incorporating both and revising our approach to physics and our world-view of nature. While a critical test is preferred to critique alone, in the case of the wave-particle debate, where sufficient technology and theoretical understanding are absent to establish a critical test, critique alone serves as the best alternative.

   Critique also serves another purpose, that of bringing to light a contribution, be it innovative or initiative in origin. Without critique, contributions in journals and academic seminars would not be valid forms of presenting works, and the time lapse that would occur from the contributions' presentations to reaching their targeted audiences might well render them entropic through disuse. In this case, critique examines contributions for their significance in their problem areas, perhaps establishing guidelines for setting up critical tests for determining their viabilities. In situations where technologies are still inadequate for proper testing, debate based on critique can stimulate ideal experiments–such as those that seek to counter Heisenberg's uncertainty principle–which can often substitute for critical tests, providing that they are accepted by those working in the area. Hence, while critique cannot be a replacement for a critical test, it can provide the basis for an ideal construction of such a test, leading, perhaps, to an imaginary experiment that in itself may be decisive. By bringing to light contributions that may have gone unnoticed, the problem areas are much more subject to the dynamics of inquiry and change.

The question of the critical test and its reliability remain to be treated. This is relevant for both periodic and social gestation. For periodic gestation, the critical test can determine which of the competing initiations is most viable for the theory and which of the competing theories provides the highest utility for the problem area. In the latter case, there may be more than one theory of high utility, with each possessing its own benefits which others lack, and each with its own deficiencies which the others may also lack. In cases of critical testing being decisive, this will result in the other contributions being abandoned–except by those that are adhered to for the reasons of anxiety stated earlier–or they may be strengthened with higher utility and reentered into the competition. For social gestation, the culmination of critical tests may bring the entire complexity of theories into question, showing that their utilities have been reduced and thereby paving the way for another historical era to begin.

Further comments on social gestation must be made before the critical test can be discussed. Social gestation results when periodic gestation occurs in most problem areas due to saturation, together with the lack of innovations of sufficient utility to make impacts on their problem areas. It is also a social time when the foundations of a new era are being established. In economics, for example, all the neoclassical macro theories assumed full employment. When the Industrial Revolution came to a close with high unemployment and unused capital, during the transition period from the Industrial Revolution to the beginning of our era, J. M. Keynes attacked the full employment assumption as stated in A. C. Pigou's *Economics of Welfare*, a work that Keynes considered to be of great clarity and elegance.[19] In physics, developments in relativity and quantum mechanics continued, but technological advances necessary to exploit this knowledge in terms of releasing and harnessing atomic energy only came about during the war and in our contemporary era.

Here is where the uniqueness of social gestation lies. Periodic gestation has been treated in terms of competition within areas, in which changes are made and in which established theories fall and new ones are formulated with such high utility that they attract attention. Without this influence, the current theories will remain fairly stable, within their competitive positions; without this utility, the current theories will be subject only to internal changes and the dynamics of initiation that are necessary for correction. This situation will continue until the areas shift radically, or until the theories become heavily entropic, or perhaps a combination of both. Social gestation is thus a macro social condition in which the dynamics of periodic gestation for the manifold problem areas are no longer relevant. This is because the culminative conditions of social gestation cannot account for the dynamics of the aggregate body of theories–in the same way that the Dark Ages could not account for the developments in the sciences and the arts, in the same way that the Renaissance could not account for the applications of science to production, and in the same way that the Industrial Revolution could not cope with the emphasis on knowledge as a commodity in a theory-oriented social situation. Hence, social gestation sets in when the trends of the theories are no longer applicable to the realities of society.

An example of a theory that had great influence but did not relate to the trends in society is communism. The difficulties between workers and employers encountered during the Industrial Revolution were relevant enough for the development of socialism and the formation of the communist movement, expressed intellectually by Karl Marx in *Capital*[20] and somewhat emotionally by Marx and Friedrich Engels in the *Communist Manifesto* (1848). The theory of these thinkers was important for the workers, for industry tended to a form of centralization unknown previously, commanding greater control over resources including that of labor. As the Industrial Revolution expanded and the labor movement rose and became political as a result of its determination and strength, the writings of these and other such thinkers found less and less support in the industrializing societies. During the Great Depression, echoes of socialist and communist thought reverberated with some strength but out of frustration with the ability of industry and its incapacity to pull out of the depression. However, since the problems of the Great Depression have been resolved, in our era the writings of the socialist and communist thinkers find little support, because the problems in our era are vastly different from those of the previous era. The significance of their writings is historical and to some extent economic. They showed the problems of the growing pains of industrialization, with Marx's economic writings serving as the watershed between classical and neoclassical economic theory.

The general shift in problem areas and their theories brings about social gestation and the decline of an era. Problem-area shifts on a macro scale render the era entropic, and the theories that are innovated within the context of this decline are directed to the new problems, as defined by these shifts. The great artistic and scientific contributions during the Renaissance were vastly different from the artistic and philosophical works of the Dark Ages. The very problems of science during the Renaissance led to the philosophy of science, a discipline that was nonexistent during the Dark Ages, even though the fundations did exist in the writings of Buridan, Duns Scotus, and William of Occam. These writers, however, were not so rigorous with respect to *scientia* when compared to Bacon and Descartes. Their problem areas differed significantly from those of Buridan et al., who were still steeped in the thinking of the Dark Ages, as Bacon and Descartes were in the historical context of the social time of the middle Renaissance.

From the argument stated in this section, it can be seen that periodic gestation can occur in each problem area. For the duration that the problem areas do not deviate radically in the aggregate, the historical era remains intact. Radical deviation brings about the decline of an era and the beginnings of a new one. The theme of the era depends on the general direction of the problem areas, and this direction is established by the construction of problem areas on the basis of the old era. Thus, in history, while there is change, there is also continuity, as the new comes from the old. Social gestation issues from aggregate specific gestation, and the innovations that will establish the patterns in the new era are those that capture the imagination of participants in the old theories, where strict imitation is predominant, initiation is minimal, and innovation is not acceptable unless it is of the quality to introduce a new era.

THE CRITICAL TEST AND THE THIRD APPROACH: THE CRITICAL ASPECT

A historical era is defined and delineated by its problem areas, and our era is unique because of the impact of its theories on society. The extent of this impact is a determining factor in assessing a country's standard of living. For example, in Nicolai Ceusescu's Romania, government permission was required to obtain a typewriter, for the government was afraid of the communication of new ideas and sought total control over their expression. That government has since been overthrown, and the new government is attempting to bring the country into our era. This is just one example of the effects our era is having as the dynamics of inquiry leading to developments in knowledge and the formulation of theories penetrate countries that were previously closed to the expansion of knowledge and remained impoverished for it. They are now opening up and seeking assistance to be brought fully into our era. This topic is discussed further in Part III.

Theories, be they alone in their domination of an area or in rigorous competition, are subject to critical testing. Critique and the critical test must be analyzed from two approaches: (1) the validity of critique and the critical test must be considered with respect to other critiques and tests, and their relevance must be assessed over time; and (2) the significance of critiques and tests must be considered with respect to one another when they pertain to the same theory and its initiated restructuring as it relates to its problem area. These approaches are discussed here with the aid of historical examples in which critiques and critical tests were formulated.

Consider, for example, the discussion on the spontaneous generation of life. Louis Pasteur (1822-1895) claimed that life comes only from life, while his opponents, Joly, Pouchet, and Musset, argued that life comes about spontaneously. Each side developed critiques of the other's position, and to settle the argument each agreed on terms for a critical experiment. Each side filled flasks, with Pasteur using a yeast-based broth, while his opponents used a broth made from hay. Each side boiled the contents of its flasks and went to great lengths to expose the flasks to extreme situations–Pasteur on Mount Blanc and his opponents on the Pyrenees. Each side opened its flask, and Pasteur's opponents found life in their flasks, demonstrating that Pasteur was in error. The critiques began, as Pasteur found no life. Even sarcasm was used as a weapon of argument, and *ad hominum* arguments were presented, albeit with a degree of professional sophistication.

This test, being inconclusive, was refined further when Pasteur's opponents challenged him to a public experiment before the distinguished audience of the French Academy of Sciences. His opponents maintained that if one single flask would fail to grow microbes after it was opened for an instant, they would admit their error. Performing their experiments before the Academic Committee, the flasks were examined and then opened. The judges came down on the side of Pasteur and proclaimed that life can only come from life and that the argument of spontaneous generation has no place in science. This decision was taken after the Committee noted that Pasteur's experiment and that of his opponents were of the most perfect exactitude.

The difficulty with this critical test was found by John Tyndall, a British scientist, who discovered years later that as Pouchet and his associates used a broth of hay instead of yeast like Pasteur, hay holds tiny stubborn seeds of microbes that withstand hours of boiling. Tyndall finally resolved the debate by pointing out that because there were different broths, and because of the tough microbe seeds in the hay broth, the results of that critical test were inconclusive, although the spontaneous generation argument is most likely in error. For critique, the issue being debated can be approached from different points of view. Given our state of knowledge, it seems perplexing that the spontaneous generation argument that had endured for so long could be dismissed so readily, given the acceptance by most astrophysicists of a Big Bang account of cosmic creation. For if life only comes from life, as Louis Pasteur maintained and demonstrated, what is the origin of the first life? With our highly advanced technologies and methods for testing and analyzing, perhaps better theories and critical tests can provide scientific understanding of this puzzling question.

Another historical situation refers to the theory of evolution. Since Lamarck, A. R. Wallace, and Darwin, several serious contributions have been made to the accepted Darwinian theory of evolution. One of Darwin's followers, R. A. Fisher, discussed evolution and sexual attractiveness. For the male peacock, he wrote that plumage development, and the preference for such plumage in the female

> must thus advance together, and so long as the process is unchecked by severe counterselection, will advance with ever increasing speed. In the total absence of such checks, it is easy to see that the speed of development will be proportional to the development already attained, which will therefore increase with time exponentially, or in geometric progression.[21]

Richard Dawkins explains that Darwin accepted female whims as given. Their existence is an axiom in his theory of natural selection, a prior assumption rather than a point to be held and explained in its own right. Dawkins states that, partly for this reason, Darwin's theory of sexual selection fell into disrepute, until Fisher rescued it in 1930. He further states that, unfortunately, many biologists either ignored or misunderstood Fisher's argument, citing the position advanced by Julian Huxley (1881-1975) that female whims are not legitimate foundations for a truly scientific theory. Huxley's critique of Fisher's argument was, of course, an indirect critique of Darwin's, as whims and tastes are in both theories and Fisher was a Darwinian. However, since further research has been done on the theory of evolution in the context of the genetic code, Fisher's position, which is a refinement of Darwin's theory of natural selection, has been reconsidered and refined.[22]

At the time that Darwin presented his theory, Mendelian selection had been formulated but had not had sufficient exposure for the understanding of evolution. When Gregor Mendel's (1822-1884) laws had gained recognition, Darwin's position on natural selection and inheritance was little considered because of Darwin's nonrigorous approach to the role of female preferences for certain characteristics in the male. Huxley's critique and rejection of Fisher's attempt to revive and refine the Darwinian argument resulted in Fisher's theory being neglected, only to be reconsidered, in turn, by modern evolutionists. The role of female sexual preference is now considered important in natural selection, and the reinforcement of special properties attractive to females is recognized as a sufficient factor for reinforcing these properties in the male of the species.

It can be said that Huxley and the other biologists neglected this aspect of Darwin's theory because of the lack of scientific rigor on this issue in Darwin's theory, but by so doing, they missed an important aspect of evolution. Without sexual attraction, the mating process would be reduced to the fulfillment of the sex drive, and evolution would be considerably slowed.

With respect to Fisher's approach, however, this can be critiqued from the point of view that he did not carry his argument far enough. The further advanced a species is along the evolutionary scale, the greater the refinement in selective tastes. This can be seen among *homo spaiens* for which there are no hard and fast rules accounting for physical sexual attraction. Perhaps this is why no serious studies have been undertaken to explain this aspect of human behavior: there are too many variables, and these change over time with each person.

With regard to the critical test constructed by Pasteur and his opponents, the real results were not known until Tyndall pointed out that the conclusion drawn by the distinguished Committee for that test under those conditions was in fact not established. It was only Pasteur's presentation of his experiment, together with the general scientific climate of the time which demanded measurement and derivation, that had won the case. It was scientifically sensible to accept the notion that life could only come from life and that in light of science at that time it was acceptable to question the theory of spontaneous generation. However, such experimentation conducted in our social time would require more refined criteria and control, as well as greater knowledge of the properties of the types of broths being used, given the durability of life within each broth when subjected to the testing conditions.

At that time, the critical test was conducted in the esprit of scientific method imparted by Bacon and Descartes. In this scientific climate, the concept of spontaneous generation had too much of a mystical "air," as if life depended on a nonself-generating force. This approach seemed unscientific then, and perhaps it was for its nonscientific quality that this theory was popular. Pasteur questioned it in the esprit of a scientific attitude liberated from the mystical influences of the Dark Ages, and thereby placed his worthy opponents on the defensive.

As a result, Tyndall reconsidered the experiments and the result of the critical test in a calmer atmosphere and did indeed find the tests to be inconclusive. The real results of the experiments and the critical test left the argument about spontaneous generation unresolved, with Tyndall's critique of the test and his reformulation providing the accepted answer, except for the difficulties of the origins of life in accordance with the Big Bang theory.

With respect to R. A. Fisher's argument, because of the nonexperimental nature of classical Darwinian evolution, such a nonrigorous position on the role of Darwinian sexual attraction was ignored perhaps because greater battles over Darwin's theory were being waged. For example, the popularized notion of Darwinian theory that monkeys are the evolutionary ancestors of humankind leaves much to be explained, in spite of some superficial similarities among simians and humans. Moreover, the religious argument that man was created in the image of God as used against Darwinian theory is somewhat difficult to explain, especially because the monotheistic religions maintain that God has no image and that our general behavior in this world is far from Godlike. However, Fisher's clarification of Darwin's position explains the processes of sexual attraction among animals–such as the plumage of peacocks–but does little to explain sexual attraction among humankind. A critical test can be established among animals, isolating conditions unwanted for the test and providing conditions that are required.

Such a critical test can entail the isolation of one female and two male peacocks, one with its plumage somewhat damaged, to determine which of the males the female would find attractive. This, however, will not explain sexual attraction in general, and especially not for humans. The point is that while a critical test can be established to evaluate Fisher's argument, the validity of the test is greatly limited if its results are to be generalized for all life forms.

In this case, critique is important. Such a critique should not be constructed in a style similar to Julian Huxley's sophisticated ridicule. Rather, it should be constructive critique, which points out the difficulties of the argument and the need to repeat the test using different combinations of male and female birds, and for a comprehensive theory of evolution, for generalizing the criteria of the critical test and making it applicable as part of such a theory.

These historical examples of Pasteur and Darwin, show that a critical test established to determine the viability of a contribution may be, in itself, insufficient in deciding on the contribution's status of acceptance or rejection. When considering critically testing Aristotelian physics, it is clear that this theory is inadequate and no longer relevant for explaining physical events as we know them. In this case, however, it is the single Aristotelian physical theory that is tested and rejected, and not a single statement that can be altered and evaluated for its utility without seriously affecting the theory.

For a single statement, initiation requires that a critical test be applied for its evaluation, especially where strong competition is involved. For the single statement, critique is important, but is necessary only where conditions and results of the critical test are questioned. The importance of critique in general is that it sheds light on the contribution's significance, or lack of it as the case may be.

When a theory is involved, the critical test itself may be insufficient in determining the theory's viability, and hence both critique and the critical test may be necessary. The critical test used by Pasteur and his opponents was not a test of whether or not spontaneous generation exists; it was a testing of the entire dimension of the issues, of the understanding of factors that lead to procreation, of inheritance that would be absent in those situations in which life could form spontaneously, and of course the evolution of life from other life forms. The role of critique can be seen in Tyndall's explanation that the test really determined nothing, even though the scientific community approved of its outcome. This has become a much broader question than that debated by Pasteur and his worthy opponents, and as our knowledge of astrophysics expands so will our understanding of the origins of life.

For Fisher's argument, such a critical test as posited earlier would most likely meet with critiques of the experimental conditions. For example, several female peacocks with the equivalent male peacocks, some with their plumages damaged in varying degrees, would provide a better experiment, given proper controls such as the absence of external influences and interferences with the birds' activities. This experiment could be duplicated not only with other peacocks, but with other animals as well. Were it to be inclusive, however, it would have to entail experiments with humans, for whom sexual attraction is more than just physical appearances. Personality, intellect, and the ability to evaluate the male-female situation are also considerations of great importance, and these are difficult to measure scientifically.

The critique leveled against Darwin's theory of sexual attraction by his defenders was directed at the looseness of his approach on this issue. It is an important concept in the general Darwinian theory, but as Darwin presented it, its lack of rigor as compared with the rest of his argument in light of his extensive research led to the neglect of this aspect despite the strong defense of his greater argument and the controversy it generated.

Hence, although Darwin's position on sexual attraction was dismissed because of the critique against it, Fisher restated the position and allowed for further analysis by way of critical testing. The critique against Darwin's position by his detractors was part of their assault on his theory of evolution. The critique by his defenders was more of an admission that they had the important business of counterarguing against his detractors and could not be so concerned by a theory that was nonrigorous within the context of his general theory. Fisher's restatement of the Darwinian argument presented it in a different light. Concerning Fisher's argument, should a critique be presented, it would not be against the theory of evolution as such, but against the conditions of the experiment and perhaps the conclusions that Fisher's supporters could derive from it.

With respect to initiation, when two or more contributions are competing as resolutions to an entropic statement within a theory, a critical test is important in determining which initiation will be accepted. Critique may then be offered to raise questions about the test's validity, which can be evaluated. Either the critique of the test is accepted and performed again in light of the critique, or the critique is rejected and the test's results are maintained. Both the test and the critique that may be raised must be conducted within the theory's utility, for it is on this basis that initiations compete, and the one with the highest utility is selected.

The critical test must therefore be constructed on what is known about each of the competing contributions, their similarities and their differences. With regard to the similarities, these will not be the issue of the test, unless they affect the contributions' dynamics within the theory. The main focus of the test will thus be with respect to the contributions' differences, assessing the possible dynamics that each contribution may generate. At first, this assessment will be conjectural and may provide the basis of critique after the test is conducted and the decision is made concerning which initiation is to be accepted. In critique, arguments made for and against the accepted innovation may result in retesting, if it can be demonstrated that the absence of sufficient rigor in the testing resulted in the acceptance of a contribution of lesser utility.

With respect to innovation, the entire theory stands to be accepted or rejected on the basis of the critical test. This is because no single entropic statement is in question, but the theory itself is. If Eddington's eclipse experiment showed that light did not bend as a result of gravitational pull, then Einstein's theory would have been rejected, leaving the problems raised by his theory unanswered and perhaps to be taken by other theories, should they be innovated.

The critical test is far more decisive for innovations than for initiations. Either Einstein's theory behaves as expected, or it does not; if not, then it is rejected, with its utility remaining viable only in the sense that it will be used until another and superior theory is developed. In the controversy concerning the Big Bang versus the Steady State theories of cosmology, if a critical test were to be established to determine the validity of either of these theories, the other would decline in utility and become entropic to the extent that its only use would be in the incorporation of some of its statements into the surviving theory, adjusted to meet the theory's probability requirements.

Repeatability of the test provides the basis for acquiring the results obtained from the test. When the test is repeated in the event different results are obtained, as was the case with Tyndall's repetition of the experiments of Pasteur and his opponents, either the experimental testing did not follow the exact procedures of the original test, or the original testing results were inaccurate, as with those of Pasteur and his opponents.

By way of experimental repetition of the critical test, scientific accuracy can be evaluated, and each repetition of the critical test is thus an evaluation, reconsidering the validity of a theory or its statements corrected by initiation, as the case may be. Acceptance is reached when the people assessing the contribution with respect to the results of the critical test agree, and this is done in terms of the contribution's utility, either as an innovation or initiation. If experimentation is carried further, it is for demonstrating and clarifying the theory or the statements, and for showing how the critical test provides the reasons why the test results have been accepted.

Consider the critical test for initiation. The operational and area statement $o_d a$ in theory $D*_t$ has become entropic because of linguistic infiltration from another theory that differs in domain, but is related in conceptualization to that of its users in $G*_t$. An example could be the adaptation of a physical concept into a sociological theory, such as Heisenberg's uncertainty principle into the prediction of mass group and individual behavior within the group, given specific conditions under limited control. The statement in $D*$ has become entropic because the adaptation of linguistic information from the other theory has altered its information content within the theory, thereby reducing its utility. If such an alteration is significant in the sense of either strengthening the theory or weakening it, $D*$'s utility will be effectively reduced until necessary adjustments are made within the theory so that its utility can be restored.

In this case, there will always be some form of competition, even if only a single initiator is involved. In this situation where only one initiator is involved, the competition is in finding the best alteration of the entropic statement within the theory's context. For example, as the contribution must fit within the theory's probabilistic consideration, the contribution of, say c, must fit within the probability equation: $P(cA^*_t) \equiv [I(\Sigma c_d a)]_t$. This means that the contribution must fit within the theory, given the sum of the information content of its operational and area statements, without generating any further shifts into entropy at time t. Since its utility within the theory is measured in terms of its probability, given its information content and how it relates to the theory, as D^*_t is equal to the sum of all its statements, the contribution may have a fairly low but still acceptable probability rating. Thus, while acceptable within the theory, yet another contribution would be able to provide a higher rating, thereby inspiring the initiator to seek another contribution.

This may also be the case for the initiator positing several contributions before going public with the one he or she considers to be of the highest probability. Once selected, its utility within the theory must be measured, and this is done by placing it within the utility equation: $Uc_t = [P(c_d a) = I[(c_d a)]_t$. With c as the contribution with respect to the entropic statement, if, after several contributions the initiator considers this to be of the highest utility, it will be submitted for others to evaluate. Since this is the single contribution, it will be accepted if the imitators consider it worthy.

This consideration will be based on whether the imitators determine that the initiator's utility assessment is correct, with the critical test being conducted according to the conditions stated by the initiator. After close examination, if the imitators agree, the contribution is accepted; if they disagree, then critique of the initiator's method may become an issue, with the test being held again, until a majority of imitators accept or reject the results. Should the results be accepted, the contribution will be included according to the theory's probability requirements and utility criteria. Should they be rejected, then either the critique will come into play and the critical test will be undertaken yet again to determine the cause of discrepancy between the initiator's findings and that of the testers, or the contribution will be rejected outright.

Consider the situation in which two or more initiators are competing for a solution to the entropic statement. Each initiator may submit one or more contributions, each meeting the probability and utility standards. The initiators in this case will select the contribution that each considers the best representative of his or her work to be tested. While the competing contributions will have areas of agreement among their contributions, it is on the basis of their differences that they will be tested. These differences set each contribution apart from the others, making each unique.

The probability requirements and utility criteria are met for each contribution, which is why each is being considered. The problem, therefore, is to determine the best contribution. The theory's imitators have to test each contribution for its differences and must not only assess the probability and utility. They must also project onto the theory the influences that each of the contributions will have once they are incorporated into the theory.

This is accomplished by establishing critical tests among the contributions, with each imitator assessing the contribution and placing it on an agreed-upon scale of measurement. In cases where two or more contributions are assigned the same place on the scale, critical testing can be undertaken to determine which of these contributions has a higher probability and is of higher utility within the theory when the theory's dynamics are considered. This includes considering which contributions will bring about the lesser amount of entropy. As this is a projection into the future, time-series equations must be established on the basis of these future projections. In situations that are undecidable, critique can be employed to establish the method and the considerations that brought about the contributions, with this information being incorporated into the decision-making processes. If the situation is still unresolved, then the other contributions will be considered, and the contribution that is chosen will compete with all others until one is finally accepted.

With respect to projection into the future, standard mathematical techniques are inadequate. Given the dynamics of the theory, nonlinear analysis is to be applied in the dynamic sense of not considering the past or present, but relying on the basis of the past and the present to project into the future. Such nonlinear analysis can be based on models. Considering the competition among the contributions, given $c_1, c_2,...c_n$ (with n being a reasonable number of competing contributions), the model can take the form: $c_t+1\varepsilon\ A_t{\sim}1$, $c_t+2\varepsilon\ A_t{\sim}1,...\ c_t+n\varepsilon A_t{\sim}1$, as the maximum utility of 1 is approximated. With these contributions included separately in the theory for testing, their effects can be analyzed with the use of time-series equations. For example, with c_t+1 included in the theory, $\Sigma(c_d a)t{\sim}\Sigma(c_d a)_t+1$, and the same for the other contributions. If the contribution suits the theory as it stands, then it is acceptable, even though this is an approximate "fit" due to the uncertainty concerning the influence of other unknown circumstances in the future that might affect the theory.

Consider the situation of competitive innovation. This situation exists when there is a known problem area for which there are either no theories or the theories are inadequate and are being used only until better theories are formulated. When the problem area is already known, and as the current theories are inadequate, the problem area has become static. The dynamics occurring within the theories are only semantic adjustments initiated in light of linguistic attempts to come closer to working with the area. While affecting the theories, these adjustments have no dynamic influence over the problem area.

An example of competitive innovation is the search for the genetic construction of insulin that took place at Harvard University, the University of California at San Francisco, and the City of Hope National Medical Center. Stephen S. Hall, in his fascinating book, *Invisible Frontiers* (1987) documents this contest, as well as that of the competing pharmaceutical companies that became involved with financing and otherwise supporting the search for recombinant DNA insulin. As Hall states:

> It was not a seminal meeting, at least not in the usual sense of the word. No shattering new natural laws were proposed when a group

of biologists gathered in Indianapolis in the spring of 1976, no cherished long-standing dogmas were challenged. When this particular meeting began on May 24, the scientists did what they usually do at these affairs. They reported, one by one, on the latest results coming out of their labs, and each report provided a kind of pointillist dot of information; if you stood back and took it all in, you could begin to connect the dots, discern a pattern. And when the meeting concluded one day later, some of the scientists went home convinced that they could achieve something that had never been done before in the history of biology. With the eager and clumsy fingers of human curiosity, they planned to reach inside a living cell and tinker with its innermost mechanisms, manipulating the machinery of heredity in a way inconceivable even five years earlier.[23]

This was the beginning of the race for the recombinant DNA insulin, and it established genetic research as a field unto its own.

The point is that competitive innovation is not evaluated in the critical test on the areas of similarity among the competitors, but the areas of difference, and given the future projections of these areas of difference, the best among the competitors can be determined. If no choice is made, then critique can produce a review of the procedures and the claims of each competitor; this should clarify the situation and perhaps lead to a conclusion. If not, then another critical test can be set up, this time taking into account the results of the previous test and the critique generated thereafter.

Yet another consideration must be mentioned in the context of competing innovations: the time factor in the presentation of the innovations. These are not necessarily placed before their audiences for their evaluation at the same time, and while the first innovation usually makes a significant impact on the targeted audience, this is not an indication that other innovations will have a less significant impact on the same audience. Although the time factor is important, it is not necessarily the determining factor in the acceptance or rejection of a contribution.

The time factor is important because it permits other innovators to reconsider their contributions, to analyze the areas of similarity and difference, and to make appropriate adjustments in their innovations when necessary. Thus, while the innovation first presented generates excitement and perhaps attracts followers, it is not necessarily the one accepted for general use. Given the time discrepancy in the presentation, each innovation may be valid and have supporters, so that the critical test, when formulated and executed, may not determine which innovation is superior, even with the critique included after.

In this case, the competition will continue until either a critical test is established that will finally determine which contribution is superior, or the competition will continue until either one contribution or all of them become entropic and decline in utility, being eventually replaced by a different conceptual groundwork on which new contributions are formulated. The competitive process will continue in this new framework.

Consider the situation in which an innovation is formulated for which there are no competitors. This occurs when theories are formulated for a problem situation in which previous, perhaps competing theories, have been proven to be inadequate. An example is Newton's theory, in which the theories of Galileo and Kepler were unified into a single theory. Galileo, in his famous *Dialogues*, pointed out the difficulties with Aristotelian physics and noted the superiority of his own. Kepler simplified Copernicus's astronomy by eliminating the epicycles and placing the planets in elliptic orbits around the sun. The competition that these theories had was therefore minimal, only because they still had adherents. Newton reformulated Galileo's and Kepler's theories into a unified theory: those areas that became entropic due to the unification were either corrected or cast aside. For example, Galileo's relativity is limited to earth physics and does not include astronomy, whereas Kepler's theory of planetary motion does not account for the sweeping pattern of the sun, nor does it include the dynamics of relativity among the heavenly bodies. While both Galileo's and Kepler's theories relied on mathematics–a conceptual revolution brought about by the freedom thought of the Renaissance–neither theory accounted adequately for infinitesimal motion or for the changes of relative motion among differing celestial and earthbound bodies. Hence, Newton–and Leibniz–invented the calculus to account for these motions. A new physics was formed which endured until Max Planck, a staunch Newtonian, established the groundwork for the new theory of relativity.[24]

An example in which the competition is inadequate and thereby leads to a new theory is that of the state of economic thinking during the Great Depression. In light of Marx's theory, economics developed from its classical form, in which the theory of Adam Smith was expounded and developed, to the theory of the firm and to general economic business cycles. Of course, within these different approaches there were theoreticians who stated their own approaches, and competition existed among them as their arguments were debated and tested critically with models. These tests led to critiques and further tests, as well as to new theories that went through the same processes. As a body of knowledge, the various branches of economics have their own specific problem areas, such as monetary theory, the theory of plant location, urban economics, and international trade, just to name a few. But it was the Great Depression that brought the focus onto the issues that Adam Smith originally raised, those of the nature and causes of the wealth of nations.

The theories that were formulated to treat the Great Depression were mainly neoclassical in origin, and the assumption of full employment was either stated explicity or assumed to be a theoretical "given," with all attempts to deal with the crisis in terms of a fully employed labor force. Economics is both a theoretical and an empirical science, and empirically, the full employment assumption did not hold. In his work, *The General Theory of Employment*

Interest and Money, John Maynard Keynes pointed out both the empirical and theoretical difficulty of the full employment assumption. He formulated his own theory based on employment, consumption, and interest and money, thereby tackling the real issues of the Great Depression.[25]

Newton's theory, which reigned for some 250 years, was brought into question by Planck's findings and gave way to Einstein's theory–becoming a special case, operating only in a three-dimensional conceptualization–and to the micro realm of quantum physics. Keynes eventually had opposition from the monetarists. In contemporary economic conditions, his theory is no longer adequate for its depression economics do not deal effectively with the economic issues as they exist in contemporary societies.

In each example given earlier, the resulting theory became entropic and gave way to a theory that was effective. The consequences of Einsteinian relativity still have to be worked out. Its weaknesses are where uncertainty in is applications exist, such as black and white holes in space, and the nature of gravitation, which may be treated by adding another dimension to the Einsteinian space-time continuum. This will be discussed in Part III.

Having stated the conditions under which critique and the critical test can be used together, and under which critique in place of a valid critical test can be used to clarify the status of a contribution, it can be seen that the decisive ability of such a test is wanting. The difficulty is that we need to impose our outlooks and our wills on a world that exists independently of how we consider it. This is our limitation and is the basis for our search for the ultimate truth that proves elusive, moving away from us as we approach it. Philosophy on its own has been unable to reach this truth, and so science has branched off from philosophy. As Newton demonstrated, this separation is not permanent, and scientists have become philosophers when discussing the method of scientific inquiry.

In light of the dual role of scientists as philosophers, further comments are in order comparing critique and the critical test with Karl Popper's crucial experiment. In a footnote to Chapter X of his *Logic of Scientific Discovery*, Popper says of the crucial experiment:

> It should be noted that I mean by a crucial experiment one that is designed to refute a theory (if possible) and more especially one which is designed to bring about a decision between two competing theories by refuting (at least) one of them–without, of course, proving the other.[26]

In his *Conjectures and Refutations*, Popper stresses a point made in the *Logic of Scientific Discovery*, that Pierre Duhem's famous criticism of crucial experiments, made in *The Aim and Structure of Physical Theory*, "succeeds in showing that crucial experiments can never establish a theory. He fails to show that they cannot refute it."[27] The issue at hand is whether crucial experiments can indeed refute a theory on its own or in competition. Therefore, the status of the crucial experiment with respect to critique and the critical experiment has to be explored.

Considering Pasteur's confrontation with his esteemed colleagues, this was a situation in which an experiment was designed to bring about a decision between two competing and opposing theories. The theory of spontaneous generation was refuted by the results of the test as it was understood, but these results, de facto, did not meet with Popper's criterion of refutation. Pasteur's results were accepted by the distinguished board of the Academy, but in fact–as Tyndall was to point out–according to the results, neither Pasteur's nor his colleagues' experiments proved in any sense its own case, nor refuted the other.

If, in this case, a Popperian crucial experiment was conducted, then this had to be an either-or contest: either Pasteur's position was correct and his opponents' wrong, or his opponents' position was correct and Pasteur's wrong, but not both. Given the actual terms of the experiment, had Pasteur's experiment been conducted differently using the same broth as his opponents and having heated the broth for a sufficiently long time, the results would have been conclusive and final. With the retrospective view of history, we know they were not conclusive and final, even though the Academy ruled decisively in favor of Pasteur. In this case, the results of this experiment demonstrated that the Popperian crucial experiment did not hold.

But the results were consistent with the critical test, as critique–in this case Tyndall's–shed light on the experiment. It demonstrated that although the Academy accepted Pasteur's experiment, thereby rejecting that of his opponents, historically, the results were indeed insufficient to determine the outcome of the experiments. Critique is not part of the Popperian crucial experiment, but it is necessary in the processes of the critical test. Tyndall's critique of the experiment shed the necessary light on the situation to decide that, given the conditions and terms of the experiment, Popper's crucial experiment cannot hold.

When theories compete, usually the either-or criterion does not exist. Each theory in its own right has utility with respect to the problem area; otherwise it would not be in competition. The measuring of utility then is the sole objective basis for determining acceptance or rejection. In this situation, the acceptance of a theory does not necessarily mean the absolute rejection of all other competitors. It merely means that the accepted theory, at the time of acceptance, has a higher utility rating and that the other theories can have their utilities increased to the point of being equal or superior to the accepted theory, relegating the accepted theory to the status of competitor once again. In this situation, given the dynamics of competing theories within their common problem areas, the processes of correcting entropy and, through initiation, increasing utility will continue until the theories or their common problem areas are changed radically from their original positions and become too entropic to salvage.

This differs from the competition in which the areas of difference among the theories are decisive, with the theories of the highest utility being accepted and all others cast aside. This is an either-or type of competition, but still the crucial experiment is insufficient. There is no room for critique in the concept of the crucial experiment, no opportunity for correction and for reentering the competition. The critical test allows for critique, with perhaps the findings of the type that Tyndall came across. The crucial experiment is decisive and absolute in its judgment, leaving no possibility to correct ambiguities that may have entered the experiment. The critical test allows for such considerations through critique.

Because of the difficulty of proving or refuting a theory of high utility for problem areas because neither proofs nor refutations are absolute, the critical test with its accompanying critique determines the acceptance or rejection of a theory, be it in competition or strictly innovative.

The Popperian crucial experiment is too extreme, rendering it unable to deal effectively with the complexities of experimental situations. As science has become technically oriented and many-faceted, it has become impossible to establish an experiment that provides conditions for absolute theoretical refutability and that when applied can be refuted experimentally. Theories of high utility do not yield to this type of condition, and in science, it is utility or the lack of it that is important. Aristotelian physics is not used in physical computations because as a theory of physics it has no practical applications and its utility has ceased to be. It is significant only in the context of the history of ideas and as the basis of an opponent in Galileo's dialogue establishing his earth physics. Aristotle's physical theory was not refutable in the Popperian sense of the crucial experiment; it was just discarded. Neither Copernicus's nor Kepler's theories have been overthrown by crucial experimental refutation. Instead, they have been discarded because of their extremely low utilities and their incorporation and adaptation into Newtonian theory.

Popper is correct when he maintains that "the striving for knowledge and the search for truth are still the strongest motives for scientific discovery."[28] His approach to scientific discovery, however, is limiting in this search, as knowledge is theory-bound. Information moves among theories, and where relevant, the information is altered to conform to the theories' utility requirements. In this manner, theories are altered and knowledge is changed. Because sciences are practiced by using theories, the ultimate goal of science, that of finding permanent and enduring truth, may remain elusive, always beyond our intellectual and technological reach. But we have knowledge in our theories, and although we understand that the utility of this knowledge will eventually decline, it will be replaced by other knowledge that is of greater utility, subjected to the same probability and utility requirements to which all theories are subjected. Our theories stand or fall–maintain their utility or decline into entropy–according to the relevance of their information and the status of the problem areas for which they are formulated. In the search for ultimate truth and wisdom, scientists are aware that their theories are not permanent and enduring, but are changing due to entropy and the initiative changes made to restore utility. Nevertheless, the pursuit of this elusive truth and wisdom remains the ultimate objectives of scientific research. Critique and the critical test provide the manner by which theories and initiative contributions are evaluated.

Crucial experiments were perhaps valid in the earlier stages of scientific development in which strict proofs and refutations were considered important. But these were either-or situations that were limited in their experimental scope, and they lacked the sophistication of such experiments as Pasteur's and those of his esteemed opponents. Hans Christian Oersted's experiment, in which electric current passing through a wire brought about the deflection of the needle of a compass, can meet the requirements of a crucial experiment. This experiment led to the development of electromagnetism, and it is repeatable, with the same results occurring. In this type of experiment, critique has no role, and the knowledge contributed to science because of its development has been tremendous. But even in its consequences the critical test has proven superior to the crucial experiment in the sense that Maxwell's equations have been replaced by Einstein's field theory in the macro realm of physics, which is valid within transformational fields. Einstein's theory is valid for the duration of its utility.[29] With respect to crucial experiments between two competing theories, Popper states that between these theories for which the crucial experiment is to decide, we must take each of the two theories together with the background knowledge involved with these theories. Then we must decide on the systems of background knowledge that differ concerning the theories under investigation. Popper maintains that

> we do not assert the refutation of a theory as such, but of the theory *together* with that background knowledge; parts of which, if other crucial experiments can be designed, may indeed one day be rejected as responsible for the failure.[30]

With this emphasis on the refutation of a theory together with its background knowledge, the Popperian crucial experiment cannot fare too well in competitions among theories in the real world of scientific inquiry and development, such as in the contest between Pasteur and his esteemed opponents. According to the crucial experiment, Pasteur's refutation of his opponents' theory would thus result in the casting aside of the background knowledge of temperatures and the boiling point of hay seeds, together with the duration of the boiling period for killing the microbes. Having decided the issue irrevocably, and as Tyndall demonstrated, erroneously, the consequence was not only the victory of a faulty argument, but also perhaps in the permanent inhibition of knowledge concerning microbes and the development of life. While this may have been reversed in the future, the conclusiveness of this erroneous position would have diverted research from the problem.

Although the critical test is decisive, it is also more reasonable. It is more liberal and hence not so condemning, allowing for information to be incorporated according to its probability and utility. Thus, Tyndall's findings are acceptable according to the critical test, and his analysis led to the revival of knowledge about spontaneous generation and the continuity of life in a theoretical context of far greater utility than Pasteur's experimental findings could yield. The either-or criterion of the crucial experiment could not permit Tyndall's reconstruction, but this is legitimate for the critical test.

The ultimate goal of science is to find permanent and enduring truth. But science, *scientia*, is knowledge, and so it is not enduring and permanent, but theory-bound and ultimately incorrect, to be replaced by knowledge in other theories. Hence, the truth and wisdom that are the goals of scientific and philosophical search and inquiry *are* static, as they must be if they are to be permanent and enduring. Knowledge is not static, and as it is theory-bound, it often contains many nuances, indeed corresponding to the nuances of its theory's languages. It is therefore not usually subject to the either-or criterion of the crucial experiment. The very dynamics of knowledge, as theory-bound, changing, and eventually entropic, renders it qualitatively different from the wisdom and truth, the achievements of which are the ultimate goals of philosophical and scientific pursuit. But while philosophers and scientists seek to achieve these goals, they work with theories that are dynamic and hence subject to the conditions of utility and entropy. Until these ultimate goals are achieved, the philosophical and scientific knowledge that provides the tools with which the practitioners of these disciplines work will remain subject to the dynamics of entropy and utility. Strict imitators will continue working out the dynamics of theories, and explorative imitators will continue revealing problems to be resolved by initiators. Innovators will bring their theories to be critically tested by their public, and the processes of critique and the critical test will be employed to evaluate the initiative and innovative contributions.

Throughout the development of philosophy and science, great and dominaing theories have become entropic over time, declining and being replaced by theories of higher utility. In this way, knowledge has developed and will continue to do so until the enduring and permanent wisdom and truth are found. Theories have been developed to account for phenomena, while other theories have been formulated to generate phenomena. Chaos theory has been developed for both purposes. It explains phenomena with the conceptual tools of nonlinear reasoning, and it generates phenomena–such as computer models–using equilibrium dynamics. The social, physical, and economic situations that chaos theoreticians seek to explain using their nonlinear and equilibrium concepts do not in fact behave according to chaos theory. They behave according to crisis theory, as is explained in Part III of this work.

NOTES

1. Frederick L. Will, "Reason, Social Practice, and Scientific Realism," in *Hermenutics and Praxis*, ed. Robert Hollinger (Notre Dame, Ind.: University of Notre Dame Press, 1985), p. 124.

2. For example, from the statement "It is raining now and not raining now" can be

added the statement "therefore, the sky is green." This is nonsensical but logically valid. Consistency is lacking, and for a scientific theory, while such nonsense statements would not exist, the existence of inconsistent statements can yield unwanted, and indeed unexpected, results, until the theory is damaged or until the problem area no longer responds.

3. See, for example, Morris Kline, *Mathematics* (New York: Oxford University Press, 1982), for the development and uncertainty in modern mathematics.

4. See, for example, Gary Zukov, *The Dancing Wu Li Masters* (New York: Morrow Quill, 1979).

5. For example, mass-behavior patterns can be predicted with an accepted degree of accuracy, but the prediction of the behavior of a specific individual selected at random in the masses cannot be carried out with any degree of expected accuracy, just as positions of particles can be determined, but the position and velocity of a single particle cannot.

6. An outstanding historical example is Archemedes. His brilliance would not allow him to work with standard procedures for very long, and he always searched for and found new methods for working out new approaches to solve difficult and often seemingly unsolvable problems. For a discussion on original thinking and creativity, see David Z. Rich, *The Dynamics of Knowledge* (Westport, Conn.: Greenwood Press, 1988).

7. Gerald Feinberg, *Solid Clues* (New York: Touchstone Books, 1985), from the Introduction, p. 22.

8. See Arthur S. Eddington, *The Mathematical Theory of Relativity*, 2nd ed. (Cambridge: Cambridge University Press, 1914).

9. The Kabbala has a great deal to say about the seven days of creation and the creation of earlier worlds. For interesting insights on this, see Arieh Kaplan, *The Light Beyond* (Brooklyn N.Y.: Maznaim Publishers, 1981).

10. See Søren Kierkegaard, *The Sickness Unto Death*, trans. Walter Lowrie (New York: Doubleday and Co., 1954).

11. See Rollo May's essay, "Contributions to Existential Philosophy," in *Existence*, ed. Rollo May, with Ernst Angel and Henri F. Ellenberger, contributing eds. (New York: Simon and Schuster/Clarion Books, 1960), pp. 37-91. See also Ludwig Binswanger's essay in the same book, "The Existential Analysis School of Thought," pp. 191-213.

12. Particles can still be considered as vortices of energy moving through a "neoether," which may be a gravitational field, generating a wavelike effect in the atomic structure.

13. One of the important breakthroughs in computation is the Turing machine. See Martin Davis's essay, "What is Computation?" in *Mathematics Today*, ed. Lyn Arthur Steen (New York: Vintage Books, 1980), pp. 241-267; see also George Boole, *Laws of Thought* (New York: Dover Books, 1961).

14. See Strobe Talbott, *Deadly Gambits* (New York: Vintage Books, 1985).

15. The Impressionist, Expressionist, and Surrealist schools that developed during the Industrial Revolution were qualitatively different from the artistic interpretations of the schools developed during the Renaissance. See Bernard Berinson, *Aesthetics and History* (New York: Doubleday Anchor Books, 1953), especially Chapter V, "Art History Specifically," and Conclusion, pp. 231-272.

16. Concerning Social Darwinism, Thomas Sowell wrote:

Lazy amorality might be the "fittest" quality to survive a sufficiently extreme welfare state, for example, or ruthless ambition in a sufficiently *laissez–faire* economy without adequate law enforcement. Darwin himself did not make the political applications known as "Social Darwinism." It was Herbert Spencer in England and William Graham Sumner in America, and countless disciples in both countries who turned the Darwinian principle of biological change into a political principle satisfying the status quo.

Quoted from Thomas Sowell, *Knowledge and Decisions* (New York: Basic Books, 1980), p. 345.

17. See Alan Guth and Paul Steinhardt, "The Inflationary Universe," *Scientific American*, May 1984, pp. 116-120.

18. For a discussion on the Michelson-Morely experiment, see Robert K. Adair, The *Grand Design* (New York: Oxford University Press, 1989), pp. 78-80; and J. T. Frasier, *Time, the Familiar Stranger* (Redmond, Wash.: Tempus Books, 1978), pp. 229-230.

19. A. C. Pigou, *Economics of Welfare* (London: Macmillan, 1920), and J. M. Keynes, *The General Theory of Employment Interest and Money* (London: Macmillan, 1947). Keynes was referring to the fourth edition of Pigou's book, which appeared in 1932, during the Great Depression.

20. See Karl Marx, *Capital* (Moscow: Foreign Languages Publishing House, 1961).

21. See R. A. Fisher, *The Genetic Theory of Natural Selection* (New York: Oxford University Press, 1930). Fisher's quote is from Richard Dawkins, *The Blind Watchmaker* (New York: W. W. Norton, 1987), p. 199. No page number is listed for Fisher's quote.

22. For a further discussion on Fisher's contribution, see Richard Dawkins, *The Blind Watchmaker*, p. 200.

23. Stephen S. Hall, *Invisible Frontiers* (Redmond, Wash.: Tempus Books, 1987), p. 3. This is a fascinating book on the development of biotechnology and genetically engineered insulin.

24. Newton formulated his calculus to explain physical concepts, while Leibniz's formulation was a strictly mathematical concept. Since both theories were formulated at the same time, but independently, a feud arose over priority.

25. See John Maynard Keynes, *The General Theory of Employment Interest and Money*, and for a critique of Keynes's theory, see David Z. Rich, *The Economic Theory of Growth and Development* (Westport, Conn.: Praeger Publishers, 1994), pp. 137-143, and 160-169.

26. Karl R. Popper, *The Logic of Scientific Discovery* (London: Hutchinson, 1962), p. 277, n. 2.

27. Karl R. Popper, "Three Views Concerning Human Knowledge," *in Conjectures and Refutations* (London: Routledge and Kegan Paul, 1963), p. 112 n. 2; italics in the original.

28. The full sentence reads: "Although it can neither attain truth nor probability, the striving for knowledge and the search for truth are still the strongest motives for scientific discovery" (*The Logic of Scientific Discovery*, p. 278).

29. Concerning James Clerk Maxwell's equations, Edna E. Kramer states that since these famous principles are expressed as a set of partial differential equations, instead of recording the abstract mathematical form as Maxwell stated them, one can give their physical interpretations as follows:

(1) The electric flux across a closed surface is zero.

(2) The magnetic flux across a closed surface is zero.

(3) A variable field generates an electric field (Faraday's law of induction).

(4) A variable field generates a magnetic field [Maxwell's hypothesis formulated on the grounds of symmetry with (3)].

Kramer states further that Einstein's field equations to which his space-time continuum was to conform control the possible distributions and changes in what is to be called the "gravitational field" and were the gravitational analogue to Maxwell's equations. See Edna E. Kramer, *The Nature and Growth of Modern Mathematics* (Princeton, N.J.: Princeton University Press, 1982), pp. 244-246; quote from p. 244. Although these equations are analogous to Einstein's equations, they are Newtonian in orientation, and as Newton's theory is a special case of Einstein's, so Maxwell's equations are included in the Newtonian special case.

30. Karl R. Popper, "Three Views Concerning Human Knowledge," p. 112.

PART III

CRISIS THEORY AND ITS APPLICATIONS

CHAPTER 9

Introductory Comments

But when we have to include an endless number of deductions in one formula, when we are face to face with the infinite, the principle of contradiction falls down just as experience proves itself to be insufficient. This rule, then which is unattainable either by experience or by analytical proof is an exemplar of a synthetic judgment a priori. Why does the judgment force itself upon us with irresistible evidence? Because it asserts nothing about the nature of things but only about an original faculty of the mind. For the mind recognizes its capacity to repeat a certain act continually, once it has become convinced of the possibility of such an act. But the mind does have an immediate intuition of this possibility; experience only affords the opportunity to employ it and so to become conscious of it.

Henri Poincaré,
"On the Nature of Mathematical Reasoning"[1]

For theoretical constructs in which logic does not prevent the possibility of an infinite number of deductions, the possibility of an infinite number of statements does indeed exist, with the breakdown of the logic because the law of contradiction enters the process. With crisis theory, the first part of Poincaré's statement is ruled out as the law of contradiction is irrelevant because the number of deductions is confined within the theory. Since the strict relationship between a theory and its problem area prevents the infiltration of the infinite, only by becoming entropic can the theory decline, and only by reestablishing utility can the theory be restored, albeit in somewhat different form. Although this part of Poincaré's statement can be removed as a worry for imitators and innovators of theories, the second part of his statement, with modification, remains a challenge to scientists and philosophers alike.

The modification is that it is not the rule that the principle of contradiction fails, for out confrontation with the infinite is no longer a problem because of the strict definitive and delineating relationship between a theory and its problem area. The difficulty is that we are bound by the theory as if it really does relate to reality and is not part of our mental construction, although we understand that theory is knowledge-oriented and is not based on truth or wisdom. While this is skepticism, it is positive and necessary for both theoretical construction and imitation, because it allows us to recognize and appreciate the barrier that exists between us with our fallible knowledge—one that we seek to break down—and the universe as it exists and is manifested in enduring and permanent wisdom and truth. Given this skepticism, we still assert our right to work repeatedly with a theory as strict imitators, to challenge theoretical statements as explorative imitators, and to be bold enough to develop new theories as innovators, employing the rule of contradiction as we proceed.

In the preface of their book, *The Collapse of Chaos* 1995, Jack Cohen and Ian Stewart discuss a paradox. The more we learn about the universe, they state, "the more complicated it appears to be, but we have discovered that beneath the complexities lie deep simplicities, laws of nature."[2] Their position is that simplicity in nature is generated from chaos and complexity—a view not held by the present writer. If nature—and indeed any scientific discipline—appears to have simple laws, it is only because of our imposing theories on specific problem areas, thereby placing them within our grasp and providing us with the conceptual tools to work with them. These laws of the nature of our disciplines therefore appear simple, for we have isolated the problem areas, removing them initially from influences we consider unnecessary and irrelevant to the issues being treated. But this is our imposition, and in terms of the natural or social disciplines, our impositions may be invalid—as with previous impositions such as the ether-drag or the Ptolemaic-cum-Copernican theory of astronomy.

Hence, the argument presented here is that our "laws of nature," or whatever our discipline may be, are theory-oriented and are our own constructs for dealing with our specific problem areas. The difficulty here is that we relate to our problem areas, and the more we work with them, the more our behavior tends to become instinctive, indeed somewhat reflexive. This, however, is imitative, for we act this way as strict imitators.

Consider our understanding of biology. In our search for biological laws regulating nature, we have unraveled the genetic code to a large extent, revealing influences that we have inherited for generating our appearances, and we are searching further into the genetic "bag" to find clues to our personalities. Basing all of nature on genetics alone, even though this is a promising field of inquiry, is, however, insufficient. Although genetics is important, so is psychology, and this is the combination of our genetic makeup and our contact with the world as it is and its influences on us. It can be argued that because each of us has a specific genetic composition, each of us is affected differently and reacts differently in our encounter with the world. This shows, however, that neither psychology nor genetics alone is sufficient for understanding human behavior. A combined discipline–call it "psychogenetics"–will, when worked upon, yield difficulties through explorative imitation that will generate new contributions, conflicting innovative theories, and shifts in specific problem areas within the general psychogenetic field. This is the way of the development of knowledge. It is as consistent as the human desire for knowledge, and it is as complex as the very people who are involved in the pursuit of wisdom and truth.

With regard to Cohen and Stewart's work, they combine chaos theory and complexity to derive simplicity, but they maintain that the key to understanding this lies in the interaction of featured with different spaces for the possible.[3] My own approach differs in the sense that while there is interaction of featured, these featured are the theoretical statements as they relate to the designated problem area. When the theory is constructed, no room exists for possible spaces, because no such spaces can be realized owing to the isomorphic relationships among the theoretical statements and the problem area. Where change does come about, it is either within the theory, or the problem area, and sometimes both. There are no different spaces of the possible for crisis theory because of the relationship between the theory and its problem area. Thus, any changes that develop within this relationship are due either to entropy, which can be corrected by restructuring the affected statements, or to area shifts, which can be corrected by corresponding theory shifts.

The complexity that does exist in crisis theory is due to the theoretical languages, and this complexity vanishes with the understanding of these languages. It is the complexity of learning anew, to acquire the use of the theory and its terminology. Once this is accomplished and the necessary skills for working with the theory are acquired, the complexity vanishes. This corresponds to the simplicity of the laws of nature discussed by Cohen and Stewart. These laws are simple because they are understood, and they are laws only within their theoretical context. While the theory endures, so will its laws; when the theory fails, these laws may be relegated to a different status, as is the situation with Newton's three laws of motion within the broader context of Einsteinian relativity.

With regard to the role of chaos theory in the simplicity of the laws of nature, this simplicity exists with respect to equilibrium. This is a throwback to a cyclical approach of the world and its laws, for just as the seasons are cyclical and just as time is cyclical, so are the other natural processes. We are born, live, and die, yet the dynamics of life continue. This is also cyclical in the dynamics of life, and even in the field of economics and commerce there are cycles. These and all other cycles are based–in the case of economics, erroneously–on the dynamics of bringing the cycle into equilibrium.[4]

Arguments against chaos theory were presented in the first part of this work, and although equilibrium and chaos theory are rejected here (and with them catastrophe theory), equilibrium cannot be dismissed entirely in the dynamic procsses of the universe. Time is indeed cyclical, and so are the seasons; and if life and death are to be considered cyclical, then so be it. However, the cyclical aspects of these enduring conditions tell nothing about them. There may be warm winters and stormy summers, short springs and lengthy autumns, so that these seasons are "unseasonal." Even though time is cyclical, there is time that is fulfilled and time that can be better used. The point is that the cyclical aspects of our world shed only the most limited amount of wisdom and truth, even though they are theory-bound within the context of the Newtonian-cum-Einsteinian conception of planetary motion with its concept of time.

Crisis theory is not cyclical, and it pertains only to theories and their specific problem areas. Although chaos theory is closed in the sense that it accounts only for the dynamics necessary for the system (and these dynamics may be internal or external, but they must be applicable as part of the system), crisis theory depends on the internal dynamics of the theory in terms of the workings of its statements, as well as external dynamics as they affect the theory or its problem area. Chaos has its dynamics built-in; crisis theory is so structured to account for its internal theory dynamics through use and for whatever external dynamics that might come into play. Chaos theory has its external dynamics operating as part of the system; crisis theory responds to external dynamics as entropy entering the system, and it is corrected by altering the affected statements through initiation. Chaos theory is closed; crisis theory is open. Chaos theory functions entirely on its built-in conditions; crisis theory functions with respect to its internal conditions and is responsive to external conditions to the point that these conditions can be absorbed into the theory without affecting its utility.

The sharp alterations of catastrophe theory that are so much a part of chaos theory are accounted for in crisis theory as external influences and are treated accordingly, with respect to initiation. Because there are no open spaces in crisis theory, and because the dynamics of catastrophe theory are rejected and replaced by the dynamics of explorative imitation and initiation, crisis theory is far more effective in dealing with issues than is chaos theory.

The set of operational and area statements within crisis theories make them more realistic than chaos theories. For crisis theories, the mapping of operational statements onto area statements allows each statement to be analyzed separately, which is important when entropy sets in and one or more statements affected are undetected. For example, in a given theory, $C^*_t \sum_1^n (o_d a)_t$, several statements have been influenced by terminologies from other theories. Finding these statements is the task of explorative imitation, because strict imitators may not be aware of the defective statements, considering them to be functioning according to the theory's probability and utility requirements. This is conducted by partially differentiating each statement, separating it from the others to analyze its specific dynamics as an independent statement, as well as one within the context of the theory. This takes the form of

$$\partial C^* t / \partial \Sigma (o_d a) 1, 2, \ldots n_t.$$

Or the case may be that defective statements are indeed known, as they are obvious as such within the theoretical context, but most imitators, accept them because they consider their theory to be the most effective way of working with the problem area and are unwilling to give serious consideration to any alternative approaches. Such is the situation with some schools of thought, whose proponents recognize deficiencies in their innovator's contributions, but accept the innovations as they are, until other contributions of much higher utility are presented, or until initiators provide solutions that correct the deficiencies without lowering the innovation's utility as it was when first accepted, and perhaps increase it. In either case, changes will be attempted, and in light of the competition among the initiators, those of the highest utility will most likely be incorporated, given the critical tests and critique that will ensue. Chaos theory does not allow for these dynamics, as the dynamics of each chaos system are built in and are not subject to personal intervention in the sense of explorative imitation, initiation, or innovation.

Since partial differentiation is used to isolate a statement or groups of statements, the sudden and often radical changes experienced in catastrophe theory can be accounted for in crisis theory. Statements become entropic. Indeed, theories become entropic, often fairly swiftly, as with Newtonian theory after Planck's findings.

The situation with catastrophe theory is that it is either-or in the sense that either one position is achieved, or another one will be, but not both, thereby relying on the principle of contradiction. In its uses in catastrophe theory, the principle of contradiction does not allow for the nuances that theories of science require. The problem areas of the sciences are many-faceted, with nuances that cannot be accounted for with the strict catastrophe either-or, such as matter and antimatter, and an ambidextrous universe in general.

The principle of contradiction is necessary in the processes of logical reasoning, for it prevents contradictions and ambiguities from entering into the reasoning processes. Hence, it is necessary in crisis theory. But its use in crisis theory differs from that in catastrophe theory, because in the either-or situation of catastrophe theory no allowances are made for repair. Statements in crisis theory that are rendered entropic because of the infiltration of other languages do indeed portray properties similar to catastrophe theory, in the sense that either they fit into the theory and function as they are required to, or they are inappropriate and must be removed or corrected. For crisis theory, each statement is constructed on the basis of its probability assessment and its utility within the general context of the theory as it relates to its problem area. Hence, the either-or situation similar to catastrophe theory enters in the sense that either the statement performs according to the theory's probability and utility criteria, or it is defective. However, because the statement did have importance prior to its entropic condition, the dynamics of initiation are employed to restore the statement, perhaps strengthening it as a result of competitive initiation. Of course, if it is demonstrated that the entropy is too extensive and restructuring cannot be carried out, then initiation ceases and the defective statement is removed, perhaps being replaced by a new statement of high utility.

This is not such an easy process because the defective statement has status as an integral part of the theory. As initiators work to restructure the statement, there is the process of the critical test, and the critique that follows, to determine which, if any, of the contributions are viable within themselves and are of utility with respect to the theory. If, after this entire procedure, it is decided that none of contributions has sufficient theory-oriented utility, only then will the statement be removed. But since there is no practical time limit on initiation and since the theory remains dynamic, then other statements may be brought into focus as being entropic. The process will continue until the theory itself approaches entropy and declines to the point that it is no longer used, but perhaps retains its utility only in a historical context. This can be due to competitive innovation bringing the theory down, or perhaps to a shift or decline in the problem area to the extent that neither the area nor the theories working with it are functionally viable.

The dynamics of crisis theory differ, therefore, from those of chaos and catastrophe theory. Chaos theory is closed in its dynamics, unreceptive to influences that are not built into its system, and catastrophe theory is oriented to strict either-or conditions that allow no flexibility for incorporating changes within the theory. Crisis theory considers the influences from other theories, including the either-or situations, and the dynamics of these influences that the imitators believe to be viable, after the necessary adjustments are made allowing these influences to be incorporated into the theory without lowering its utility.

One more point needs to be clarified before we explore the dynamics of crisis theory, and this pertains to nonlinear analysis. Interpreting the dynamics of a theory in terms of nonlinear analysis and strange attractors is here considered erroneous. This judgment is based on the methodological merging of two different concepts of dynamics: one is the dynamics of the theory itself, and the other is the dynamics of its application. This means that both the theory's internal dynamics and those of the problem area have to be considered, given the isomorphic relationship between each of the theory's statements and their corresponding parts in the area. Hence, the significance of the "t" in the C^*_t formula, for the factor of time is necessary when discussing and working with these relationships. Reverting back to a central–strange attractor–point in tracing the development of a dynamic process as with chaos theory only demonstrates that the dynamics being considered are not the multidimensional time-oriented dynamics of crisis theory. For while chaos theory allows for the plotting of dynamic paths over time, it plots these paths in a one-dimensional cyclical motion, in which time is considered in terms of movement and direction, but not in terms of content. Both time and content are important in crisis theory.

For crisis theory, nonlinear analysis holds; it is oriented not to a strange attractor, but to conditions that *resemble* attractor positions, which in fact are circumstances that may bear some similarity to events that have occured in the past. Although we observe cycles in the processes of nature, we seek out cycles in history, economics, political dynamics, and in the physical sciences. We look for the regularity of events, their recurrences, in a world in which regularity provides us with consistency but in content tells us nothing. In our search for enduring and permanent truth, we seek natural laws on which we can be certain and can build. But the laws of chaos and catastrophe theories are of little assistance in our search. Only when we relate theories to their problem areas in a crisis theory context does theory take on meaning, allowing us to work with our problem areas and to exploit their dynamics.

Cyclical motions, such as they may be, and strange attractors that generate such motions are not relevant for crisis theory. For crisis theory, nonlinear analysis does not bring the theory back to a starting position, or to equilibrium, with respect to its problem area. Rather, it brings the theory into a new position with respect to its internal dynamics and its problem area. This position may be cyclical or it may be continuous, depending on the problem being considered.

For economics, the patterns are cyclical but different from the long-term cyclical approaches. For political dynamics, the patterns are not cyclical but are broken and yet still continuous in the long run. For sociopolitical dynamics, patterns may or may not be cyclical, depending on each situation. For the biological sciences, the cyclical patterns are those of the species' life cycles. It is not these cycles that are important, but how these lives are lived that provides meaning to all levels of life forms. Our planets move in cyclical patterns, but our understanding of our solar system is theoretical, and the conditions for testing our theories are extremely difficult.

In the development of our theories, we need a schematic with which to work. Such a schematic should allow us to relate specific theories to specific problem areas without the "baggage" of equilibrium-oriented chaos theory concepts, and without the either-or logic of catastrophe theory in our world, which is far too complicated to behave according to the logic of either-or. The logical concepts that the world in all its complexities does relate to are those of crisis theory, with its linguistic nuances, imitation, initiation, innovation, and the competition of contributions.

The emphasis is not, therefore, to be placed on strict logic or on the necessity of equilibrium. The emphasis is to be placed on the adaptation of languages to theories for which probability and utility are the concerns, in a context of dynamic disequilibrium. This is shown in the chapters that follow.

NOTES

1. Henri Poincaré, "On the Nature of Mathematical Reasoning," *The Review of Metaphysics and Morals* (Paris: Hachette et Cie, 1984), pp. 371-372. Quoted here from Ernst Cassirer, *The Problem of Knowledge*, trans. William H. Woglom and Charles W. Hendel (New Haven, Conn.: Yale University Press, 1974), p. 79.

2. Jack Cohen and Ian Stewart, *The Collapse of Chaos* (New York: Penguin Books, 1995), p. 1.

3. This is discussed in their work *The Collapse of Chaos*; see, for example, p. 442.

4. For a critique of equilibrium and a discussion on disequilibrium in economics, see David Z. Rich, *The Economic Theory of Growth and Development* (Westport, Conn.: Praeger Publishers, 1995), Chapters 7 and 8, pp. 135-311.

CHAPTER 10

Crisis Theory and Long-Run Business Cycles

On controversial scientific questions for which there is a scarcity of empirical data, scientific opinion sometimes shifts back and forth like changing women's clothes. The skirt is low in one decade, high in the next, and then back down it goes again.

Martin Gardner,
The New Ambidextrous Universe[1]

GENERAL COMMENTS

In science, fads are sometimes effective in motivating research, even to the extent that the fads become the focus of serious scientific effort. Determining which subject matter–serious or otherwise–had its origins as a fad depends on the interest and scholarship generated after the initial endeavor.

Economics is not subject to fads as such. As a serious discipline, it has various branches for research and theorization. However, together with subjects such as welfare economics, business cycles, price theory, the theory of plant location, and urban and international economics, another aspect, long-term business cycle theory, is being developed. This theory is meant to show how the long rhythms of economic activity affect current economic positions, to determine long wave patterns in rising and declining prices, to asses whether building cycles, transportation cycles, or any other long-term cycles exist, and, if so, how current economic situations can best be treated with respect to these cycles.

In keeping with Martin Gardner's sentiment, the question is, can the search for long-run business cycles be considered a fad? This search does not come and go as do the styles in women's clothes. Indeed, it has been a concern–albeit a minor one–among economists since 1847, when Dr. Hyde Clark published a paper in the *British Railway Journal* describing a fifty-four-year long wave from

1793 to 1847 which included five apparent cycles, each ten to eleven years in length. Brian J. L. Berry mentions that the idea was reinstated in 1901 in a pamphlet written by "Parvus" (Alexander I. Helphand) and soon after by two Dutch socialists, J. van Gelderen and S. De Wolff. Van Gelderen, writing under a pseudonym "J. Fedder," discussed a cycle including a quarter-century of slow growth, followed by a "new springtime," a surge of new growth. De Wolff focused on the causes of depressions, attributing their regularity to the effective depreciation rate of long-living fixed capital, or capital infrastructure.[2]

Although not the first long-run cycle theorist, Nikolai D. Kondratieff was one of the most influential of the early contributors. The question associated with his work is as follows. Given annual growth rates and fluctuations within these rates, can there be long-run accelerations and decelerations, covering at least fifty years, of the underlying growth rates of prices around which the annual movements oscillate? One way to answer this question is to smooth out the year-to-year oscillations by computing the averages of standardized products, as W. W. Rostow suggested in his book, *The World Economy*. However, as E. E. Slutsky pointed out in a 1937 article, the averages of moving prices for standardized products can be compared to moving averages applied to random numbers, generating cyclical fluctuations where none existed before.[3]

Long-run cycle theory has not entered the mainstream of economic theory, for two reasons. One reason is the gathering and interpreting of statistical material, assigning them the correct weights with respect to their times and to our own. Each economic period has its own weighting, such as refrigerators in the 1920s and in the 1990s, with the emphasis on the types of refrigerators and their cooling systems. Certainly, the weights of these commodities during these different time periods show the difficulty associated with this long-run cycle approach. Although some goods and services that exist now existed then, they were different, and their weights in the consumption of goods and services relative to liquid income have changed. With the technological advancements in communications technology, much of liquid income is directed to the purchase of communications equipment, where in the previous historical era and the social times up to our present, no such consumption existed. We could, of course, weigh only those goods and services common to the time periods being considered, but this would ignore the dynamics of the economic periods, their markets, their production and consumption patterns, and the functions of money and liquidity in each period. The weighting problem is difficult, and perhaps unresolvable.

The second reason resembles Slutsky's argument. Flattening out the year-to-year oscillations by computing the averages of standard products is also not without its difficulties. Slutsky's argument, correct as it is, is not complete because not only are cycles generated in this method, showing the price fluctuations of these standardized products over time, but also this approach fails to show the reasons for these fluctuations, brought about by the products unique to each period, as well as the value of money in terms of inflation and aggregate liquidity. No knowledge is gained from this approach, and although long-run cycles for these standardized goods and services may be shown to exist, the explanations for these cycles will be lacking.

The comparisons of standardized products over different time periods can never be accurate because the products being compared have changed over time. Standardized products such as automobiles, refrigerators, and other durables such as washing machines and dryers, have changed over time. Comparisons among them in the contxest of standardized products thus becomes inaccurate because, while these products remain similar in their very basic functions–hence the standardization–they are extremely different in the ways they perform these functions. Automobiles manufactured in the 1950s or 1960s did not have computer technology or the safety features that are standard equipment on automobiles manufactured in our social time. Hence, although durable goods maintain their classifications over time, they are, in fact, unique products in their functioning and in the conveniences they provide.

BUSINESS CYCLES AND METHODOLOGICAL APPROACHES

For those who are not trained in economics, this field of social inquiry and policy making is baffling. Economics deals with the generation of wealth and the allocation of scarce resources among competing factors. The purpose of this allocation is to present a strong industrial base that provides employment and promotes the general well-being of the populace. However, in light of the business cycle's fluctuations, during which wealth is seemingly generated as the cycle moves upward to prosperity and taken away as the cycle declines into recession, to the untrained person economics may appear to be a discipline in which discussions held among its practitioners have no influence on conditions as they are, so that the process of business cycle activity continues regardless of what the professional economists say or do. For example, government leaders formulate proposals for generating growth, yet business cycles come and go as if they were immune to these proposals. Because of this, Kondratieff and other economists have sought to understand long-wave cyclical dynamics for exploring economic phenomena. One difficulty is that economists, even when employing advanced economic models, are often thrown off guard by the intensities and influence of the cycles. A speech by a leader of a big corporation, or the sudden illness of a national leader while visiting an economically competing foreign country, can send shock waves through the economy, thereby influencing activity in ways previously not considered. The activities and policies of a foreign country can influence the home economy's markets in ways that economists can understand only after they have taken effect. The extent of their secondary influences is often evaluated only after they have made their impact on the economy.

Given these built-in uncertainties, the layperson may be puzzled that economists consider their discipline to be a science. The layperson may open an academic text on economics and find that its advanced mathematics seems to endow economics with a semblance of being scientific. But then the person reads about poverty, unemployment, the struggling emerging and developing countries, the breaking apart of a once-mighty empire, a severe foreign trade deficit by the world's leading economic power, and the homeless walking the streets of the world's great cities–the daily material in the newspapers and magazine. These events raise questions about the validity of economics as a scientific discipline.

The layperson should understand the economist's position, however, for economics is not unlike the study of medicine, a discipline in which a degree of uncertainty exists in both diagnosis and prognosis. In medicine a patient's well-being often depends on the physician's abilities, sensitivity, and understanding in prescribing geared to that patient's particular needs. A person who is ill may affect other people nearby, including loved ones, but this does not determine the well-being of the entire society. Nevertheless, economic activity, with its uncertainty, is a general social phenomenon, and the isolation of a single economic malaise cannot be conducted on a single economic sector because of the dynamics it generates. It must therefore be done on a large scale, embracing several sectors. Understanding the causes of the malaise depends on the economist's training and skill and on sensitivity when treating a given problem.

Since the Great Depression, economists have become increasingly aware of the difficulties of their discipline, especially the business cycle and its causes. During the Great Depression which signaled the end of the Industrial Revolution, economists argued among themselves over the issues of full employment and economic growth and development. Perhaps only Keynes pointed to the real problem: The neoclassical assumption of full employment as the basis of economic policy–a position that Pigou stated eloquently earlier–was inadequate and invalid. The lessons of the Great Depression have been learned well, so that taxation is now adjusted and social security payments are provided to ease the economic burden, governments have assumed the role of economic protectors of the banking system, and unemployment insurance buffers against personal poverty. Nevertheless, as the layperson will readily point out, poverty in the world's economies still exists and is debilitating both personally and socially. In the postindustrial societies as well as the emerging and developing societies, taxation is a burden, social security and national insurance systems provide little assistance in providing living standards reasonable in our time, and unemployment insurance and welfare payments are far from adequate as a means of combating the ravages of personal poverty. Granted, these measures are better than none, as was the situation prior to and during the Great Depression, but they are insignificant in our contemporary era for societies in their various stages of development.

The evaluation of these measures requires the amassing of empirical data on labor, employment, housing, health services, and education, as well as specific economic information in the economies' various sectors. These data, gathered by economists and statisticians, are supposed to clarify the current situation in every economy and to provide material for economists to project into the future and provide theories and methods for treating the economy. This information differs both qualitatively and quantitatively from that used by physicists and other natural scientists. Economists are nevertheless scientists in the sense that they seek to provide a theoretical and projective basis for their economies in general and their various sectors in particular. As scientists, economists have to consider the overall operations of business and the role of government as regulator, and construct theories for their specific branchs of concern. They can apply them either in competition with other theories or as paradigmatic constructions dominating the defined and delineated problem areas of concern. Unlike the natural sciences, however, economics cannot be restricted to a laboratory, because it deals with the social dynamics involved in the allocation of scarce resources among competing ends, the alternative uses of resources in manufacturing processes, the investment of profits in industry, and, in the macro realm, the efficient uses of national resources for the betterment of the general economy. Indeed, the problem with testing economic theory in the same manner as the theories of the natural sciences is that, for economists, there is a marked absence of laboratory conditions. This results in theories being tested for their internal logic and their contributions when compared to other corresponding theories in the body of economic knowledge.

Economics, like the natural sciences, is somewhat esoteric, understood in depth mainly by its practitioners. Although laypeople may study these disciplines as hobbies or acquaint themselves only in passing interest, the practitioners of these disciplines find audiences mainly among themselves, and they are concerned professionally with the problem areas and their theories. Economics is somewhat different, however, because their discussions include their colleagues, as well as businesspeople and officials on all levels of government. As Wassily Leontief has stated:

> We, I mean academic economists, are ready to expound, to anyone ready to lend an ear, our views on public policy, give advice on the best ways to maintain full employment, to fight inflation, to foster economic growth. We should be equally prepared to share with the wider public the hopes and disappointments which accompany the advance of our own desperately difficult, but always exciting intellectual enterprise. The public has amply demonstrated its readiness to back the pursuit of knowledge. It will lend its generous support to our venture too, if we take the trouble to explain what it is all about.[4]

Leontief's sentiment is difficult to put into practice, even for the most receptive nonprofessional audiences, because of all the academic disciplines, economics most directly touches peoples' lives. Yet the ways in which economics operates are widely misunderstood, if not utterly confusing. Moreover, there is a reluctance to discuss economics seriously with professional economists when it is realized that the debates among economists themselves do not seem to result in resolutions, and the economy continues its cyclic movements regardless of what the economists say or do.

Our contemporary social and political situation provides material for much heated debate among economists. Not only is the geopolitical world undergoing great and dramatic changes, but during all these changes basic economic needs must still be fulfilled. In our era, the European Community is coming together, and the Eastern European states are pulling apart. Great political uncertainty exists in Russia, and Communist China is moving toward becoming a dominant economic power. Common bonds are being forged in Indochina, yet competing countries there are striving to achieve economic and political dominance. The changing situation in South Africa gives it an ambivalent position of power with respect to the rest of the continent. South American countries are attempting to deepen and expand their economic infrastructures in order to improve their industrial output and combat unemployment. And the Middle East, still a center of turmoil, provides some hope as peace talks are being conducted, providing conciliation for long-warring sides. Economists have to consider events in these areas and their influences on domestic economies when discussing policies and formulating theories. These areas are extremely dynamic, and hence unpredictable, which creates a severe handicap for economists, as predictability is an important tool of the natural and social scientist.

Although there are prevailing uniting and dividing tendencies among the nations of the world, a common business cycle is becoming a factor in the world's domestic and international economic activity. For the emerging and developing countries, this type of cycle is manifested in the amount of aid available. As the amount of funds for aid declines, economic activity slows down, and these countries experience their own minicycles, moving around the big economic cycle that moves in turn throughout the postindustrialized world.

The economist as scientist lacks the luxury of a laboratory with the technology for constructing sophisticated experiments and subjecting them to various controls. Nevertheless, a laboratory is available to the economist. This laboratory is the world's economies, which are subject to economic, political, and, in some cases, natural influences—such as major floods, earthquakes, or volcanic eruptions—and the consequences that result. The policies of one country often affect the policies of others, such as the breaking up of the Soviet Union and the Iraqi invasion of Kuwait and the Gulf War that followed.

The economist as scientist has another tool for inquiry: the econometric models of the various economies based on available statistical inputs subject to each country's built-in variables. But as Leontief stated:

> Without making a misplaced methodological analogy, the task of
> securing a massive flow of primary economic data can be compared

to that of providing high-energy physicists with a gigantic accelerator. The scientists have their machines while the economists are still waiting for their data. In our case not only must the society be willing to provide year after year the millions of dollars required for maintenance of a vast statistical machine, but a large number of citizens must be prepared to play, at least, a passive and occasionally even an active part in actual fact-finding operations. It is as if the electrons and protons had to be persuaded to cooperate with the physicist.[5]

The control in the applications of economic theory is the squaring away of the theory with economic behavior according to these statistics and their interpretations, as well as with econometric predictions according to these statistics, in order to assess the economy's performance as correlated with the theory's dynamics.

Thus, we can understand the difficulties economists have in practicing their discipline in its many forms. The point is not whether economics is a science. In the framework of the natural sciences this issue is debated, as the lack of a laboratory prevents the theoretical and experimental precision that exists in the natural sciences. But as the study of the allocation of scarce resources among competing ends for the purpose of generating wealth and economic growth and development, economics is definitely a science. It has theories that are confirmed or refuted by the experience of economic activity, and its models are tested against reality as assessed by the gathering of statistical data and the interpretation of its information. It differs from the natural sciences in its inability to control economic conditions for testing. But this is a statement for the human spirit that rebels against controls. After all, it was the great economist Adam Smith and the political theorist Thomas Jefferson who argued against controls, for to control the economy, to impose on it laboratory conditions, is to control the people who are the businesspeople, the consumers, and the workers, and their influences on both domestic and foreign markets both individually and collectively. It is they who generate and direct economic activity and growth. Such control may be possible for a while, but it cannot endure. Its imposition results in great suffering and economic loss, as the demise of the Soviet Union and the declarations of independence among the former Soviet states signify. The aim of economic theorists is not to impose economic control, but to understand economic activity and to provide theories that can best explain its dynamics. Long-term cycle theory is such an approach, and the use of chaos theory as a scientific tool has led to some interesting insights. But, as will be argued in the third section of this chapter, long-run cycle theory is an invalid approach, given crisis theory and the economic situation in our contemporary era.

COMMENTS ON LONG–RUN THEORY

The study of business cycles goes back at least to Adam Smith, who, in his *Wealth of Nations* discussed cyclical fluctuations in markets for goods and services. Although in Smith's time the business cycle was not very sophisticated, his treatment did show how the subtle fluctuations in demand regulated supply. Following Smith was J. B. Say, who with his famous law of markets, argued that in the long run, the markets are in equilibrium as supply generates its own demand. Moreover, in 1860 Clement Juglar espoused the study of various long-run aspects of business cycles, in which common traits in the economic sectors can be shown through the various cyclical phases. While Juglar was not the first economist to study business cycles, he is perhaps the first to emphasize cyclical similarities, an approach that was to be undertaken by other economists.[6] Juglar was particularly interested in investment cycles, and he compiled statistics to show the frequencies of these cycles. These cycles are related to production, as investment in capital and plant is undertaken for manufacturing. Declining investment is due to increasing production, with employment increasing to meet the demand for production. As inventories are cleared, the cycle declines with unemployment increases until the inventories are sufficiently low to warrant reinvestment in inventories, bringing the investment cycle up once again. Juglar's work is significant for his emphasis on the study of the various cycles within the general business cycle, showing how the general cycle is influenced by the smaller cycles moving according to their own patterns.

Another long-run cycle theorist was Nicolai Kondratieff, a respected economist during the Stalinist regime. Kondratieff sought to understand the resilience of the capitalist system, a program that the Stalinists rejected. But he found that in the capialistic system, the business cycle moves over long periods, with minicycles occurring within the greater cycle, just as Juglar found. Hence, the capitalist system will always recover from its depressions in the long run, and in the short run, distortions will always exist. Capitalism, Kondratieff argued, would always survive because of its inner cyclic dynamics; for his conclusion, he was executed.

As Brian J. L. Berry reports, Kondratieff discerned three empirical patterns in the cycle and suggested that they might aid in the study of long-wave cycle theory. In one pattern, prior to and during the beginning of the rising wave of the long cycle, a society's economic life undergoes considerable changes. Thse changes are usually seen in production and exchange techniques preceded by significant technological discoveries and inventions, gold production and money-circulation conditions, or involvement of new countries in worldwide economic relations.

The second pattern concerns the period of the rising long-wave cycle, and is characterized by a far greater number of social upheavals and radical changes in the society. But in Kondratieff's view–and this is the third pattern–downward waves of the long cycles are characterized by prolonged and serious depressions in agriculture.

Kondratieff concluded that the historical material relating to the development of economic and social life as a whole conforms to the hypothesis of long cyclical economic waves. On this basis, he argued that the strength of the capitalist system lies in its ability to exploit the long wave, to develop new technologies, to cope with the social upheavals and radical changes, and to bring the depressions in agriculture to an end through the new technologies and social changes. Berry focused on these points in the following manner:

> 1. Prosperity and depression, with all their profound social implications, are tied to the upswings and downswings of the long waves.
> 2. During long-wave downswings, agriculture suffers an especially pronounced depression.
> 3. During long-wave downswings, a large number of important discoveries and inventions in production techniques and communications are made, but to be fully implemented these must wait for the upswing.
> 4. Worldwide gold production increases on the wave's upswing, and the global markets for commodities and manufactured goods are enlarged by the assimilation of the new national territories and colonies.
> 5. It is during the rise of the long waves that the most disastrous and extensive wars and revolutions occur, as a rule, because of the period of high tension caused by expanding economic forces. In addition, the rising long wave is associated with the replacement and expansion of basic capital goods and the radical regrouping and changing of productive forces and the allocation of resources in society.[7]

But as Leontief indicated, statistical information about countries, unlike data in scientific laboratories, is obtained with difficulty. Moreover, as Joshua S. Goldstein has demonstrated, statistical interpretations differ, yielding differing theoretical conclusions among economists concerned with this area.[8]

Another aspect of the long-wave cycle approach considered by Kondratieff and now of great importance to long-wave cycle theorists, is the consideration of noneconomic factors and their influences on the economy. One such factor is war, which, according to Kondratieff, comes on the long-wave rise and is due to the high tension among the expanding economic forces. War, political efforts toward world hegemony, regional domination and the conflict for world domination, and the tendencies toward world unification as well as its fracture into socioeconomic units that stand in economic competition (perhaps to the extent of verging on military confrontation) are now being studied by long-wave cycle theorists as influences on the long-wave cycle. The justification for these inclusions is that while economists have to isolate their specific branches of inquiry with the ceteris paribus clause, in the real world economics cannot be separated from politics and ultimately from global cooperation and conflict.

To a certain extent, this is indeed the case. But political events in far-away countries have little impact on the microeconomics of the firm in domestic compeition. The difficulty with the long-wave theorists is that they are macroeconomic in orientation when they discuss their subject, but not in the traditional sense that has existed since Keynes. Their problem area is not of the national economy in isolation from other countries' economies–although the Keynesian economists who worked with trade theory first broke with this economic tradition.[9] The problem area of the long-wave theorists is the long-run cycle, including elements of economic growth, and the economic, political, and social changes resulting from the wave's motion. The consequences for the single competitive firm in the long wave's motion are like the personal history of a family circle during a great epoch. The family is influenced by the events that occur, and indeed, some of its members may rise to the occasion to shape these events. The individual competitive firm may expand and grow, occupying a major role in its markets over the long run, and this may be significant for micro and macroeconomists for study and analysis, and for those hired to advise. But this, in a sense, is being inside the economy and looking out: the method of the long-wave economists is based on the general overview, with glimpses into the economies to obtain statistics and other information, such as the political shifts within countries, their military alliances, and economic shifts resulting from significant changes in production, distribution, and marketing techniques. Using the statistics and the other information, they formulate their theories.

The search for the long-wave cycle is part of the scientific endeavor undertaken to place economics on a more solid foundation, so that an understanding or both the past and the present can be achieved more clearly, and projections into the future can be made on a firmer basis. The modern long-wave cycle theories differ from Kondratieff's because he sought only to examine the long wave in order to understand and explain the viability of the capitalist system. In his investigations, he found that the Marxist call for workers in the capitalist countries to unite in conflict against the owners of the means of production was unrealistic on a grand scale. What Kondratieff found was a system that, from the Industrial Revolution's inception to World War I, had an internal strength to overcome its difficulties, incorporating the necessary accommodations that would allow for its continuance and guarantee its strength.

The modern long-wave theorists have another set of problems to consider. These include the unification of Europe in the Common Market, the decline of the Soviet Union as a world force, and the rise of the Commonwealth of Independent States, the struggles for markets among the great postindustrial powers, and the struggles on the African and South American continents. Indochina, with its vast population and inner strengths, is awakening after the nightmare of the Vietnam War, and the region is beginning to embark on serious economic activity. The Middle East is still smouldering from its many wars, but with the U.S. hegemony now established in that region, peace talks are under way. There are real chances to tame the passions that run high there and to introduce reason based on economic needs and requirements. Given the near-harmonious phases among the postindustrialized economies, and the influences of these economies on the emerging and developing countries, the study of the long wave has taken on a significance other than that which Kondratieff ascribed to it.

In the interest of the science of economics, although long-run cyclical trends may indeed be discerned, their relevance for specific business cycles is somewhat questionable. Granted, even during the pre-Industrial Revolution era, there were business cycles of sorts. These took the form of market surpluses that drove prices down and market shortages that resulted in high prices. Such cycles operated within the framework of classical economic theory in which high prices resulted in increased production and competition, so that surpluses of products were achieved, resulting in falling prices to clear the markets. They differed from the industrial business cycle that relies to a large extent on new products and methods of production, and their imitations. Moreover, whereas elements of classical economics still exist, the dynamics of classical economics do not prevail today, but another type does, which will be discussed in the next section.

Another economist who studied long-run cycles is Simon Kuznets, who posited an approximate twenty-five-year building cycle in the capitalist countries based on waves of migration, the allocation of monies for mortgages to meet the demand for building, and the general impact of immigration on the economies, including the shift of resources to the extent of accommodating the newcomers. This cyclical consideration does not, however, take into account, declining imigration due to improved conditions in the home countries, the official decline in accepting periodic large-scale immigration, the influences of other phases of the cycle on such long-run cyclical dynamics, and the allocation of resources to other objectives, thereby eliminating whatever long-run building trends may have existed previously.

Even if Kuznets had indeed described a cyclical phenomenon, using statistics that had been compiled accurately, he described a situation that lacks the necessity for its continuation. Kondratieff described the capitalist system in general, and he predicted that the capitalist system's resilience would maintain it, no matter what difficulties it confronted.

This is a far cry from the program undertaken by Kuznets and other modern long-run cycle theorists to find a cyclical pattern that can be argued to exist in the past and the present and to project it into the future. Kuznets, in his lecture on capital formation, stated that for long-term trends, the records of capital formation are poor.[10] From this, it can be surmised that with these poor statistics, a theory is involved by which these statistics take form. As with all scientific theory, one object is to predict into the future. Kuznets's theory offers valuable insights into the workings of economics, but can offer no reliable predictable power. Statistics and theories that yield long-run cycles but cannot be applied with an acceptable degree of accuracy into the future are interesting in the history of economic thought, but of little value for economics as a viable science.

Long-wave cycles in agriculture, building, and construction, and geopolitical shifts cannot be traced here and analyzed in depth, but some comments must be made on their methodological pursuits. Berry, for example, showed similar cyclical patterns over the years 1790 to 1990.[11] Although such patterns may demonstrate great similarities, they differ in one important point: the general economic (and sociopolitical) infrastructural changes that have occurred during this 200-year period. Cycles are formed by patterns, such as depressions and prosperity, and although such events occurred during the time that Berry was considering, the economy of 1990 would be unfamiliar to a person who lived in the 1880s. The cyclical patterns may be similar, but their economic contents are extremely different. This is true even for the period 1945-1955 to 1985-1995. The approach to bussines cycles to be presented here differs from long-cycle theory in two aspects. One aspect is the application of chaos theory to the long-wave cycle; the other aspect is the consideration of the cycle as traditionally four-phased. The argument to be presented here is that the four-phase cycle is no longer de facto, but the three-phased cycle is. The consequence of the three-phased cycle is that it is not subject to long-run considerations.

THE CRITIQUE OF CHAOS AND THE
FOUR–PHASED BUSINESS CYCLE

When discussing chaos theory in economics, Brian Berry states that the use of moving averages is chaos theory, which he describes as a circumstance under which the "dynamic mechanism may be simple and deterministic but the resulting time path is so complicated that it passes the standard tests for randomness."[12] If a system can be shown to be chaotic, he observes, there is evidence that endogenous mechanisms are at work, which is important for prediction. A chaotic system offers prediction to the extent of time dependent on the chaotic conditions. For Berry, then, economic systems are chaotic, but with a lot of "noise" to disrupt the strict deterministic mechanisms of chaos and to add the element of uncertainty due to the complicated time-path.

Granted, there are external influences on a business cycle, such as entering into military conflict, assassination of a world leader, and the contagious uncertainty over the stock market's performance in light of possible government policies. These exogenous influences on the business cycle are to be considered so only within terms of chaos theory, for they interrupt the dynamic mechanisms to maintain the cycle in motion. This means that the cycle that conforms to the principles of chaos is a business cycle only with respect to an economic model, which can be constructed to be complicated over its projected model-oriented long-wave time span, given its built-in conditions.

Models are abstractions and hence representations of aspects of the real world. As such, they cannot be subjected to the real dynamics of the real world. In the chaotic model, noise is ruled out for the dynamic mechanisms to function according to the laws of chaos. The snowflake performs on the computer screen according to the programmed instructions, and the computerized model of the released gas moves according to the conditions ascribed to it. The same holds for the economic model, which is programmed to behave according to the instructional input.

Although economic models are often necessary for viewing an economic situation, they cannot operate on information that is not within their instructions. Therefore, they lack the flexibility to cope with changes that the real economies have. As the long-wave theorists have demonstrated, models of the long-wave kind are constructed to explain the past and perhaps to offer clarification of the present. But as these models have been shown to perform, they cannot account for the future cycles in any of their segmented fields, because they lack the flexibility to adjust for sudden and unexpected changes in the political, economic, and indeed climactic aspects of economic activity. Berry acknowledges this notion when he states that while underlying mechanisms do exist, with deterministic chaos "rapid and unexpected changes are possible, and thus, predictability and therefore [individual] choice exist only within bounds."[13] This type of reasoning contains an inherent paradox. Chaos systems are deterministic, but for chaotic economic systems the time part is so complicated that it passes the standard tests for randomness. Berry's concession to chaos is to yield on determinism to a system in which prediction is possible within a limited interval of time that depends on the specific characteristics of the chaos system. Hence, with chaos, we have economic systems that are strictly deterministic. Yet given the possible "noise," the system allows us the possibility of predictability for a limited time interval that depends on the chaotic determinisitc conditions.

The strange attractor in these long-wave cycles must be discussed. This attractor is an important factor in chaos considerations, because it demonstrates the equilibrium properties of the chaotic system. In long-wave economic theory, the strange attractor is that position in which complicated paths, either starting in its neighborhood or outside of it, are attracted. This is the cycle's equilibrium position and refers to specific cycles within the general business cycle, as well as the business cycle itself.

To consider these positions as reflecting the cycle itself is erroneous. What these equilibrium positions indicate are the various growth rates during the considered cycle's path. Cycles have their own unique momentum while riding the general cyclical wave; this wave, too, has its own momentum, depending on the economic conditions prevailing during its lifetime. Growth rates indicate motion and the extent of this motion; they do not, however, indicate content within the cycle. Growth rates cannot show, for example, the types of goods and services within the economy that make the cycle unique with respect to other cycles–and it is held here, as will be demonstrated, that each general cycle is unique. Hence, the strange attractor is that growth position which is in equilibrium during the cycle's motion. Its moment is of very short duration, for the cycle is dynamic. Apart from inidicating these equilibrium positions and the time periods in which they occurred, they offer no light on cyclical dynamics. As an economic description on its own, the strange attractor has value for indicating an equilibrium position in the growth rate of the subcycle and the general cycle. As a factor of chaos theory, however, it has as much value in the discussion of economics as does chaos theory itself.

The business cycle has changed in our era from being four-phased to three-phased. This renders invalid the arguments of long-wave cycle theorists who base their reasoning on the neoclassical four phases. Hence, the theories of Juglar, Kuznets, and the other long-wave theorists are somewhat out of date when these arguments are related to the situation in our contemporary era.

The cycle changes from the classical and neoclassical four phases of prosperity, recession, depression, and recovery because the depression phase has been ruled out by governments' active participations in an economy's various markets. This was done to avoid the repetition of conditions similar to the Great Depression which brought an end to the Industrial Revolution and resulted in World War II. Recessions have become severe enough, but they still lack the severity of depressions. The Great Depression was so severe in its intensity and duration because of the level of industrialization that existed. Given the current levels of industrialization among the postindustrial and developing countries, a depression would be devastating, perhaps to the extent of altering the industrial bases of the afflicted countries. Active monetary and fiscal government participation, even in the stock markets–as the October 19, 1987 stock market crash demonstrated–restores confidence in an economy that has been severely weakened.

The question we may now ask is, how does this relate to crisis theory? Since chaos theory is inappropriate and the strange attractors have been interpreted as equilibrium positions without information content, can crisis theory be constructed for economic problems? If so, can such a theory be relevant for long-run cycles?

This situation has to be approached differently from long-wave theory, because long-wave cycles do not exist, and any similarity among various cycles over the continuous three-phased general cycle is due to the existence of similar problem areas for these cycles over time. The completion of the three-phased cycle period brings into the economy an infrastructure different from that of the previous cycle period, even though similarities may exist. Agricultural cycles may show that problems of crop rotation, marketing, price fluctuations due to the supply and demand for produce, weather conditions, and government policies affect farmers and their calculations in their uses of their lands. Building and construction may still be influenced by demographic shifts, the types of materials available and demanded, the availability of workers, and choosing between building and renting. Industrial planners have to consider competition, the availability of liquidity, and the allocation of resources for new products, as well as maintaining competitive products and phasing out those products that bring in reduced profits. Industrialists have to consider plant location and transportation of its products, as well as placing plants in regions with access to raw materials for production. Other relevant factors are the labor force and government policies, for both industrial output and within their own spheres, with labor trying to achieve its best interests and government trying to maintain the economy so that it does not become overheated or underutilized.

Two issues are relevant here. One is the decision-making processes of the firm's management, and the other is the broader view of the effect of decision making on the macroeconomy with respect to industry, government, labor, and the business cycle. Because of the various problem areas that confront management in business, government, and labor, decisions are taken and policies are made. The exogenous factors affecting the policies are those that are not taken into account in the expectation of decision making. This may be due to insufficient information or to factors that previously did not exist. If the policy is to be considered as the theory for the working problem area, then the policy must be flexible to account for exogenous factors. If not, then the policy becomes entropic and will fail. The problem area itself changes due to influences that are not controlled by the isomorphic relation of operational statements onto the area, for outside influences affect the area, bringing about changes within it. If management decides to continue working with the area, the policy has to be altered accordingly; if not, then the policy will be abandoned and the resources utilized differently.

Management defines the problem area with respect to the situation and purpose of the organization being managed. For example, for the firm as the source of economic activity, the area may be a specific market established by management for a new product. The product is designed and researched, and then tested on a select sample of the intended market. If the response to the product meets management's expectation, then it is put into production according to the policy and is marketed accordingly; if the product fails expectation, then entropy has set in, leaving the option of either reconstructing the product or abandoning the policy. In each case, the amount of resources and the availability of capital for further policy development have to be considered.

In terms of crisis theory, the establishment of a new market is competitive innovation, because it brings into the market a new product, requiring the shift in resource allocation from other products, and perhaps the keeping of other plans on hold until the short and medium profits are registered. Another example of competitive innovation is that of producing a good intended for markets that are already established but with the intention of taking consumers from these markets. An example is that of electrically powered vehicles, to compete with fossil fuel-powered vehicles. Experiments are being conducted with this method of private transportation, and the company that can produce this product successfully will capture a god percentage of the market.

In terms of crisis theory, strict innovation is the establishment of a plant to manufacture a product that is unique, in the sense that no close substitutes exist. For example, in our social time the antismoking campaign has successfully resulted in the introduction of smoking substitutes, such as nicotine patches, chewing gum, and psychologically oriented programs to wean smokers from their habit. In light of the linkage between smoking and heart disease and cancer, the first of these projects was a strict innovation, followed rapidly by close substitute imitators.

Imitation, in terms of crisis theory, refers to policies within the firm and to those outside it. Within the firm, strict imitation occurs when the firm's policies are being carried out according to the official plan, without deviation. The policies are carried out according to the plan, but the markets may not respond as expected. As long as strict imitation is being conducted, there is no deviation from these policies.

Explorative imitation is the process that brings out discrepancies between the policies and the market's performance. As these are noted in revenues, explorative imitation is the follow up of the products' progress The products may be very successful, with revenues as expected, or perhaps greater for a specific duration of time. However, the market signs may indicate that, because of strong competition, the products are no longer being consumed according to expectations. Explorative imitation reveals this, bringing the situation to management's attention. If convinced, management will act to initiate changes in the products, marketing, or pricing policies, making their products more competitive. If sufficient revenue is accrued through sales, they may phase out some or all of the products, using the liquidity to finance new products.

These are policies of initiation, and if initiation is undertaken, there will be competition with the best policy undertaken. Critical tests will be used in arguing for these policies with critique being employed in evaluating them.

The firm performs in this manner, whether its markets are domestic or international, or both. Although a firm exerts a degree of control over its domestic markets, its international markets are less controllable owing to unexpected events outside the firm's economic and political influences, according to its market share and the number of people it employs. For example, American firms trading with France exerted no control over the French markets during the general strike in December 1995, when industry, social, and government services were severely crippled.

With respect to the labor sector, labor leaders formulate policies according to their evaluations of business performance and the terms they can obtain for their members in consideration of the degree of accuracy of their evaluations. These evaluations are made on the basis of checking market results for products, whether they are competitive or strictly innovative. As unions operate in the economy's various sectors and geographical regions, their policies have to be based on the performances of these sectors and regions. The leaders of national unions have to consider sectorial and regional differences when bargaining for the financial benefits and working conditions of their members, as well as the competitive positions of the businesses in which they are involved.

Hence, with a formulated policy agreed upon by both business and labor, the policy, once established, becomes the working crisis theory. Business management will consider the policy as it relates to labor, given its operational and area languages, whereas labor will consider the policy acting on business for the same reasons so that the problem area of one side is the operational domain of the other. Since it is in the interest of both business and labor to maintain good working relations for the duration of the policy, work disputes that occur are usually reconciled with little difficulty. The policy is maintained in terms of strict imitation.

Explorative imitation occurs when specific clauses of the policy are tested, by way of extending them into domains that are not specifically clarified by the general policy. Should this result in work disputes, then the issues can be settled either through arbitration or, before official arbitration, through one or both sides yielding ground. Because explorative imitation in this sense is important for the clarification of the policy and for future policy considerations, this is necessary. Both sides undertake explorative imitation periodically. The results, through the initiation of unique approaches within the confines of the policy, can be beneficial for both sides in terms of worker-business relations and the establishment of future policy, to be worked out upon the termination of the current arbitration.

If the judgments of one or both partners in arbitration are inaccurate owing to the misunderstanding of the other's position or to the attempt to impose conditions on the other side that are against its best interest, then work disputes result. They may be resolved through arbitration, with each side perhaps moving closer to the other's position, or they may result in a standoff in which labor and business cease their dealings. In the contemporary economic world, such a situation benefits neither side, and the socioeconomic costs will have to be paid in the form of lost revenues to the business and reduced pay to the workers. Even if the union has a strike fund, it cannot pay the workers' regular salaries, and management could not survive on the basis of its profits for any significant duration. Arbitration has to be conducted on the basis of the socioeconomic situation, in which the new problem area requires a new crisis theory as an agreed-upon policy, to be worked out to the advantage of both sides.

Once the policy is agreed upon and established, business and labor will view the policy from their own perspectives, with management seeing the policy as the crisis theory to work with the problem area of the union, and the union leaders viewing it as the crisis theory to work with the problem area of business management. The attempt to reconcile work disputes without excessive action on either side demonstrates the extent of mutual need. When strikes and business management action against labor are evoked prior to the termination of the agreed-upon policy, this is a result of incorrect judgment on the part of both management and labor leaders.

If such action is undertaken after the policy's termination for a specific firm or in case of national business–such as railroads, air traffic control, or the postal system–the terminated policy has become entropic and provides no real basis for formulating a new policy. It does damage the economy and the society's social structure, both internally and internationally. The difficulties brought about by national strikes–regardless of which side is at fault–take a long time to overcome after a policy is agreed upon. The disuse of equipment, the forced unemployment of labor, and the difficulties caused to people who rely on these services are not easily restored and rectified. Much money is lost to the national sectors and to the private businesses that rely on them.

When a policy is formulated and both business and labor agree on it, the policy itself becomes the crisis theory. According to this theory, business views the policy as operating on the problem area of labor and labor views it as the crisis theory operating on the area of business management. The policy is formulated as strict innovation, taking into account the unique problems of management and the union in their relationship with each other. Strict imitation exists when the policy is adhered to according to its written and oral understanding. Deviations from this are due to explorative imitation, as various clauses are tested by both sides to see how far they can be taken. When a dispute arises, it is because the entropy that has set in due to explorative imitation cannot be resolved, for it has resulted in the clause being moved into a difficult situation that is outside the understanding of the policy by each side. The explorative clause is given a new interpretation, which, if adapted into policy by the side undertaking this exploration, will bring about a change in the linguistic perspective of the statement, as manifested in acting on the interpretation. As a result, entropy enters the policy.

Two approaches to this situation can be taken. One approach is initiation, by which contributions are offered to resolve the difficulty to the satisfaction of both sides. This may result in agreed-upon alterations of other clauses to maintain the policy as the working document. Should such explorative imitation continue, the policy's time-signature setting its duration may have to be altered. Alternatively, explorative imitation may lead to a policy that is strengthened to the benefit of both sides. Such imitation will eventually bring about the demise of the policy as it stands owing to the alterations in its formulation that initiation has made necessary.

The second approach is that of a work dispute bringing about a strike and a labor shutout. Should this outcome take place, it is because of an inaccurate judgment lay one or both sides leading to diseconomies through the loss of revenue and wages. A correction through initiation has to be undertaken as soon as possible to minimize these losses; if not, the strike and the labor lockout that occur will have unwanted and often unnecessary consequences, such as the hardening of positions and perhaps violence. Initiation may not be sufficient to restore the policy to the satisfaction of both sides, and strict innovation may be required again to construct a policy that will reduce the conflict situation and permit work to continue. The working policy between management and labor is intended as a crisis policy, because with each side protecting its own interests there will always be the potential for crises between them. Crisis, however, is not conflict. When the policy breaks down and conflict results, a policy that will eliminate the conflict and restore a level of crisis without conflict is the preferred way of conducting management-labor affairs.

With respect to the government sector, its monetary and fiscal policies are structured to maintain acceptable growth rates and to lessen the impact of cyclical downturns. The determinants of acceptable growth rates and impacts of cyclical downturns are established by the government's monetary and fiscal agencies, and are based on the economy's past, present, and projected future performance. Here, again, statistics are important, and for the developing and postindustrial economies, the performances of the stock exchanges serve as a barometer for growth, even though their performances are in nonproductive and paper markets. Yet, investors in these markets take their cues to a large extent from how the governments view their activities and the impact on these policies on the liquidity rate and for monies available for investment in productive industries.

Fiscal policies, such as setting budgets, establishing tax rates, and investing in the public sectors of defense and space projects for the involved postindustrial countries, as well as subsidizing education when appropriate, usually last a year and are revised annually in accordance with political pressure groups and the authorities' understanding of the countries' needs and requirements. Monetary policies, consist of establishing interest rates, setting taxes on investments as a restraint, floating government securities at favorable interest rates to reduce the competition for goods and services in the private sector, increasing or decreasing building by providing or reducing subsidies, and regulating the interest rates that banks levy on loans by requiring the banks to pay higher or lower rates to the government.

Although these two policies are directed toward different objectives, they are, in fact, different aspects of the same overall policy objective–that of effectively regulating the economy so that growth is maintained in the long run and recessions are minimized in both intensity and duration, thereby making them short run. Kondratieff's point that the capitalist system has a built-in resilience is thus not only well taken, but has also achieved greater significance since the Keynesian revolution during the Great Depression. Governments have become active, using countercyclical policies for correcting overheating and underutilization within the countries' economies.

The combination of fiscal and monetary policies as an overall policy is the government's crisis theory. It allows corrections in the economy to be undertaken when necessary. The economy is thus the problem area, and the combined policies serve as the theory relating to this area. The theoretical language relates to the economy and, in the case of monetary policy as the short-run aspect, is altered when the area conditions are altered. With fiscal policy in the longer run, structural changes are introduced to allow government spending in light of the present and projected annual economic conditions.

With respect to the long-wave cycles of the type discussed by Berry and the other theorists, the crisis theory approach negates their existence, bringing the focus on the cycle itself as it performs. This is because the cycle is now three-phased, with depressions ruled out by the combination of monetary and fiscal policies used to regulate the economy. In terms of crisis theory, firms and unions operate within the cycle, responding to its peaks and troughs. New business projects are usually not undertaken during recessions when money is tight, with firms relying on existing revenues from existing projects for the realization of other plans. New projects may be in various stages of planning, awaiting implementation when consumers are freer with their liquidity to engage in purchasing new products. One reason for the cycle's decline is the near-market saturation brought about by strong imitative competition among firms producing close substitutes for the same markets. The results are declining revenues for each competing firm, declining liquidity, and a corresponding reduction in investment in new projects.

This situation has an effect on labor's position, for unemployment looms owing to the aggregate decline in sales. With profits down and wages fixed by contracts, when these contracts expire labor is faced with unemployment. The government becomes active, providing unemployment compensation, and in more extreme cases, welfare payments, these being part of fiscal policy. This is the recession phase, which lasts long enough to reduce the supplies of existing goods and services, and allows firms to invest whatever liquidity is at their disposal through profits or easy-term loans backed by the government's lowering of interest rates to encourage economic growth.

Once reinvestment begins, labor is reemployed with the unions, providing for the welfare of their members and actively seeking the best contracts possible for them. This provides a socioeconomic guarantee for consumer liquidity for consumption, and the recovery phase begins. This moves the cycle upward into recovery, and prosperity is achieved as markets begin to develop and sales increase. Monetary policy is enacted to reduce interest rates on loans by reducing the rates the banks pay to the government. During this period, fiscal policy is geared to reduce unemployment payments and welfare benefits, as more people are being employed to enable industry to meet the increasing demand. Union contracts are signed to protect workers' rights and benefits, and to guarantee management-worker harmony in the industrial sector so that production can continue with a minimum of conflict.

As competition increases, recovery moves into prosperity, and with more people entering the labor force, sales increase with the increased consumer liquidity. Competition results in greater sales and the moving of inventories due to the lowering of production costs and sales prices and the incentives such as strong guarantees and servicing warranties on merchandise, discounts such as for favored customers and on volume sales, and easy payment terms.

With sales increasing and the demand for consumer goods rising, the cycle moves from recovery to prosperity. This continues at an increasing rate until aggregate consumer liquidity begins to diminish as near-consumption saturation is approached. The decline in consumption produces a cutback in orders, and unemployment results as stocked inventories are moving slowly and manufacturing is reduced. At this phase, monetary policy results in higher interest rates, and fiscal policy, depending on the political climate, leads to higher taxes. Because there is always a time lag in monetary policy and because fiscal policy is stated annually, the response to the cycle's fine-tuned movements is always late. Nevertheless, these policies are enacted to provide a rapid cooling process, and this results in the cycle's turning downward with some control. It would have turned down anyway due to the decline in demand, but this would have been reminiscent of the type of policy enacted prior to the Great Depression. In the present situation, depressions are ruled out. The economy is brought into its recession phase, and the cyclical mechanism resumes its inner dynamics, aided by the government.

Crisis theory is appropriate here for two reasons. First, when business managers plan their strategies, they draw up their projects and target their markets. Innovation is brought to the fore when new products are considered. Strict innovation pertains to entirely new products, and the preparation of markets is required for introducing the product. Competitive imitation refers to introducing a product to compete with others, but the new product has unique characteristics that make it original, even though it is formulated to compete in existing markets. Strict imitation is the maintaining of the product as it is, with the market orientation and publicity held constant. Explorative imitation is the bringing of the products into new markets, and initiation refers to the introduction of changes in the product or in its marketing to enter into new markets. If the product successful in terms described in the firm's policy of achieving its sales and realizing the projected revenues, then the policy is of utility and is maintained. If the product is not successful, the initiation occurs for corrections, and critique enters to provide a balance against initiation. If this fails to achieve the policy's aim, the policy is altered or eliminated as the entropy is considered irreparable.

Riding the business cycle, of course, influences the product's success or failure. Innovating during recessions may or may not result in profits. If the product is successful, it may assist the cycle's movement upward, depending on its impact in the national economy. Imitations are not usually undertaken during recessions, unless they are unique and can draw out available consumer liquidity, but this can be determined to a certain extent only after intensive market research.

As for unions, crisis theory is established when the leadership formulates its policy and terms for contracting with management according to their understanding of their strategic positions relative to management's. However, management's understanding of its business requirements concerning labor also enters into the contractual bargaining process. The management policy has labor as the problem area in this instance, whereas labor refers to management and the business in question as the problem area. Policies are thus formulated by each side. When agreement is reached and the contract validated, the document providing the terms and conditions of employment for both sides is in force.

Innovation for each side is the formulation of a unique policy that will guarantee good worker-management relations with as little friction as possible. Innovation is important because the terms of the previous policy are no longer relevant owing to the changed conditions brought about by the business cycle (a point to be discussed later in this chapter). Although previous concepts may still remain, they must be placed within a new conceptual understanding that takes into account the conditions of the social time and the economic environment.

With the agreed-upon contract as the working policy, strict imitation is the enactment of the policy according to the understanding of each side. This refers to working processes established in the spirit of the policy, as well as management's meeting its obligations concerning working conditions, wages, and benefits. Explorative imitation is the process of investigating the policy to determine its leeway for maneuvering provided by the agreed-upon clauses policy. This may be necessary due to circumstances in labor-management relations that were not hitherto considered important, but because of current conditions these clauses have to be examined by one or both sides working together. It may also be due to one side or the other seeking ways to change the spirit of the contracted policy without altering the policy as such. In each situation, if explorative imitation requires the consideration of changes to make the policy more effective, then the processes of initiation and critique that both sides engage in will continue until a suitable initiation is accepted. The difficulty here is that each side has its own interests to consider, even though this means considering the other side's position.

The natural conflict of interest between management and labor, together with the necessity for agreement, often makes this crisis situation somewhat volatile. Each side tends to reject the initiations of the other side, and yet each side recognizes the need to compromise and return the policy to its working utility position. Once entropic clauses are corrected, the policy will continue to be of utility until another explorative imitator finds difficulties, or until the policy's time duration expires and the bargaining between labor and management results in a new crisis theory policy being formulated and agreed upon again.

With respect to the government's position, the problem area of the crisis theory is the economy itself. The government formulates its financial and monetary policies with the intention of maintaining growth and eliminating as much economic and social disruptions as possible. However, as the control over the economy is far from strict, socioeconomic factors and influences cannot be contained, and the government's policy must be adapted to meet with the unexpected changes. This is the situation in which the problem area is altered, and the corresponding operational language must be corrected to maintain the theory's utility. This situations is conducted through monetary policy, which is ad hoc, relating to the situation as it has developed and exists. Seeking to reduce aggregate demand when the cycle is moving to its upper peak, and to stimulate demand when the recession phase is becoming too steep, the government raises or lowers interest rates, and may devalue the currency to stimulate foreign consumption and curb domestic consumption. Alternatively, it may revalue the currency to reduce the domestic consumption of foreign goods and services, so that by consuming domestic production, the added demand will stimulate domestic industry and reduce unemployment.[14]

The fiscal aspect of government policy is of longer duration, with monies relegated to the various socioeconomic sectors of the economy as the government deems necessary. These include welfare programs, defense and education, medical programs (such as national health care in its various forms), national transportation (such as national airlines and rail), and the provision of financial assistance to states or counties. This is usually an annual allocation and depends on the government's resources and the means for controlling inflation, preventing national or regional strikes, reducing unemployment, and relating demand to the business cycle by way of the monetary aspect of the policy. Here, again, the problem may change due to increases or decreases in welfare payments, or the increased or decreased burden felt by the various nationalized or civil service sectors that raise the strike threat to increase their benefits. These problems are handled by monetary and fiscal policies joined into a unified crisis theory policy for dealing with the expected and unexpected in socioeconomic problem areas.

This is crisis theory because the monetary and fiscal policies are innovative, even though this policy may be similar to past policies or to those of other governments. Competitive innovation has no role here, for the government, in terms of its fiscal and monetary operations and obligations, is the ultimate controller of the economy. Its fiscal policy is formulated annually, and the skills and understanding of the economy and the rapidity of the cycle's movement and direction must be such that monetary policy can be implemented to overcome all economic difficulties over the period until the next fiscal budget is considered.

By strict imitation is meant enacting the fiscal aspect of the policy to the letter, whereas explorative imitation is examining aspects of the fiscal policy to determine the extent of their utility as the economy responds and develops within its cyclical motion in terms of this policy. Should these aspects, as clauses, be found to be entropic, then initiation, with critique, is necessary for their correction.

Because the fiscal part of the policy cannot be changed, the initiative changes have to come about within the context of the monetary part, which may entail printing or recalling currency, charging higher or lower interest rates, or devaluating or revaluating, or some or all of these measures in varying degrees as may be required. Initiation here is competitive, as the central bank formulates a position–itself initiative and competitive among its members–and the treasurer (or exchequer, as the case may be) formulates its position. Proponents and opponents of these positions engage in debate until a final position is reached and agreed upon. Critique is important here, for it helps clarify the issue in question and sharpens the acceptance and rejection processes. Time is also a factor. As the economy is dynamic and as the defective clauses indicate, a policy of high utility is required to correct the defects. As the economy continues its development in its cyclical movement, further clauses become entropic given the current economic conditions, and the processes of initiation and critique continue. This will not bring the general fiscal and monetary policy into a condition of entropy, because the fiscal policy will serve the economy for its annual duration, with entropy corrected on the policy's monetary side.

Second, crisis theory is appropriate here as well, because in contrast to long-wave theory, the events of the previous cycle have an impact on present cycles, the recession phase is a clearing process in which the conditions of the present cycle cease. The influence of these conditions on future cycles are relevant only within the contexts of current cycles, so that long-wave building cycles, for example, are long-wave only from the perspective of history, while each building cycle is in fact part of the current business cycle and is subject to the cycle's current monetary and fiscal conditions. The manner in which government officials and businesspeople relate to these conditions depends on their respective crisis theories.

Because of the Great Depression, governments have undertaken permanent commitments to eliminate economic depressions, thereby relegating the business cycle to its three phases. The contemporary business cycle is thus a combination of the product cycles and liquidity positions of the many firms in society. During recessions, when the utility of production is low, the commitment of funds to the low-profit potential of imitative and innovative products is not readily forthcoming. Similarly, when the cycle is in recovery and moving into prosperity, funds are readily allocated for imitative and innovative projects, depending on their projected utilities. Contrary to long-wave cycle theory, the combination of product cycle for the contemporary business cycle refers to those specific cycles generated within the three-phased business cycle.

This is significant, for economic activities such as construction, agriculture, and the manufacture of such durable goods as refrigerators, automobiles, and washing machines and dryers, when considered historically, have long-run cycles, in spite of their periodic refinements and improvements. Tracing their development over time shows long-wave cycles of high levels of consumption as well as production gluts.

Although these are cyclically generated, and in terms of their histories are long-wave, their long-wave condition is ambiguous. The ambiguity is brought about by invalidly combining two different perspectives. The historical view of construction, for example, does show what can be considered to be long-wave building cycles, just as the historical view of the automobile and other durable goods, and indeed of agriculture, shows apparent long-wave cycles. This, however, is as if a country's current political situation depends solely on its historical circumstances, at the exclusion of all else. This is not to belittle history, for it is important for understanding current situations, as shown in the conflicts in Eastern Europe, the Middle East, and Africa and Asia. But in terms of the apparent long-wave influences of past epicycles for the various products, for our three-phased contemporary cycle, the apparent long-wave influences of the past have little, if any, influence on the present.

Present economic conditions are due to the present phases of the cycle. When liquidity is available in recovery and prosperity, consumption increases; when recession causes liquidity to be low, consumption is restricted, and this influences construction, agricultural consumption, and the purchase of durable goods. The long-run–in place of the long-wave–influences on these and other sectors within the economy are not cyclical but historical. The current economic conditions present within each phase of the cycle influence the manner in which consumers allocate their liquidity. When the cycle moves into recovery, liquidity increases due to the industrial sector's demand for more labor and the contracts signed by unions and management to ensure the rights of both sides. With the cycle moving into full recovery and into prosperity, employment increases still further, with a greater increase in output resulting from the applications of the viable technologies developed over the previous and present cycles, and the current cycle's phases are used in the manufacturing processes. Technologies that are no longer viable are phased out, with the viability of the technologies depending on the products being manufactured and the competitively innovative and imitative changes introduced for existing products, so that to a large extent, even technologies are cycle-oriented. The ambiguity is thus removed when the two perspectives of the business cycle–the historical and the current cyclical–are separated.

The strange attractors that Berry pointed out in long-wave cycle theory still have to be considered, for this is a genuine aspect of chaos theory, and this is the second relevant issue. Since chaos theory is both dynamic and equilibrium-oriented, the long-wave cycles of the various economic sectors tend toward equilibrium in their growth through their historical movements in business cycles. Hence, strange attractors are equilibrium positions in stable yet dynamic economic systems, to which economic activity beginning in their neighborhoods in the cycle tends to gravitate. This refers not only to rates of growth, but also to price levels. Profitable imitative products tend toward competitive price levels, fluctuating only marginally according to the supply and demand for these products, and the need to clear inventories. Prices will not fall below cost, unless this is advantageous to individual retailers, such as for bringing customers to purchase, but these losses are recouped by marginally higher prices on other items.

With respect to the growth rates of these products around the strange attractors, these are restricted by the dynamics of equilibrium and would certainly be the case if the economy is dynamic-equilibrium oriented. This is not the case, however, and even in the early stages of industrialization, this equilibrium orientation did not strictly hold. Adam Smith's "invisible hand" and its refinement by J. B Say into his law of markets were models of economic activity that had little bearing on the industrial process that was and is dynamic, in which innovation brings about change and imitation follows to reap the profits. This is even sharpened when international trade is considered, as new products are introduced into foreign markets to stimulate consumption and gain profits. This very disequilibrium dynamic, which is so necessary for economic activity and indeed for growth, was the factor that Kondratieff considered when he discussed the resilience of the capitalist system.

The dynamics of market innovation and imitation serve as the basis for economic growth and development in the emerging, developing, and postindustrial economies. Kondratieff did not know of the Keynesian revolution during the Great Depression, nor was he familiar with the subsequent economic theories that emphasize innovation and imitation in the development of new and existing markets. Long-wave theory and its strange attractors cannot account for these developments, but crisis theory can, for innovation and the subsequent imitation in market development are the generators of economic growth.

The ambiguity of product pricing and growth rates between long-wave theory and its strange attractors and the crisis-theory business cycle approach can be removed, again, by considering the historical and cyclical prespectives discussed earlier. In terms of the historical pricing of products, their equilibrium points—or for chaos theory, strange attractors—to which they "gravitate" are only those portions of their specific cycles to which competition has brought them. These are the aggregate price levels that the products have reached in order for them to be sold. Such equilibrium positions are far from static, but are highly dynamic, as some firms phase out these products because it is of greater utility for them to invest their liquidity elsewhere, while other firms maintain their current production levels until the utility of this approach declines. Still other firms may enter into production, and the volume of their output and advertising may reduce the products' general price levels even more.

With respect to equilibrium—that is, the strange attractor—pricing, the dynamics of change are registered in Berry's graphs. While there is a tendency toward equilibrium pricing, this process is very short-run-oriented within the general business cycle. Tracing these products—should they still be marketed over many business cycles—shows no long-wave cycle but different demand schedules, each reflecting the composite of consumer liquidity for spending. Historically, showing the cycle of a single product over several business cycles merely demonstrates that the product, in its general form, has survived competition. It is not the same product it started out to be, however, as the cycles of the automobile and other durable and nondurable goods readily demonstrate.

With respect to growth rates for products and the strange attractor, historically "gravitation" is not toward an equilibrium position, but toward a decline in production corresponding to a decline in consumption. Here, nonlinear equations are necessary, for they show changes in consumption that have not yet been registered in production. When competition declines, this is registered only after a time lag sufficient for producers to become aware that their goods are not moving as they did previously. The first response is to initiate price reductions to encourage sales. If the decline in demand should be for noncyclical reasons such as shifts in consumer interest and liquidity or better purchasing conditions for other products, price reductions will stimulate sales.

If after the price reductions sales are not affected or increase only marginally, in the aggregate this is a sign that recession is approaching, for consumer liquidity is being restricted mainly to necessary purchases. For each specific product cycle, however, this situation may indicate that either innovation or competitive imitation is necessary to stimulate sales. The projects then undertaken are to be within the consideration of their utilities and entropies of the current conditions.

Product growth rates and pricing are therefore cyclically oriented even when viewed historically, for those products survived several cycles of competition. From the historical perspective, equilibrium prices are those that reflect the short-run conditions of price stability for the products being considered, and equilibrium growth rates are those that reflect declines in production. In the aggregate, production is far from stable as new products are introduced and old products are phsed out. Those that are competitive over several cycles are different owing to changes brought about through competition. Those few products that manage to remain unchanged, though still competitive, have done so because of their quality and the changing advertising within the cycle.

The long-run view of these products indicates, therefore, not the strange attractors of chaos theory, but the dynamics of their respective production cycles within the general business cycles over time. Chaos theory cannot provide an understanding of long-run cycles, as each business cycle is unique. The cycles of those products that have endured the dynamics of the business cycles have done so because their firms have adapted to the conditions of each cycle, initiating changes and competing imitatively where necessary in terms of the dynamics of disequilibrium-oriented crisis theory.

NOTES

1. Martin Gardner, *The New Ambidextrous Universe* (New York: W. H. Freeman, 1994), p. 165.

2. Brian J. L. Berry, *Long–Wave Rhythms in Economic Development and Political Behavior* (Baltimore, Md.: Johns Hopkins University Press, 1991), p. 3 n. 1. All references to Berry are from this work.

3. See Berry, p. 12; see also W. W. Rostow's work, *The World Economy* (Austin: University of Texas Press, 1978); and see E. E. Slutsky, "The Summation of Random Causes as the Source of Cyclic Processes," *Econometrica* 5 (1937): 107-146.

4. See Wassily Leontief's essay, "Theoretical Assumptions and Nonobserved Facts," in his book of essays *Essays in Economics* (New Brunswick, N.J.: Transaction Books, 1985), p. 282.

5. *ibid.*, p. 280.

6. See Adam Smith, *The Wealth of Nations* (New York: Modern Library, 1937); J. B. Say, *Treatise on Political Economy,* trans. C. R. Princip (London: Longman, Hurst, Rees, Orme and Brown, 1821); and Clement Juglar, *Des crises commerciales et de Leur Retour Périodique en France, in Angleterre, et aux Estats Unis* (Paris: Librarie Gilliaum et Cie, 1860), and also the 1869 edition of this work.

7. See Berry, pp. 39-40. Berry's points have been restated somewhat for brevity. See Nicolai D. Kondratieff, *The Long Wave Cycle* (New York: Richardson and Snyder, 1984).

8. See Joshua S. Goldstein, *Long Cycles* (New Haven, Conn.: Yale University Press, 1988), Chapters 1-7, pp. 1-172. In Part 3, "History." Goldstein looks at the political and economic cycles from 1485 into our present era and projects his vision into the future. Also see his comments on Kondratieff's long-run cycle on pp. 81-82.

9. For a discussion on this point, see Ingrid Rima's essay, "Neoclassicism and Dissent," in *Modern Economic Thought,* ed. Sidney Weintraub (Philadelphia: University of Pennsylvania Press, 1977), pp. 7-22.

10. See Simon Kuznets, Lecture IV, "Capital Formation Proportions–A Cross-Section View," in *Six Lectures on Economic Growth* (New York: Free Press of Glencoe, 1961), p. 81. See also Kuznets's work, *Secular Movements in Production Prices* (New York: Augustus Kelly, 1967), a reprint of the 1930 edition.

11. See Berry, Appendix A, "Price Dynamics: The Growth Rates of Prices Smoothed by Successively Longer Moving Averages," and Appendix B, "Growth Dynamics: The Moving Growth Rates of Real Per Capita GNP Smoothed by Successively Longer Moving Averages," pp. 199-211. For both appendices, the time span is from 1790 to 1990.

12. Berry, p. 14; emphasis in the text.

13. Berry, p. 186. The choice spoken of here is individual choice by the economic performer.

14. However, changes in foreign currency rates are of short-term benefit only, if at all. See David Z. Rich, *The Economics of International Trade: An Independent View* (Westport, Conn.: Quorum Books, 1992), pp. 53 and 134.

CHAPTER 11

Crisis Theory and the Rise and Change of Nations

The development of a political community is most readily demonstrated by interest group activity. In a developed economy federated into a supranational system, those whose interests are affected by the decision-making institutions, adversely or otherwise, will organize to lobby at the supranational level to influence particular decisions.

John Spanier,
Games Nations Play[1]

GENERAL REMARKS

A political community is a sociopolitical community because of the social interactions on the personal and professional levels within the community. Because the professional level is also the economic level, the political community is therefore an economic sociopolitical community. While considering the sociological, political, and economic aspects of a community, it is convenient to emphasize the aspect under discussion, so that the community may be a society, a political entity, or an economic entity, as the case may be. This is merely a conceptual manner for treating an extremely complex body politic, each of which is unique in its history, cultural inheritance, and nuances of its social, political, and economic aspects–no matter how similar they are to other such systems from which they may have developed or share a common history.

Because the body politic is extremely complex, with each socioeconomic polity being unique, discussions on the economics, sociology, or politics of any one country must entail a discussion of the history of that country's development. When discussing these aspects of countries in general, comments can nevertheless be made that can be tested for their validity for each country within the realm of discussion. Hence, to discuss postindustrial countries in general is to discuss common properties among these countries, regardless of the qualitative and quantitative differences that exist among them. The same holds for the developing and emerging countries.

The terms "postindustrial," "developing," and "emerging" indicate to some extent the political systems of the countries that these terms fit. For example, a postindustrial country is one that has a democratic political system, while developing countries tend toward democracy but may indeed be monarchies, or semidictatorships, and the emerging countries may be monarchies or strong dictatorships. The fact that the postindustrial countries are democratic attests to their stage of sociopolitical development, whereas the developing countries may not yet have achieved this degree of sophistication. The number of dictatorships among the emerging countries attests either to their lack of sophistication or to the need for strong government to enact programs necessary for economic growth. The purpose of using this growth is to bring the country under consideration to the level of sociopolitical sophistication needed to attain postindustrial status.

Although each country within these classifications has its own unique dynamics, generalizations can nevertheless be made. For example, Professor Spanier's generalization holds for the postindustrial countries and for those developing countries in which the democratic process has become established. But this matter requires further comment.

Because the postindustrial countries are democratic, they are both supranational and regional. The supranational aspect is the seat of federalized government, located in the countries' capitals; the regional aspect is representational and is expressed in the seat of counties, provinces, or states as the case may be. Interest group activity gives political expression to the opinions of the group members, and although these may be of political influence, they are not static, as people shift from group to group and from opinion to opinion. These interest groups may be political parties or lobbying committees seeking to exert their influence on political parties.

The interests of these groups are affected by the decision-making institutions, either adversely or otherwise. If these groups are the political parties in power deliberating and making the decisions, their choices are made on the basis of the utility and entropy of deciding to change or of leaving the considered situations as they are. Their decisions are also made on the basis of projected utility and entropy, after analyzing the situations and formulating crisis theories to deal with them. The ruling parties will then be influenced by the directions of their decisions, just as their directions have influenced the decisions taken.

Of course, situations are not static, and as they are the problem areas to which the decision-making processes relate, they are influenced and changed by events that occur that are not considered within the problem area when the crisis theory is formulated. Policy is innovative, and at the federated level it is supranational and therefore affects the countries' regions to the extent that the crisis theory policy is applicable. Thus, strict imitation guarantees that the policy is carried out as it is supposed to be, while explorative imitation will yield shifts in the understanding of the policy as well as changes in the problem area of those regional sectors to which the policy is applicable.

Supranational policy for regions can be lobbied at the supranational level to influence particular decisions and their enactments into policies. As regions also have their seats of government, and levels of government are still further removed from the suprational level, local governing bodies also enact policies to enable their concept of government to prevail. Lobbying can also occur at these levels, as interest groups may be affected adversely by decisions taken on these levels that have no relevant bearing on supranational policies. Lobbying can be for or against a policy; indeed, the advocates of the pros and cons of a policy may meet in protest and in lobbying. The democratic system of governing makes allowances for voicing these types of differing views.

Regional and local policies may also conflict with supranational policy–such as with the Southern American states not complying with federal desegregation orders in the early 1960s–resulting in the pro and con demonstrations for local and regional, as well as supranational positions. The democratic process assures the right to these expressions of support and dissent, provided they are carried out within the countries' laws.

For the developing and emerging countries in which the roots of democracy have not yet taken, monarchies and dictatorships set the policies and neither street-level protest, interest group involvement, nor respectable political opposition is tolerated. The developing countries have a firmer socioeconomic base than the emerging countries, and their move into genuine democracy occurs when they move from the developing to the postindustrial stage. The monarchies and dictatorships in the emerging countries have a different set of problems. Their countries are highly unstable and prone to coups and political infiltration from hostile neighboring countries, as well as to seeking glorification in the eyes of their citizenry to protect their power bases. They also wish to maintain their standards of living, even if it is at the expense of the welfare of their peoples. This is why emerging countries are generally unstable, and their peoples' awareness of this condition is a prime motivation for rebellion and collusion with hostile neighboring countries, whose governing bodies may not be that much better toward their citizens.

Economic growth, needed to move the emerging and developing countries into the postindustrial and developing stages, respectively, is controlled by the ruling powers. Where both government control and the play of the market forces operate within the economies, growth occurs, albeit in a controlled and inefficient manner. This is why some of the emerging countries have moved into the developing stage but at great cost to industrial output, industrial labor relations, emigration, and the uses of resources to correct social discrepencies.

This is also why the postindustrial countries are politically democratic, because this is the most effective system for ensuring social development and economic growth. The political maturity required to maintain democratic systems in required not only by the citizens, but also by their rulers. That in democratic systems these rulers are chosen by popular consent as expressed through voting attests to the voters, sociopolitical awareness and ability to evaluate. The democratic process encourages economic growth as a result of the right and ability to establish businesses in chosen locations, to enter into markets and phase out products that are not profitable, and to make other business and economic decisions without government interference. This means that government licensing when necessary will be considered for whatever the scope of the business–local, state, or country or province as the case may be, or national or international, as long as the social and legal requirements are satisfied. The right to do business is therefore granted without harassment and legal interference, providing that businesses do not infringe on citizens' rights.

Granted that the forms of government and social dynamics in the emerging, developing, and postindustrial countries differ, the question to be addressed now is as follows. How can the postindustrial countries, federated into supranational systems that are subdivided into lower and more localized government forms requiring vast bureaucratic organizations that occasionally conflict with one another, and with vested interests in the form of lobbies or consumers acting in concert but independently, maintain reasonable rates of economic growth and general prosperity? The general trend is toward emigration from the emerging and, to a lesser extent, the developing countries to the postindustrial countries, regardless of the restrictions each postindustrial country places on immigration. People "vote with their feet" to obtain better lives, emigrating from the emerging countries and some developing and postindustrial countries. When necessary, they find ways to cope with the immigration laws in order to achieve political freedom and economic security.

Because of the nature of the democratic processes in the postindustrial countries, their political communities are most active on all levels in the demonstration of interest group activity. In these countries, democracy permits the expression of individual and interest group opinions, and where there is sufficient economic and political influence, these groups can exert great influence in their respective fields. Labor unions and business, being naturally antagonistic, seek through the exertion of political pressure to achieve their aims, just as political groups that are naturally antagonistic use their influence to gain popular support for their objectives. Democracy allows for majority rule and the minority to voice its opinion on all relevant issues, again with the consideration of the rights of the countries' citizens. Should these rights be in jeopardy or be violated, then the democratic processes are threatened and the governing bodies have the legal right to act on behalf of those citizens so affected to curtail and even suspend all lobbying and other such activities.

OLSON'S PARADOX

In his book *The Rise and Decline of Nations* (1982), Mancur Olson discusses a paradox which he believes is inherent in the bargaining processes of interest groups in the postindustrial countries. The paradox is based on the assumption that if the individuals in groups or firms have some interest in common, then the group will tend to seek this interest further. Each individual in the population is in one or more groups, and the vector of pressure of these competing groups explains the outcomes of the political bergaining processes.

Olson explains that if the logic of this is considered, it will be found faulty. If individuals spend money and time to organize to lobby for legislation they consider favorable, what will this sacrifice of money and time obtain? At best, the individual will succeed in advancing his or her cause to a small, often imperceptible degree, and in any case will receive only a minute share of the gain from this action. Olson states that the very fact that the object of interest is common to the group or is shared by it entails that "the gain from any sacrifice an individual makes to serve this common purpose is shared with everyone in the group."[2] Moreover, as he states, "the number of people who must bargain if a group-optimal is to be obtained, and thus the costs of bargaining, must rise with the group."[3] Olson argues that the significance of his logic can best be seen by comparing groups that have the same net gain from collective action, if they could engage in it, but vary in size. He gives the example of a million individuals who would gain a thousand dollars each, or a billion in the aggregate, if they were to organize effectively and engage in a collective action that had a total cost of a hundred million. He argues that if his logic is correct, they would not organize or engage in effective collective action without selective incentives, owing to the absence of actual gain.

Olson suggests that, although the total gain from collective action and the aggregate cost of a hundred million remains the same, the group is composed instead of five big corporations, or five organized municipalities, each of which would gain two hundred million. Even in this case collective action is not an absolute certainty, since each of the five "could conceivably expect others to put up the hundred million and hope to gain the collective good worth two hundred million at no cost at all."[4] Yet, he maintains that collective action, perhaps after some delays due to bargaining, seems very likely indeed, as in this case, he argues, any one of the five would gain a hundred million for providing the collective good, even if it had to pay the whole cost itself. The cost of the bargaining among the five would not be great, resulting in an agreement sooner or later being worked out among them providing the collective action. While Olson states that the numbers in his example are arbitrary, roughly similar situations often occur in reality. The contrast between his "small" and "large" groups could be illustrated with many diverse examples.

The significance or Olson's argument shows up in another way, with the comparison of the operations of lobbies or cartels within the jurisdictions of vastly differing scales, such as a modest municipality on the one hand and a big country on the other. Olson argues that within the town the mayor or a city official may be influenced by a score of petitioners or a lobbying budget of a thousand dollars. A particular line of business may be controlled by only a few firms, and if the town is distant enough from other markets, only these few are needed to create a cartel.

In a big country, the resources needed to influence the national government ("supranational" in Spanier's terms) are likely to be far more substantial. Unless the firms are gigantic (or, to contribute to Olson's argument, of great importance despite their size), many of them would have to cooperate to create an effective cartel.

Olson then supposes that the million individuals in the large group in the previous paragraphs were spread out over a hundred thousand towns or jurisdictions, with each jurisdiction having ten of these individuals, along with the same proportion of citizens as before. He assumes that the cost-benefit ratio remains the same, with the billion dollars for all jurisdictions, or ten thousand dollars in each, the cost is still a hundred million dollars for all the jurisdictions, or ten thousand dollars in each. Olson maintains that it no longer seems out of the question that in many such jurisdictions the groups of ten or subsets of these groups would put up the thousand dollar total needed to get the thousand for each individual. "Thus," he states, "we see that, if all else were equal, small jurisdictions would have more collective action per capita than large ones."[5]

Olson lists nine implications of his argument; they are restated here and considered, in turn, within the reference of crisis theory. His first implication is that no countries attain symmetrical organization of all groups with a common interest and thereby attain optimal outcomes by way of collective bargaining. This, of course, is correct to some extent, because in the real world changes of opinions and positions with respect to collective bargaining can exist, and there is no guarantee of symmetrical organization of all interest groups in the real world. Clashes of opinions expressing vested interests will remain as long as society exists as a supranational organization. Whether these differences of opinion expressed in the lobbying procedures are allowed to be realized depends on the nature of the clash and the type of ruling body holding the power. If legislation is passed to enable lobbying and negotiating, and if this legislation is upheld as the law of the land, then the lack of symmetry will exist and collective bargaining and lobbying will be maintained according to the crisis theory positions and utility considerations of the groups involved. After all, it is the sharing of common crisis theories that unites groups, enabling them to lobby and engage in collective bargaining.

Lobbying and collective bargaining are based on the crisis theories of the respective sides involved. In Olson's two examples, if the computation shows that the individual rewards equal ten times the financial layout if the collective action is successful, this may or may not allow for the compensation for the time spent, as greater profits can be gained by spending time otherwise. This decision, however, is an individual one, even though it can be argued that once the individual becomes part of the collective grouping, this commitment obligates the placing of $100 for a $1,000 compensation. But if the individual accepts commitment to the grouping as his or her crisis theory, this commitment also means dedicating sufficient time which could perhaps be used more efficiently and profitably to assist in achieving the total group's goal. This commitment is made only after the individual's consideration of its viability.

Whether these groups are individuals within a single jurisdiction or several jurisdictions in nearby regions is irrelevant. What is important is the utility of their approach, just as the cartel established in Olson's second example demonstrates. This type of cartel can be broken by temporary boycotting of their products. With the profit motive still operating, each cartel member will then reduce its price to outsell its former competitor.

Olson also argues that if the million people are spread out too much, the chances are that they will not partake in this type of action. This implies a very loose organization motivated only by the financial gain of $1,000 per member. Loose organizations become tight rapidly where money is involved. If a "roof" were to be placed on this organization in the form of management, these people could become united regardless of their geographical dispersion, and indeed use their power again for other such financial gains. This depends on how they view their common crisis theory position with respect to the problem area of maneuvering for financial gain.

Olson's second implication is that stable societies with unchanged boundaries tend to accumulate more collusions and organizations for collective action over time. However, this depends on what is meant by "stability." If it means a type of political system that allows for bargaining and receives its mandate from the country's enfranchised citizenry, then this merely provides a general description of all postindustrial countries, without their dynamics. Stable political systems are necessary for continual postindustrial development, but conditions that are stable in the dynamic socioeconomic and political circumstances of our contemporary era are extremely rare.

In every postindustrial society, periodic circumstances interrupt the seeming social stability and show the underlying instability. The assassination of President Kennedy in the United States, the war in Vietnam, and President Nixon's involvement in the Watergate scandal are just a few examples of the instability in the United States in recent decades. France's problems with social unrest as the 1995 general strike demonstrated, along with problems of terrorism and its program of nuclear testing together with the protests this program has generated throughout the world demonstrate French instability, while Great Britain's is illustrated by its difficulties with Irish terrorism, the scandals of some of its members of Parliament, and its obsession with the personal lives of the royal family. Similar examples can be cited for Japan, Canada, and the other postindustrial countries such as Italy. Stability is not, therefore, a factor on which organizations engaged in collusion and collective action can rely.

As for unchanged boundaries, they are important because they allow the law of the land to be understood to hold within these fixed geographical boundaries, so that organizations for collusion and collective action know just where the jurisdiction of their influence extends. Of course, international organizations may have their own de facto or understood charters that set out their purposes and objectives. Still, these organizations must adhere to the laws of each country as established within each country's geopolitical borders.

The point is, however, that organizations for collusion and collective action are formed in the postindustrial countries, regardless of the stability or the lack of it in these countries. These organizations are formed on the basis of the understanding of common policies and objectives among their members, and these policies are formulated into working crisis theories. Membership may increase according to the theory's domain of interest and, given suficient interest, to the theory's utility in working with the problem area for which it was formulated.

Such collusion or collective action may be a destabilizing influence in society. The establishment and domination of cartels, for example, may provide price stability for the product in question, but as this price is not competitive, greater consumer liquidity is channeled toward the product than would be under normal competition. This leads to an inefficient use of resources and can easily result in a consumer boycott, causing disruption throughout the economic sector. In this case, the cartels' crisis theories are of low utility and tend to irreparable entropy should a boycott occur. In postindustrial economies, there are substitutes, so that if a boycott is against one product, other products–perhaps with marginally less consumer satisfaction–can take their places. This also generates diseconomies as the less preferred products are price-oriented and not consumer first choices. Thus, while acting as substitutes, their quality will most likely not be improved and may even decline because of their demand as substitutes.

All such policies formulated into working positions as crisis theories are subject to the dynamics of changes within their operational and area languages, and this is independent of stability or the lack of it. Geographical boundaries are important and necessary for determining the extent and effectiveness of the law of the land where these crisis theories are formulated, either for collusion or for collective action. Nevertheless, the utility or entropy of each crisis theory depends on the viability of the operational language or its corresponding area language. Given the dynamics of change, the people working with these innovated theories, as strict and explorative imitators and as initiators when necessary, will relate to the theories within the geographical confines to which the theories relate and for which they hold.

Olson's third implication is that members of small groups have disproportionate organizational power for collective action, with this disproportion diminishing but not disappearing over time in stable societies. The point is that group size is not really a criterion for organizational power where collective action is concerned. The Teamsters Union has a considerable organizational base on the local, regional, and national levels, and enjoys support from other such international unions. Its membership gives it tremendous resources, making the union extremely effective in collective actions.

Size in itself provides no basis for power, disproportionate or otherwise. Small groups exhibit disproportionate organizational power in collective action only if their crisis theories are of very high utility, requiring that their problem areas be extremely well defined and their operational statements viable. These theories provide small groups with the necessary organizational power to establish the necessary organizational structures for taking on issues requiring collective action. Small groups, like the large national groups, are effective in organizing for collective action only if their organizational strength is proportional to the utility of their crisis theories.

As these theories are innovative, the problem areas will undergo changes owing to the shifts caused by explorative imitation and by the infiltration of nuances from other theories, bringing these theories into entropy. For these small groups to remain viable, the necessary initiation with the accompanying critique must be undertaken, with the accepted initiations being incorporated into the theories. Over time, provided that these changes do not allow for too much deviation from the original theory, the groups will remain viable.

Given stable societies, these groups will remain viable for the duration of their problem areas. Too great a deviation will render these groups entropic, and they will disband when they are no longer able to retain their viabilities. The stability of the societies in which they exist will not guarantee their endurance. Only their abilities to remain viable with respect to their problem areas, with their membership understanding the conditions of entropy engaging in initiation and critique to eliminate these conditions, can guarantee their permanence. Thus, for both large and small groups, their ability to remain organized depends on their maintaining viable crisis theories to meet with the conditions of their problem areas.

Olson's fourth implication is that, on balance, special interest organizations reduce efficiency and aggregate income and make political life more divisive in the societies in which they operate. Several issues must be considered here. One issue is the right of "natural" monopolies as forms of collusion. Necessary social functions such as police agencies, fire-fighting services, and other groups, such as sanitation workers, can operate collusively, because they have complete control of their markets, allowing them to determine their wages within social limits through collective bargaining and to exert their special status to prevent competitors from entering their fields. These are natural monopolies in the sense that they provide services that are required by society, and they do so exclusive of all competitors. Their unions are effective in representation and in collective bargaining. Nevertheless they exert a marginal influence on the utility of money inasmuch as their services are paid for by taxation, with increases in salaries and benefits made possible by tax increases. These monopolies are socially oriented, employed by the municipalities with the consent of their citizens.

Other "natural" monopolies such as telephone and electric companies have acted as self-interest groups and because of their monopolistic positions. These positions are justified on the grounds that competition in these fields cannot effectively be undertaken because if so, they would result in redundancy in equipment such as telephone and electric cables, thereby rendering their services inefficient. This argument has been shown to be false with the introduction of competing telephone companies, imposed by judicial ruling. Rates are competitive, services improved, and the consumer gets a better product than before. The electric companies have yet to be confronted with this type of competition, which would reduce consumer costs and make the electric companies more efficient by investing more resources into improving the product and passing these improvements and cost-reductions onto the consumers. This will provide consumers with a form of loose collective bargaining by allowing them choices of electric companies, just as consumers have choices concerning telephone companies.

"Natural" monopolies have maintained their positions by way of their argument that they provide efficient services at the lowest possible costs, given the nature of their services. Defending their positions as natural monopolies, public utilities such as electric, gas, and, previously, telephone companies argue that they supply their consumers their services in situations where competition would only hinder their operations. For example, it is maintained that more than one gas company would use available resources to duplicate their services, resulting not in greater efficiency but in a reduction in efficiency due to this duplication. The gas companies, for example, lay down their lines to supply their customers. With two or more such companies there would be a crossing of lines, yielding to the reduction in each company's services due to the interference with other companies' lines. Similar arguments have been posited by the electric companies, which claim that competitors will reduce the general capacity to supply their products. These are natural monopolies because they have been developed to fulfill their functions and obligations to their consumers and therefore have no need to meet the challenges of competition.

As special interest groups wielding economic power, these natural monopolies tend to exert the political power needed to maintain their monopolistic positions, while maintaining their pricing policies, even though their responses to consumer complaints often leave much to be desired. As long as the crisis theories of these and other such monopolies remain intact, they can preserve their influence over society.

As with the telephone companies, however, it is society itself that alters the problem situation, imposing forced and legal competition on them. The telephone companies were deemed monopolistic to the extent that they hindered the development of telecommunications. They were thus ordered to divest themselves of some ot their subsidiaries. Long-distance telephoning became the domain of other companies, resulting in the development of improved telecommunications technology. The new companies entering the communications field stimulated competition, leading to new products such as computer-based telecommunications, the wide use of fax machines and cellular phones, and experiments with television, leading in turn to the development of satellite dishes and telephone screens to view a communicating partner. As the new information entered the telephone companies' problem areas, they shifted their operational languages in order to remain profitable, adapting with great efficiency to the new requirements of competition.

As for the argument that these groups will reduce efficiency and aggregate income, thereby making political life more divisive by introducing competition, efficiency has been enhanced as these groups provide innovative products and improve on imitative products through initiation in order to compete effectively. Aggregate income is not reduced because the pressures of competition require that employment increases but only to the extent that it performs with utility in the context of crisis theory.[6] Political divisiveness is necessary within the postindustrial democratic societies, exemplified by competitive political parties vying for power. In this process, these parties exploit the situations of interest groups, which themselves are answerable ultimately to the citizenry.

On balance, then, special interest groups acting in collusion are viable only for the duration of their respective crisis theories. Shifts in the problem areas of these theories require corresponding shifts in the area statements for these groups to survive. Given these conditions, their survival is to the benefit of the societies in which they operate.

Olson's fifth implication is that encompassing organizations have the incentive to make the societies in which they operate more prosperous. They also have the incentive to redistribute income to their members with as little excess burden as possible, ceasing the redistribution unless the redistributed amount is substantial in relation to the social cost of the redistribution. The contrast here is between encompassing and narrow interest groups, with the narrow interest groups acting in the interest of their members only, while the encompassing group's existence is justified by the range of its membership. In the first instance, income distribution among its membership is justified only if it is within its crisis theory; in the second instance, income distribution is necessary to maintain the group's cohesiveness. This redistribution makes the societies in which they exist more prosperous.

For example, coalition governments rely on maintaining the balances of power among the participating political parties, and this balance is maintained by providing political payoffs, either in the form of grants or positions of power to the coalition partners. Cartels provide payoffs in terms of pricing, so that each member reaps its rewards for its participation. Union branches collect dues, part of which are channeled into strike funds for their membership within the specific regions when needed. The minimal excess burden in redistribution is due to the condition that such redistribution is necessary to maintain the organization.

Therefore, Olson's point that the redistribution will cease is correct, unless the amount redistributed is substantial in relation to the social costs of maintaining the encompassing organization.

This, however, depends on the crisis theories of the various members within the organization. If it is to the advantage of one or more members to demand more income because of their bargaining positions, then other members may accept this and remain quiet. Alternatively, they may also exert their influence and demand greater share. Depending on the roof organizaton's position, greater all-around funding may be granted, but this "extortion" may pave the way for still further funding. If so, then the entire organization may become entropic and collapse. Such income distribution must be granted with viable constraints, but once extortion is shown to be a viable policy, entropy has set in, and the demise of the roof organization is imminent, leaving each member to go its own way. Hence, the amount redistributed is substantial only for a specific time framework, with entropy built into the encompassing organizational crisis theory. As a consequence, the member groups maintain their cohesion within the encompassing group for the duration that it suits their specific crisis theories.

Olson's sixth implication is that distributional coalitions make decisions more slowly than the individuals or firms composing them. They also tend to have crowded agendas and bargaining tables, and to fix prices more often than quantities. These coalitions move more slowly because they must consider the opinions and needs of their members, where each member–be it a firm or individual–has only to consider its own interests, including retaining its membership in the coalition or to withdraw from it. The heavy agenda and bargaining tables are also due to the composition, whereas each firm or individual only has to consider its own agenda and bargaining issues.

Price fixing is easier for these coalitions than quantity fixing, owing to the easier agreement reached on prices than on output. If output is not regulated but prices are fixed, then given the inelasticity of demand schedules and the absence of close substitutes, greater aggregate profits will be reaped for each coalition member, thereby maintaining the coalition's viability.

The difficulty here is that with each member realizing that greater profits can be made by increasing output and lowering prices, the agenda of maintaining the coalition has to be a constant issue, with internal bargaining among the members and external bargaining for outside markets conducted by the coalition's representatives. Customs unions and cartels, such as the Organization of Petroleum Exporting Countries (OPEC), are confronted with these difficulties, but unlike the American farmers who get paid by the government for not farming portions of their lands, customs unions often have to confront internal opposition to their policies. Moreover, OPEC is not a stable organization, with each country tending to bargain in the open markets for its own best interest, yielding to cartel policy when suitable. The crisis theory of each coalition member dictates the orientation of policies, with the coalition being viable only while it provides utility to its members' positions.

Olson's seventh implication is that distributional coalitions slow down a society's capacity to adopt to new technologies and to reallocate resources in response to changing conditions, thereby reducing the rate of economic growth. New technologies are produced either by members of coalitions or by independent individuals or firms, innovated to meet the requirements of problem situations. The adoptions and adaptations of these technologies depend on programs and production policies according to their crisis theories. When these policies are guided by strict coalition policy, Olson's comment is valid. However, with the profit motive as a major stimulant for production, in general, viable new technologies are readily adopted and converted to the firms' uses, even at the risk of violating coalition policy.

As for the reallocation of resources, firms' crisis theories dictate the manner in which they use resources. Should they consider coalition policy to be more viable than independent action, they will abide by this policy, complying with resource allocation according to the coalition's considerations. Should they consider their own objectives in terms of independent decision making and growth, they will act accordingly. Economic growth depends on both the implementation of policies that require new technologies and the reallocation of resources, but given that these policies are of utility within the crisis theory, their viability is largely dependent on the phases of the business cycle. If the phase is recessive, then adherence to coalition policy may be the better choice. If the cycle is moving from recession into recovery, perhaps the choice for independence has the greater utility. This choice, however, depends on each firm's crisis theory with respect to its profit position and objectives, and this requires a managerial staff that is capable of generating innovation, imitation, and initiation when necessary.

Olson's eighth implication is that once distributional coalitions are large enough to succeed, they become exclusive, seeking to limit the diversity of incomes and values of their membership. When cartels reach maximum size as determined by their market strength, they have no need for further members, as they control most of the market, with nonmembers exerting only a marginal influence on price and consumption. Once effective market control is achieved, cartels tend to be exclusive, restricting membership. By so doing, they limit the diversity of incomes, focusing primarily on the profits being made from sales of the carteled product, and restricting the values of their memberships by controlling product revenues.

Cartels are as viable as economic units as long as their membership remains intact. If some member can foresee a higher rate of return from sales without the necessity of the cartel, they will become independent. Once this process begins, the cartel loses its influence and becomes entropic. The determining factors for the loss of cartel viability are market orientation and the opportunity for higher profits without cartel regulation.

Customs unions as selective distributive coalitions base their exclusiveness on the geopolitical and economic effectiveness of their competitors. For example, the European Economic Community, in competition with the United States and some Asian countries such as Japan and South Korea, has adopted a policy of including all European countries that have similar industrial bases and that can provide effective competition with the United States and the Asian countries. In this situation, incomes from revenues and the values of membership are limited to the requirements of the Community in general.

With customs unions as with cartels and other such distributional coalitions, the exclusivity of the membership and the amount of regulation on the diversity of incomes and the values of membership depend on the problem areas for which these organizations are formed. With respect to the European customs union, the problem is fixed to the dynamic economic situation and is enduring. Whether these countries will remain unified economically will depend on each country's crisis theory regarding its markets and viability as a producer and consumer. For cartels, this depends on each member's crisis theory concerning its markets and abilities to be independent. Submission to a distributional coalition that controls incomes and values will endure as long as each member finds it to its advantage to maintain its membership. Should a member's crisis theory–given its ability to innovate, imitate, and initiate–indicate that independence is of greater utility than membership, then independence will be opted for, reducing the coalition's viability and utility with respect to its problem area.

Finally, Olson's ninth implication is that the accumulation of distributional coalitions increases the complexity of regulation, the role of government, and the complexity of understanding, and changes the complexity of social evolution. Every society, be it emerging, developing, or postindustrial, has interest groups representing their various causes. These causes–problem areas– may be innovative in the sense of being formed as issues by the groups' organizers, or they may be innovative in the sense of defining real issues external to the group that were articulated and given format and program as crisis theories by the organizers. The increased complexities in the regulation and understanding of these distributional coalitions have to do with the increased complexities of the defined problem areas and the crisis theories posed by these groups.

These distributional coalitions affect the direction of social evolution, but without valid problem areas these coalitions could not exist. As responses to these problems, these coalitions are formed, and their duration depends entirely on their viability. Coalitions exist due to innovation, and viability of the innovative coalition depends on its utility as a functioning organization. Without utility as determined by the working relations between the area and operational languages, the coalition will rapidly decline into entropy. The complexity of regulation refers both to internal regulation necessary within the coalitions, and to external regulation which is social and if necessary, government controlled on the local, national, or international levels. Coalitions multiply in number and expand with respect to their problem areas. This increased complexity usually results in greater government control to maintain the coalitions within their expressed domains and to prevent or limit infractions against personal and social liberties.

This last comment requires clarification, for in the emerging countries, those ruled by dictatorships would not allow the formation of distributional coalitions without government consent, and in many of these cases personal and social liberties are not the prime concern. Such coalitions may be formed by these governments to exert further control of their citizenry. These are examples of governments in the past-oriented stage of development–a topic to be treated in the next chapter. Those emerging countries that are democratically oriented may have to confront distributional coalitions that engage in the de facto unsurpation of power, innovating problem areas and using propaganda to generate a following. Emerging countries, by their very lack of contemporary amenities and opportunities, are often the prey of other countries or nongovernmental factions seeking power. Distributional coalitions in the form of political organizations often take advantage of these countries' positions to install themselves as dictators.

Developing countries that already have established democratic traditions do not have this difficulty. Political distributional coalitions are formed within these countries to compete in a nonrevolutionary manner for economic and political power. Here, they often differ from these types of coalitions in the emerging countries, where the distinction between political power for rule and economic influence over the marketplace is usually well-demarcated.

Regardless of the qualitative and quantitative differences among the emerging, developing, and postindustrial societies, the dynamics for distributional coalitions are the same: they are organized based on the well-being of their members within the context of their organizational purposes. Within the context of their respective sociopolitical orientations, both the leaders and members of these distributional coalitions must consider their organizations in terms of their activities and their objectives for the rest of their respective societies. Should these coalitions be supported directly by the country's political leaders, it means that they have vested interests in maintaining these coalitions and retaining their influences within the country. In postindustrial societies, political leaders have to maintain their professional distance from such coalitions, for this hinders the democratic process by providing political weight for some coalitions without regarding others equally. The political leadership in developing countries often finds it to their professional advantage to support and be supported by such coalitions, especially when democracy is still not firmly rooted in the political processes. The leadership in many emerging countries often lacks the firm political support necessary to govern effectively and must solicit such support from whatever distributional coalitions are effectively active.

In the cases of the developing and emerging countries, wise political leadership can reduce or remove entirely the cynicism and exploitation that such coalitions tend to have owing to their power bases and influences within their respective societies. The point is to mold these coalitions into effective social groups that have been formed and are joined for both personal and social interests. By maintaining such control over these groups, a wise leadership can help channel their objectives to the betterment of society. But this must be undertaken with great skill so as not to give the impression that the leadership effectively supports and is supported by these groups. The emerging and developing countries offer such opportunities for this to be undertaken, and such support has to be terminated once the objectives are achieved.

Consider Olson's final comments:

> May we not then reasonably expect, if special interests are (as I have claimed) harmful to economic growth, full employment, coherent government, equal opportunity, and social mobility, that students of the matter will become increasingly aware of this as time goes on? And that the awareness will eventually spread to larger and larger proportions of the population? And that this wider awareness will greatly limit the losses from the special interests? This is what I expect, at least when I am searching for a happy ending.[7]

Happy ending or no, people are both individualistic and gregarious, and as we must socialize and exist within societies, we will find common interests with other people. When we define these interests as problem areas and construct operational languages to deal with them, we then form special interest groups and distributional coalitions. If we achieve sufficient public support, we can influence the directions taken by government and by society. However, we will not be alone, for others will unite into such groups and express different, perhaps opposing, opinions, and ideological conflict may result. This is the way of social orientation and development. These groups will remain viable for the duration of the utility of their crisis theories. Once this utility declines into entropy, these groups will disband and perhaps form into other groups.

This is the way of social dynamics, and for this reason, the title of this chapter is the rise and change of nations. Nations do not decline as within a downward phase in a cycle of growth; they are changed, altered by the way their citizens formulate their problem areas and by the aggregate viability of their crisis theories formulated to deal with these areas. The postindustrial societies have attained their status through their development since the Industrial Revolution. The aggregate viability of each of these countries' crisis theories, however, determines their positions of wealth, their political influence among themselves, and their ability to influence the policies of the other postindustrial societies and of the emerging and developing countries relative to the other postindustrial societies. (This is discussed further in the next chapter.) However, as nations do not decline but are changed by the manner in which their citizenry formulates their problem areas and the crisis theories to deal with them, it can be readily understood that the wars that have raged among the former Yugoslavian states and in the Middle East, the Russian crisis, and the constant struggles in Africa are examples of crisis theories that are entropic. War, in our social time in our contemporary era, can provide no viable solution to the perceived and constructed problem areas in these regions. The countries involved in these crises have not declined, but for the most part their entry as members into our contemporary era–members with growing economies and the amenities that accompany economic growth and social development–is being postponed, with tragic consequences.

NOTES

1. John Spanier, *Games Nations Play* (New York: Praeger Publishers, 1974), p. 251.

2. Mancur Olson, *The Rise and Decline of Nations* (New Haven, Conn.: Yale University Press, 1982), p. 18. See also p. 74 for a listing of his nine implications.

3. Olson, *The Rise and Decline of Nations*, p. 32.

4. *ibid.*, p. 33. Olson interchanges the terms "one billion" and "hundred million."

5. *ibid.*, p. 33.

6. Although one large telecommunications group reduced its employment for what it considered to be an increase in competitive efficiency.

7. Olson, *The Rise and Decline of Nations*, p. 237.

CHAPTER 12

Crisis Theory and the Dynamics of Nations

There remains, then, the question whether some sections of the elite can act scientifically about political affairs. It is necessary to raise the question in this modified form, rather than about the elite as a whole, because the elite is not ordinarily a homogeneous group.

James Burnham,
The Machiavellians[1]

INTRODUCTORY REMARKS

Further to this comment, James Burnham grants that individuals can conduct their political affairs scientifically or logically. He states that an individual, with some luck, can decide to rise in the social scale and can take appropriate steps that will provide a fair chance of achieving this aim. By deliberate scientific means, he or she can rise to the top rank of social and political power.

Burnham states that the inability of the masses to function scientifically in politics rests on the factors of size, so that the huge size of the mass group makes it too unwieldy for the use of scientific techniques; on the ignorance of the masses about the methods of administration and rule; on the necessity of the masses to devote energy to making a living, which leaves little energy or time to gain more knowledge about politics or carrying out practical political tasks; and on the lack in most people of a sufficient degree of the psychological qualities of ambition, ruthlessness, and so on, that are prerequisites for active political life.[2]

Here, however, is another example of social Heisenbergian theory, in which the actions of those individuals who demostrate initiative and the ability to improve their situations are unpredictable, with some succeeding and others failing. Considered as tired working people, the masses are highly predictable in behavior, lacking the logical and scientific abilities to conduct themselves in a manner appropriate to move them to the upper reaches of social and political power.

This approach poses two difficulties. One, in terms of scientific analysis, this approach is empirical, based on observation and not on rigorous theory. Observed are the masses of people conducting their lives, working as best they can to provide comfortable livelihoods for themselves and their families, and taking, at best, passive roles in the political processes of their societies. Also observed is the fact that only a small minority of each society is engaged actively in political events, and even a smaller percentage of those seek positions of political power. When making this observation, it is tautological to state this as a fact of society. Yet, to state this scientifically, without the basis of a rigorous theory, is erroneous in terms of sociological science, for it sheds no light on the situation that is not already understood through empirical observation.

The second difficulty with this approach is its consideration of the masses as an empirically amorphous class, not partaking in the positions of social and political power. This excludes people forming into pressure groups and distributional coalitions such as those discussed in the previous chapter–for example, unions, cartels, and monopsonies to break cartels–indicating that the masses are not passive, but active when their own interests are concerned. As part of our inheritance from the Industrial Revolution, in our contemporary era of knowledge we recognize that while individuals can achieve greatness through effort and initiative, groups can exert pressure within society to protect and expand their rights. Thus, although the masses still exist and are part of every society, their power is defined in terms of their organizational abilities and the subsequent impact these organizations have on their societies.

The real issue is how much power each type of society relegates to its organizations. Consider, for example, the postindustrial societies. They are democratic politically, for only democracies allow individuals and organizations to achieve personal financial success without the direct intervention of the political powers. This does not, of course, mean that there are no legal obligations on these people and organizations, but each postindustrial country has its own concept of legality in terms of the country's requirements. Even in a postindustrial democracy such as the United States, each state has its own specific laws regulating commerce within it, which are still evolving and are given legal expression because of each state's specific conditions. Laws within postindustrial countries are expressions of requirements that have evolved and are still evolving as these countries developed and are still developing, and they are enforced by the democratic processes that maintain these countries' sociopolitical systems. Laws that are irrelevant owing to development are either ignored or repealed; therefore, only those laws are maintained that allow for these countries to sustain their dynamic growth. Within each postindustrial country's legal system, the rights of individuals and of organizations are protected, providing that neither these individuals nor these organizations threaten the democratic system.

Developing countries may be benevolent monarchies such as those in Morocco and Jordan, in which the ultimate power rests with the monarch but individual political rights are protected and the right to organize is granted as long as they do not clash with this ultimate authority. They may be benevolent dictatorships such as in Singapore which encourages individual initiative and organizations that advance the economy, again providing they do not go against the authority of the ruling power. They may be democracies in the style of the postindustrial countries, such as South Korea, in which political and social protest, free elections, and a viable Parliament to allow opposition are instilled within the system.

The emerging countries are usually dictatorial in orientation. This is justified socially by the lack of political stability that comes from a sound and dynamic economic infrastructure. However, such an infrastructure can be established only if the country has political stability. The emerging countries are formed by the coming together of various strictly unrelated sectors of a region that may or may not have been in conflict with one another. Their union is due to the mutual advantages gained and perceived in the future. But as these sectors have backgrounds prior to their union, they bring with them elements of these backgrounds, among them being the independence they had prior to the union. These elements are often combined with ideologies of outside powers that seek to exploit them for their own geopolitical benefits, thereby bringing instability into the union. Dictators can control this instability through the use of force, which requires limiting organizational and individual liberty to maintain the country's stability. In this way, eventually, it becomes possible to establish a viable political system that allows the formation of economic infrastructure and individual initiative and organizational activity, such as distributional coalitions and unions to protect workers' rights.

Although democracies in emerging countries may be impractical, the durability of dictatorships hinders the very social justification for their existence: that of establishing the basis for economic and social development. Dictators are most reluctant to relinquish their control of their countries, even to the extent that they often make no provisions for the peaceful transfer of power to a chosen successor after their demise, as happened in the former Yugoslavian countries. Yugoslavia's ruler, Marshall Tito, failed to groom a successor, and after his death, those who sought to maintain the balance of power were unable to hold the coalition of countries together. The result was the religious-oriented civil war that has shaken Europe and caused so much suffering and destruction in the 1990's. Sometimes, however, even grooming successors is insufficient, as in Haiti when the Duvalier regime came to an end even though Papa Doc groomed his son to take over. His son fled, and in the turmoil, a democratically elected regime was finally established, only to be overthrown by a military dictatorship, which itself was deposed as a result of the intervention of the United States, which reestablished the elected regime.

Burnham expressed his sentiments within the conceptual framework of the past historical era, when, in the beginning of the Industrial Revolution, people were moving from the rural areas to areas being industrialized. Education was not an important social requirement, but the ability to work in industry was. The concept of the "amorphous masses" perhaps held true then, for there was no real organization of the workers. The guilds of the previous era were made up of skilled workers who protected their interests through apprenticeship and the demand for professional standards, which they set. However, during the early years of the Industrial Revolution, organizing was for conducting business, and if cartels and monopolies were necessary for doing so, they were established. Legal restrictions against these forms of collusion were not yet formulated, but competition still reigned for purposes of gaining control of markets.

Only when industrialization was firmly established did the concept of worker organization become a reality. Samuel Gompers began the first guild-labor movement for cigar makers, and the concept caught on for other types of work. Still, the masses were unrepresented, until socialistic and communistic thinkers began considering how the fruits of industrialization could open up a new world where want, hunger, and discrimination world no longer exist.

It was within the context of the problem area of industrialization that workers' leaders considered their plight. They sought not new worlds, utopias that could never come about, but considered organizing to protect their rights within the context of the Industrial Revolution. Workers' organizations in the form of unions were established, and the conflict with industrialists resulted. It was only at the end of the Industrial Revolution that unions finally gained their full rights as workers' representatives, and the power of organizing for a well-defined cause as such became part of the sociopolitical conceptualization for all countries.

SOCIOPOLITICAL ORIENTATION

Every historical era has its foundations in the era that preceded it. Our contemporary era of knowledge began with the issues of the Great Depression still unresolved. In the aftermath of World War II, the problems of world trade loomed heavily, and the Bretton Woods conference held in July 1944 led to the adoption of the Articles of Agreement of the International Monetary Fund (IMF) and the International Bank for Reconstruction and Development (IBRD) by the United Nations. The objectives of the IMF are to reconcile expansion and balance of growth through international trade, eliminate disruptions of trade by unstable exchange rates, and abolish trade restrictions while seeking to maintain high levels of employment and real incomes within each country. The IBRD, or The World Bank, provided short-term capital for postwar reconstruction as well as long-term policies for promoting larger flows of international private investment. The World Bank was established to operate together with the IMF, with each member subscribing to the Bank's stocks and each member having 250 votes and an additional vote for each stock held.

The issues involved here were not only the reconstruction of the war-torn areas, but also the aspirations of the emerging countries, which posed a problem that had not been considered important previously. The colonizing countries, owing to their own difficult economic conditions after the war, had to yield to the colonies' demand for independence. This raised the issues of external support for these newly independent countries and the directions they would take as they developed economically and socially.

With regard to the postwar problems of the industrialized world, countries such as Great Britain, Germany, and to a lesser extent France, had suffered heavy infrastructural damage during the war and now required massive reconstruction. Once these countries regained their economic infrastructures, however, they quickly reestablished their industrial dominance. Japan had just entered the industrialization stage as the Industrial Revolution came to an end, but having been severely crippled during the war it helped wage, it had to undergo a serious reevaluation of principles. The devastation Japan suffered during the war reinforced its commitment to the new era. While maintaining its imperial tradition, Japan established democracy, and oriented its educational and industrial infrastructures to contributing to and profiting from the era.

As our era developed in its social times, the world leaders and their citizens had to make a decision of sociopolitical orientation. This decision involved not only the form of government, but also the direction these governing systems would take in light of the new era. As a result of our era, this orientation had taken three forms. The future-orientation form had already been adopted by the postindustrial countries, not so much as a matter of conscious decision, but by the nature of their strong industrial bases and the contributions they were making as a result of their emphasis on industrial output and education to meet the needs of domestic and international competition. This resulted in the paradox of industrialization, which has become part of our era and its social time. (This paradox and its consequences are discussed in Chapter 13.)

The two other forms of orientation are past orientation and present orientation, with each orientation manifested in the domestic and international policies of the countries that include them. These forms have not become so deeply embedded in these countries' individual systems that they cannot be altered and ultimately replaced by a future orientation. This is due to the influence of the future-oriented countries on those countries of past and present orientation. This is a long process, however, often entailing bloodshed, as was the case in Romania when Ceausescu and his wife were overthrown and executed. The former Soviet Union achieved a somewhat more peaceful transition from communist dictatorship to the beginnings of a genuine parliamentary democratic regime.

The past-oriented countries follow the patterns set by the future-oriented countries, as these countries generate knowledge and technology. The past-oriented countries also have to maintain competitive postures with respect to the future-oriented countries as they vie for support from both present- and future-oriented countries in their competition for influence in these countries and other past-oriented countries. Because of their past orientation and their refusal to deviate from their historical foundations, they have to acquire technologies on levels that their systems have been incapable of developing.

The importation of future-oriented technologies is a significant development and needs to be encouraged as long as these technologies have no military applications. With regard to these technologies, an internal conflict arises in which the past meets the future in the absorption and application of these technologies. The conflict is manifested in past-oriented societies, basing their sociopolitical, economic, and foreign policies on past conceptualizations while incorporating contributions from societies that–while respecting their histories– are future-oriented.

This scenario inevitably sets up a clash between past and future, with the future the winner for three important reasons. One reason is the obvious situation that the past, though important, is gone; it holds weight only as a set of circumstances, data, and relationships. The past cannot be altered and is better understood only as more information about it is revealed and clarified. The second reason, also obvious, is that the future has not yet been realized, and the events of the present will assuredly affect future development. By obtaining future-oriented technology in the present, the past-oriented societies can better understand the circumstances that help form the future. The relevant changes can then be implemented to cope with the future-oriented technologies and their implications for the past-oriented societies and the present- and future-oriented societies.

The third reason is a political one and refers to the international competition that still exists between the future- and the past-oriented societies for the present-oriented societies' alliances and alignments in the ordering of the geopolitical struggle for resources, markets, and military bases. The future-oriented societies are therefore making greater efforts to continue the development and expansion of knowledge in disequilibrium crisis theories. In addition, the clash between past and future in the past-oriented societies intensifies as they incorporate future-oriented technologies. These technologies are difficult to incorporate in the sociopolitical and economic climates in which the past weighs so heavy that little serious consideration is given to changing the orientation. Therefore, these technologies must possess a degree of adaptation to enable them to fit and be effectively deployed in these societies. This effort requires retraining and rethinking, which cannot be accomplished without loosening the reins on the spirit of inquiry. Thus, a thawing out will eventually occur; in fact, it is occurring now in many of the past-oriented countries, moving them into present orientation. Although there will be continuing conflict between the conservatives of various shades of opinion (from being reluctant to accept social change but accepting it anyway as the inevitable movement of history to the more extreme view of considering social change a betrayal of principles, ideologies, and teachings on which the society was and is still being formed) and the liberals (who, though patriots, recognize the need for social change made necessary by the adaptation of new technologies and the dynamics within the society these technologies will generate). This clash is necessary for reevaluating values and for bringing the past-oriented societies into the dynamics of our contemporary era and its social times.

The situation of the past-oriented countries in our geopolitical complex results from two apparently paradoxical strains of thought, in the form of two approaches to domestic and international politics that represent both independence and dependence. This paradox is as ancient as civilization itself: what form of government system is to be established that can best maintain control in domestic and international spheres, while participating in the commonwealth of nations in trade and political alliances? This paradox is one for the past-oriented countries because the forms of government they choose historically allow only for domestic control. This situation is explained, indeed justified, on the basis of controlling internal disorder within the country. Hence, there is the need for a governing system that can establish a conservative foundation within the country on which to build a socioeconomic infrastructure and allow the country to move into our contemporary historical era.

The paradox is manifested in past-orientated countries whose governing systems are oppressive, maintaining order at the expense of individual initiative in the political and economic arenas. With the control of politics and economics within the country, there is also the need for a less restrictive approach to international trade and relations. The two different approaches are, therefore, for internal control and foreign relations, where the internal control is repressive and the purpose of foreign relations is liberal to the extent that is acceptable to the community of nations.

The paradox is that, by assuming strict internal control, these countries can operate internationally according to the public relations image the leaders want to project, without provoking extensive internal dissent, thereby seeking to limit the damage to their countries in the conduct of their foreign relations. This Janus-faced attitude, expressed in the approaches to domestic and foreign policies, can persist for the duration of internal control. It cannot, however, persist for the duration of the dictatorship because communications with the present- and future-oriented countries, so necessary for commerce and political support internationally, expose the internal policies, leading to international condemnation. The dictatorships in Cuba, Iraq, and Lybia, and the extreme religious dictatorship in Iran are examples.

Other past-oriented countries in which dictatorships reign do not criticize these countries, for the reason that they do not want to draw attention to their own policies. They sacrifice the very assistance from the present- and future-oriented countries on which they must rely for foreign trade and financial aid. Past-oriented countries with natural resources such as oil that are in world demand do not have to rely heavily on aid, for their commodities are traded on market terms. Other countries that rely primarily on a single product that is not in great world demand–such as Cuba's sugar–are subject to competitive market conditions and their ability to compete with other countries. This competition is hindered as dictatorships enforce their policies while maintaining low-income initiatives, with resulting social problems, such as the decline in health services, substandard education, declining municipal services, and corruption as both civil servants and the other citizenry seek to protect and enhance their own socioeconomic positions.

The consequence is neocolonialism. Traditional colonialism has largely been repudiated in our contemporary era. Where such colonialism does still exist, it is with the agreement of the majority of the population in the colonial countries. Indeed, the Falklands War in 1982 was precisely about such an issue. The Argentinian government sought to claim these islands, while their people wanted to remain British. The result was the British invasion of these islands and their retaking them from Argentinian military control. In the history of our contemporary era, those colonies that have sought independence have been granted it, and the political and economic relationships between the independent countries and their former colonizers have been maintained, usually on terms suitable to both.

In contrast, neocolonialism may or may not involve previous colonies; this depends on the historical situation of each past-oriented country. This form of colonialism is manifested by the dependence which the past-oriented country imposes on its benefactors for reasons of economic support and political and military backing in the international arena. All past-oriented countries share the need for economic support, because they must build socioeconomic infrastructures for their countries to develop. In these circumstances, these countries do not permit economic support to affect their independence in their form of government, while it might affect this support in their international relations by being rejected as allies by other geopolitical blocs. The leaders of the neocolonial past-oriented countries seek sponsors and, having found them, attach their economies to those of their sponsors. Such an example was Cuba. The former Soviet Union was once the main consumer of Cuba's primary commodity, its sugar crop. Several Middle Eastern countries, such as Syria (and prior to the Yom Kippur War, Egypt), also attached their economies to that of the former Soviet Union, and as a consequence, their economies became dependent primarily on Soviet and their satellite markets. Egypt is now a recipient of annual aid from the United States, and while tourism is a heavy industry in Egypt, it is attempting to diversify its economy, seeking to trade with as many partners as it can find. Syria has sought aid from the United States, but its stance on the peace talks with Israel and its support of terrorism are serious obstacles for U.S. and other postindustrial countries' support. Its position on the peace talks has also weakened Syria among the more extreme regimes in the region, thereby hindering its trading possibilities still further.

The unique aspect of neocolonialism is that it commits the leaders of the past-oriented countries to their colonizers, so that the established markets produce a rigidity in their economies that can be changed only with the colonizer's consent. There are established crisis theories between the colonizer and the colonized country. As these crisis theories become entropic, no innovation is tolerated. Little initiation is sanctioned if it results in deviations that are too extreme from the established crisis theories' concepts, unless they satisfy the colonizing country. The uniqueness of this neocolonialism is that the leaders of the colonized countries consider their countries to be sovereign, with their own political systems and military forces for its conduct of defense and foreign policy. Yet, they are dependent on their colonizers for their markets, and since these markets are their main sources of income, their internal markets are so tied.

With regard to the case of Cuba again, its reliance on the former Soviet Union for aid and for purchase of its sugar crop placed the Cuban economy in a neocolonialist situation. While the Soviet Union remained united, this relationship held, and the Soviets were Cuba's patron, supporting its markets and purchasing its sugar crop. This allowed the Cuban leaders to base their economy on the Soviet Union's decision to make its sugar crop its economic mainstay. With the demise of the Soviet Union, Cuba has had to find new markets, and in view of the strong competition with other sugar-exporting countries, the Cuban economy has suffered from the decline of its markets. Still, its economy could be strengthened if its leaders would abandon their past orientation in the economic system and its emphasis on a single-crop policy and move into a future-oriented system of liberal internal politics and more open international relations. Relying on its version of Marxist-Leninist doctrine as the basis of its economic policies (when Russia and the other former Soviet countries are trying to move into a future orientation and when communist China is vacillating between its doctrinaire version of Marxist-Leninist policies and the future orientation of our contemporary era), Cuba's leaders are trying to maintain the economy in the face of its lack of raw materials because of its declining export position and the necessary monetary and fiscal policies to rectify this situation. With its economy in critical condition and its markets dwindling because of inefficient domestic policies, Cuba nevertheless maintains its position as the bastion of communism in Latin America, standing against the influence of the United States and continuing its rift with that country. As an example of neocolonialism, with its sociopolitical and economic system and its leaders directly supported by another country, Cuba's situation demonstrates just how precarious neocolonialism can be.

Chapter 7 stated the general schematic for crisis theories of countries that have entered our contemporary era of knowledge. It took the form $C^{**}=\sum_{}^{n} [C^* (C^*_e U \ C^*_u)]_t$. The emerging countries, because of their sociopolitical and economic situations, have not fully entered our era as generators of knowledge in the arts and sciences and are therefore not active participants in our era. Their crisis theory schematic therefore takes the form $C^{**}_{em} = \sum_{}^{n}[(C^*_{em} U \ C^*_u)]_t$, ($C^{**}_p > C^{**}_{em}$), with the subscript "p" indicating the contributions of the postindustrial countries, and the subscript "em" indicating the contributions in these fields by the emerging countries, contributions that are far exceeded by those of the postindustrial countries.

The crisis theories of the emerging countries are mainly in the fields of distributional coalitions in the realm of political affiliations and economic organizations. This is because of the political instability that permeates these countries. Prior to the demise of the Soviet Union, the emerging countries gained some stability by using the big power blocs to their advantage. They played one country against another, and shifted alliances when this was politically and economically feasible for domestic reasons and when the big powers allowed some of their client countries this flexibility.

Since the end of the Soviet Union, the geopolitical situation has changed radically. Because big power competition is no longer a major factor in geopolitical dynamics, emerging countries must rely on their own geographically strategic positions to acquire aid for their economic development and military support when necessary for fending off predator countries and maintaining internal stability. Both the institutional investment and personal efforts in developing the arts and sciences in these countries are subservient to the investment and efforts in forming governmental–and, where acceptable, private–distributional coalitions for establishing power bases in these countries. These endeavors both hinder the national contributions in the arts and sciences, and affect the programs to improve education. Hence, the educational standards in these countries are lower than those of the developing countries, and this situation influences every aspect of the emerging societies.

The crisis theories of these countries have proven to be as enduring as the governments that sanction them, and they are employed regardless of the technologies used in the developing countries. Antiquated farming techniques and outdated understanding of soil conservation and crop rotation, together with inadequate storage of grains in anticipation of poor crop years, take their toll on the emerging countries. Especially hard hit are those countries engaged in civil wars. In these countries the distributional coalitions in the form of military organizations vie for power, often destroying farmland and preventing the educational systems from functioning. In emerging countries such as Cuba and North Korea where official distributional coalitions exist only through government permission, such warring conditions never occur. The dictators controlling these countries, however, have established their countries' farming policies in terms of their official ideologies. In Cuba, for example, the sugar crop yield and harvesting are viewed as a sign of Marxism-Leninism's superiority to the West's decadent capitalism. Similarly, in North Korea the auxiliary organizations that distribute the produce, service the vehicles, process the foodstuffs, and maintain the stores that provide selling distribution points, such as grocery stores, operate according to government ideology. Otherwise, they would not be so employed.

These ideologies are justified on the basis that without strong governments based on ideology, these countries would break up into warring regimes. Only through the ideologies, as well as the governments that establish and support them, can the unity of these countries be guaranteed. This argument can be justified only if these ideologies do indeed seek to establish a basis for organization in which the countries' regions are united and working together, in order to bring them into a developing status. If, on the other hand, the argument is used to justify the governments' enduring dictatorships (as it most often is), then these countries will remain in their emerging status, continuing to seek aid from the developing and postindustrial countries. They will maintain their citizens in a state of semiliteracy in the name of ideological purity, and they will continue to be sources of geopolitical instability in their respective geographical regions as well as for the rest of the world. The situations in North Korea and Cuba attest to this state of affairs.

However the alliances of these countries shift owing to changing geopolitical conditions, the ideologies may not be sufficient to maintain country unity. In Yugoslavia, for example, Tito did not groom a successor, and soon after his death, the Soviet Union declined and the anti-Soviet ideology that had held the country together since World War II was no longer valid. With the threat from the outside no longer an issue, the historical conflicts based on religious and ethnic differences that were held in check during Marshall Tito's dictatorship now became important enough for the ethnic communities to seek to resolve. With the end of national ideological unity and with the great differences dividing all sides, the military option was deployed with devastating consequences. As a result, United Nations negotiators, the United States, and the North Atlantic Treaty Organization (NATO) have worked assiduously to secure a working cease-fire and to effect political reconciliation. With an ongoing peace process, the countries that once formed Yugoslavia may yet join the ranks of the newly emerging countries, together with Hungary, Romania, and other countries in the now defunct Soviet bloc. Only after real peace comes to this region, however, can a commitment be made to moving into the present-oriented developing stage.

The developing countries will never have to face a Yugoslavia-type situation, for they have already resolved their old, troubling internal and external issues. Moreover, the economic stakes are now too high for military ventures to be undertaken. The present-oriented countries have committed themselves to economic–and hence political–integration within their geographical regions, and as they seek ties with other developing and the postindustrial countries, their primary concern is to achieve internal socioeconomic development. The military option for resolving conflicts, though always available, will be used only when such conflicts cannot be resolved through peaceful means, for none of these countries would want to risk the destruction of their economic infrastructure.

Viable developing countries are those that have made a temporary commitment to present orientation, with the intention of moving into future orientation once they have achieved a sufficient degree of economic growth allowing them to compete with the future-oriented postindustrial societies. The crisis theory schematic for these countries takes the form $C^{**}_{dc} = \sum_{1}^{n} [(C^{*}_{dc} \cup C^{*}_{u})]_t$, $(C^{**}_{p} > C^{**}_{dc})$, with the subscript "dc" indicating the contributions of the developing countries, contributions that are exceeded by those of the postindustrial countries.

The leaders of some present-oriented countries, in spite of this commitment, seek to delay the move into future orientation in order to forestall their relinquishing of power. By yielding to the democratic processes necessary in future-oriented democratic countries, they would have to resign or be deposed. Hence, present-oriented developing countries cannot establish sound socioeconomic infrastructures and move into future-oriented conditions until they accept democracy, with each country expressing this process according to its evolved traditions.

Countries such as Singapore, South Korea, and to some extent, mainland China, though considered developing countries, have already achieved fairly high levels of economic growth. Although each is a developing country, each has its own approach to the democratic process and has made a commitment to future orientation. This commitment is reflected in each country's economic performance and in its political and economic relationships with other developing countries, as well as with the postindustrial countries that seek trade with them.

The country that is least committed to the democratic process and future orientation is Communist China. The Chinese leadership justifies this policy stance on several grounds. First, following the end of the Soviet Union and the Cold War, China has remained intact, with its former politically and militarily troublesome neighbor no longer a problem. However, even in this social time of reconciliation, because of its population size and military strength, China continues to exert sufficient influence to guarantee markets for its goods and services. Moreover, because of the size of its workforce, there is no need for high levels of technology in agriculture and other industries that other developing countries require for efficient domestic commerce and international competition. Its large population and its government control of the domestic markets more than compensate for this lack.

Another factor is China's potential and actual consumer markets for the postindustrial countries' goods and services. In some instances, branches of these countries' businesses with their industrial capital and knowledge have to be established in China; this emphasizes China's own economic strength with its vast population with respect to its trading partners. The introduction of postindustrial business techniques into the Chinese economy has not only led to a break with many traditional methods of manufacture and marketing; it has also brought a new liberty in lifestyles and the imitation of the postindustrial nation's way of life. With the military threat diminished after the Soviet Union broke apart, the new liberty led to the questioning of the communist dictatorship by the youth and businesspeople who sought relaxed restrictions on thought, reading materials, and exposure to people from the postindustrial countries. When, as a result, the communist ideology was threatened, the government cracked down on what it considered "dissident behavior." This brought China into the peculiar situation of requiring the business knowledge and technology of the postindustrial countries while being cautious about exposure to the postindustrial ethos and the liberty it implies.

Another factor concerns the Chinese government: this is the decline of world communism as a result of the changes in the former Soviet bloc. During Premier Mikhail Gorbachev's term, Japan's increasing economic strength, together with the strength of the U.S. economy in world competition, were causes of real concern. But, as noted earlier, it was the rise of the European Economic Community that finally made the Soviet leadership realize that their economy was in no position to compete effectively in the world's markets. Gorbachev recognized that the Soviet Union's trading relations with its satellite countries, such as Hungary, Poland, and Czechoslovakia, were insufficient to maintain a competitive posture with the United States, Japan, and the EEC. Through Gorbachev's initiative, the restructuring of the Soviet economy began, with the emphasis on both the quantity and quality of goods and services produced according to the quotas of the planning board. Moreover, managers were given broader decision-making power concerning their respective markets.

A new wind was blowing through the musty industry of the Soviet Union. But as Gorbachev and the Soviet leadership in general learned, economic freedom–no matter how little–cannot exist without a corresponding degree of political freedom. The programs of perestroika and glasnost that opened up the Soviet economy introduced the necessary political freedom, but they had the unexpected consequence that many of the Soviet states and the satellite countries now demanded complete political freedom to determine their own destinies. Thus, Gorbachev's reforms resulted in the dissolution of the Union and brought Russia and the other states into a confederation known as the Commonwealth of Independent States.

With respect to China, prior to World War II, the country was partitioned into areas by the warlords who ruled them, with the areas' boundaries being as flexible as the warlords' abilities to maintain power over their regions. It was under Mao's leadership and inspiration that the country, with its vast land mass and population, achieved national unity. This unity was to be guarded by Mao's inheritors, and because of the Soviet Union's experience, the Chinese distrust the type of economic freedom needed to bring the economy and the country fully into our contemporary era.

The leadership's decision to maintain China in a present orientation poses serious economic and political difficulties. Only by remaining a dictatorship can the present economic and political system be preserved, and with China's history and its vast population and land mass, no other system seems conceivable. Thus, China's crisis theories for its social and political situations are present oriented, and little serious consideration is being given to the future. China's repossession of Hong Kong in 1997 presents many problems along these lines. This once British colony is very much in the future orientation mode, and many observers fear that China's regime, not knowing how to handle future orientation, may impose its present orientation on Hong Kong's socioeconomic and political institutions.

It is the economic sphere, however, that will probably enable China to move into future orientation. Using Hong Kong as an example, we observe that the profit motive, though somewhat alien to mainland China's system, is integral to Hong Kong's system. With the postindustrial countries making an impact on China's economy and with Hong Kong's know-how in manufacturing and marketing and its reputable stock exchange, China's economic'position can well benefit.[4] Its population program, while long term, can also benefit its industrialization by allowing the establishment of a strong technological base as well as an established workforce. Over the long run, the workforce can be traded off, with technology replacing physical labor as much as possible as in the postindustrial countries.

China's conflict with Taiwan, which is ideological in origin, can be resolved without military confrontation. Military confrontation would be unwise, for it would upset the region's stability and most likely result in a cold war situation with the United States, a situation that neither country wants. Economic integration could result in the mainland acquiring Taiwanese industrial technology and marketing techniques, and Taiwan participating in developing the mainland's vast market potential. For this to be achieved, adroit leadership from both sides is required to develop appropriate and mutually acceptable crisis theories. Once accepted and employed, these theories will be a strong indicator that mainland China is willing to move into future orientation, as Taiwan is attempting to do.

Unlike China, Singapore's commitment to present orientation seems to be unchallenged by its geographical and political circumstances. Its economy is efficient and stable, growing at the rate prescribed by its leadership. Its location on the China Sea provides shipping to markets throughout the world. As a tourist-oriented country, and with its low crime rate, it provides a haven for those who accept its way of life. Singapore can be termed a benevolent dictatorship, and it is a stable country because the political leadership has no real viable opposition. Its stores are full, and its citizens are fairly content with its lifestyle. Thus, it has no reason to move into future orientation, and the country will most likely maintain this position until genuine democracy is initiated. This change to democracy will come about when the entire region becomes more dynamic economically, thereby requiring the political commitment to democratically acceptable opposition parties. Only then will Singapore feel the pressure of economic competition and develop crisis theories that are competitive and democratically oriented. Opposition parties contesting the government's policies will then be formed and, due to competition, will become effective, making Singapore a fully democratic and innovative country. Until then, its crisis theories will continue to reflect its present orientation, leaving the country in a situation for which there is no great incentive for change.

Contrary to China and Singapore, South Korea is present-oriented and is moving into future orientation. Having been occupied by Japan and having received its independence after World War II, Korea split in 1945 into North and South at the 38th parallel. The northern part of the country became communist, supported in part by mainland China and in part by the Soviet Union; the South chose democratic capitalism and, while remaining independent, received support from the United States. When in 1950 the North invaded the South, the United Nations was called on to enact a defensive response, with the United States justifying its sending in troops as a police action, thereby eliminating the necessity for a proclamation of war. After much senseless bloodshed, the conflict was temporarily resolved, with both sides meeting in peace talks at the 38th parallel; a standoff situation exists between the two states, with occasional border skirmishes.

With one historical people in two countries, the North has lost its firm communist support. The Soviet Union no longer exists, and Russia has its own difficulties and cannot afford to continue backing the North; China has also become less generous and is demanding hard currency–preferably U.S. dollars–in payment for its grains and other materials. The North is rather reluctantly turning to the United States for assistance while maintaining its present orientation. Given North Korea's economic and international political circumstances, this ideology may yield to necessity and a future-oriented attitude may yet prevail.

South Korea's cold war relationship with the North, its years under Japanese occupation prior to World War II, and its domination by the postindustrial economies since then have moved the country from being a war-torn satellite of the Western-oriented countries to a thriving democracy and economy that is providing the postindustrial countries with strong competition in its internal markets. Its political system, being democratic, allows for internal competition among both domestic businesses and internationally based multinational firms, giving expression to the contemporary concept of democracy as a system of governing that can survive only in an economically competitive country. Even though South Korea has international businesses on its soil, it has also become internationally competitive in electronics, automobiles, textiles and other products through which the postindustrial countries have previously dominated world trade.

Although South Korea tends to a future orientation, it nevertheless remains in a present orientation because of its financial defense burden and its dependence on the United States for military and financial aid in defense against its northern neighbor. Even with North Korea's difficult financial position, it still engages in periodical border skirmishes and occasionally threatens to develop nuclear weapons using technologies supplied by China and other anti-Western countries that are not within the domain of future orientation. As a consequence, the U.S.

responses has come in the form of threats and some assistance to the North, as well as support for the South, to reduce the tensions and attempt to bring the North into at least a present-oriented position. Because of South Korea's own defense burden, it must expend money and manpower that could better be used to expand its education system, industrial output, and economic and social innovations expressed in its crisis theories.

In summary, the Asian continent is a region of great potential. China's vast markets are awaiting development, but its inner dynamism is held in check by its present-oriented dictatorial government. Countries such as Thailand, Malaysia, Burma, Singapore, Vietnam, the Koreas, and Cambodia are capable of moving into future orientation. South Korea has demonstrated this potential with its democratic government, its economic output, and its domestic and international marketing abilities.

With respect to the sociopolitical orientation of the African continent, its countries are seeking their own identities, but in many instances they are plagued by tribal conflicts, often resulting in policies of genocide in our contemporary era. These countries have long known the abuses of their peoples, and their tribal heritages are deeply rooted in their cultures. Thus, when, in the aftermath of World War II, the postindustrial countries rejected classical colonialism and granted these countries independence, their past orientation was so deeply ingrained that political parties based on tribal considerations were formed to rule these countries. The difficulty is not only political rivalry, but also deep-seated hostility among the tribes, which was held in check by the colonizing powers but unleashed anew with independence. This hostility has often erupted into violence and sometimes in near-tribal genocide, as Rwanda's experience demonstrates. With the various tribes seeking to rule, and because of the intertribal conflicts this generates, their past orientation has been maintained.

The peoples of the African countries are dynamic, but with the vast African continent divided into countries on the basis of tribes, many conflicts within national borders have been generated. Because the continent has known physical and economic exploitation by other countries, the people accept tribal rule as they look within their borders for leadership that will bring them into our contemporary era. Outsiders are distrusted; leaders from within their own tribes are supported, and with several tribes within national borders, the dominant tribe often fails to give the others proportional representation. With their vast natural resources, enlightened leadership uniting their peoples and working for their betterment often comes to the fore. All too frequently, however, once a government becomes established, it is maintained by tribal favors and patronization, thereby continuing past orientation. The starvation in Sudan, the corruption in Zäire, and the tribal wars and dictatorships in many African countries are expressions of this condition, and so the inner dynamism of the majority of the African peoples is held in check.

South Africa—and to some extent Zimbabwe (formerly Rhodesia)—are the exceptions. Both countries were founded on the policy of apartheid, and both are now governed by black leaders. Because of Rhodesia's relationship to Great Britain, its policies were changed owing to the boycott of Rhodesia after Ian Smith issued a unilateral declaration of independence. After much bargaining, and because of the effects of the international boycott on the economy, the British brought the Smith government down and established a democratically elected government. The country was given the name of Zimbabwe, approved by the British, in which the rights of all citizens were to be protected. Zimbabwe's resources, having been part of a British colony, were not as developed as South Africa's. While this situation is slowly changing, since becoming independent it has maintained a present-orientation position that has allowed the inequities of apartheid to be disposed of without great social disruption. Zimbabwe has thus provided its peoples with work and opportunities for a decent education, living in a democracy and developing international relations and commerce. It has thereby provided the foundatation for the country to move into future orientation and develop unique crisis theories for its society, to be recognized as viable by other present- and future-oriented countries.

Although South Africa has also based its sytem on apartheid, its situation differs from Rhodesia's. As a country that gained its independence early in its history, after many years of hesitating, it finally yielded to the demands of the postindustrial countries and to international pressure from citizens everywhere who found apartheid repugnant, and installed a black leader who once served time in prison for his opposition to apartheid.

South Africa's diamond, gold, and armaments industries were well established during apartheid, with its diamond and gold industries based largely on nonwhite labor, which was socially and politically discriminated against under the apartheid laws. As which all such businesses in other countries, its armaments industry has been affected by the end of the Cold War and by strong competition among the current traders. It is now a marginal industry with international contracts and sales greatly reduced.

Following the abolition of apartheid, international companies are finding the economic climate suitable for investments. This is resulting in South Africa's change of emphasis from the heavy industries of diamonds and gold, and to a lesser extent armaments, to areas such as international finance, tourism, and other businesses that are domestically and internationally profitable. Its educational system is benefiting from visiting educators who had previously boycotted the country. This has long-run consequences for the improvement of the country's economy and international standing.

South Africa's abolition of apartheid has also resulted in a high crime rate; this is an unexpected result, as the effects of the economic activity are taking time to be realized throughout the country. Poverty and revenge for years of racial discrimination are the main causes of crime, induced by areas of great wealth surrounded by pockets of poverty. Thus, resources and money that could be used for education, the building of infrastructure, investment, and spending in manufacturing are going into security and the protection of property. But the emigration rate is not high, and the citizens have confidence in the leadership's ability to realize the country's promise and move from present orientation with its static crisis theories into a future orientation in which innovation, imitation, and initiation in all realms of political, social, scientific, and economic activity will eventually prevail.

Central and South America are mainly present-oriented areas. Dictatorships and corruption have plagued the countries in these regions, rendering their citizens both hopeful when democracy is restored and skeptical that it will endure. Chile's democratically elected government was overthrown, replaced by dictatorship, which in turn was replaced by a newly restored democracy. Argentina's experience has been similar, with its military dictatorship being replaced by a popular democracy. Moreover, the problems of narcotics and the corruption in local and national government that results from the power of the drug lords are not new to countries in Latin and South America. Colombia and Panama are notorious for their drug manufacturing and distribution, mainly to the North American continent, and Mexico's drug merchants have provided conduits into the southern region of the United States. Real productive industry justified by the peoples' dynamism, however, is lacking in these regions. The purpose of the North American Free Trade Act is to vitalize industry by stimulating exports from these countries as well as exports to them, and by relocating North American industries in countries with access to raw materials and new markets, where labor is efficient and its costs lower than in the northern continent.

These regions have made some moves toward future orientation, but the status quo of present orientation persists. The changes from dictatorship to democracy to dictatorship and then again to democracy have no doubt contributed to the regions' instability. The arguments for dictatorship in these countries have been based on the seeming lack of public control by democratic governments, which has resulted in the tendency for social institutions to break down. Dictatorships have thus been justified on the grounds of reestablishing order and the traditions of the countries in which they take control, but there has never been a clear definition of what the governments have to do with tradition, as government systems change all too often. But as Argentina's and Chile's dictatorships have demonstrated, the contributions of dictatorial regimes in each country are well established. With the dictatorships in these countries now out of power, the economic and sociopolitical consequences of their rules are being analyzed. The harm to their countries and the senseless loss of lives justified in the defense of their regimes are now being exposed.

The present orientation of these countries is manifested in the ways they pertain to labor relations in light of the influences of domestic and international big business. For present orientation, Mancur Olson's argument is correct; the debilitating social and economic consequences of present orientation in terms of Olson's position in these countries are readily perceived. But as industries move from the North, bringing with them the technologies necessary for efficient manufacturing, and with governments in these countries needing new industries and the benefits of employment they bring, the influences of present orientation will exist together in these countries with the future orientation brought in by the new industries. As the dynamics of industrialization become established, the necessary infrastructure, technology, and education will be incorporated in these countries, and will help strengthen their democratic systems, enabling local industries to expand and develop in competition among themselves and with industries from their regional and northern neighbors.

Three more geographical areas merit attention here, each with its special problems and attempts to resolve them in terms of sociopolitical orientation. The Indian continent is one area in which all three orientations are integrated into their societies, with each country expressing these orientations in different ways. India, for example, has its overpopulation problem and its strong diverse religious beliefs that have often resulted in conflict and bloodshed among their followers. Gandhi's historical pacifistic protest against the British, which won India its independence, led to the formation of Pakistan and eventually to Bangladesh, after the Bengali people achieved their independence from Pakistan. The conflicts within and among these countries show that their differences are far from being resolved.

India and Pakistan have strong aspects of past orientation in the form of the influence of religion on their governments, and the conflicts these influences often generate within and among their countries. The aspects of present orientation are manifested in their economic and sociopolitical orientation, as they lack the necessary internal unity and infrastructure for building future-oriented societies with strong innovation, imitation, and initiation. They have aspects of future orientation, however, because their industries are capable of moving into highly technological production and innovation resulting from the incorporation of technologies into their economic and sociopolitical structures, removing the seemingly pernicious poverty and bringing their peoples into a condition of productivity and domestic and international competition.

On the Indian continent, the Bengali people have perhaps suffered more than the others, as their claim to independence was paid for in blood. Even with all the international assistance given to the fledging country, its socioeconomic infrastructure remains inadequate for maintaining a reasonable standard of living. The influences of past orientation in this region in the form of religion–as in other past-oriented areas such as the Middle East–prevent sufficient understanding of religion's purpose in our contemporary world in which spiritual matters have become separate from material issues. The need for economic development in this country is extremely pressing. The Bengali leadership has not demonstrated the necessary skills in achieving this development at a rate sufficient to bring their country into a present-oriented condition, which will provide opportunities for future orientation and participation in our contemporary era of knowledge.

For future orientation to be established in the countries of this region, present orientation must first be firmly established. Thus, religion must come to be accepted as both a personal and a social affair to be engaged in by those who follow religious teachings; it cannot be a source of conflict and bloodshed in present-oriented societies. The diversification of religious beliefs allows people to deal with their spiritual matters in ways they find acceptable and suitable according to their traditions. The imposition of religious beliefs on others, which occurred in the Dark Ages and to a lesser extent in the Renaissance and the Industrial Revolution, has no place in our contemporary era, or in present-oriented countries capable of moving into future orientation. In addition, differences in political orientation cannot be resolved by conflict and bloodshed, but rather must be debated as rationally as possible, according to the issues involved.

This is an important consideration, for these countries with a common history of colonization cannot resolve the differences that resulted in independence through war or political hostility. For these countries to move solidly into present orientation, they must establish sufficient internal harmony to build infrastructures that will promote internal integration and competition so that the region can be united in economic competition and cooperation. The workforces in these countries are sufficient to achieve this objective, given wise political leadership for developing economic policies and effective banking systems for the efficient use of money and stimulation of competition.

Political independence without the economic viability of at least the status of present orientation means that these countries are subjected to neocolonialism. Such was the case with Eastern Europe when the Soviet Union imposed past-oriented communist ideology on them and incorporated these countries into a mercantilistic common market in which their economies were geared for production to supply the Soviet economy and were dependent on the Soviets for their main foreign markets. (Eastern Europe is discussed further in the next chapter in the context of future orientation and the paradox of industrialization.) Hence, for countries to move strongly into present orientation, they must be independent both politically and economically. Otherwise, the neocolonizers will impose their own orientations on these countries, and as was the case with Cuba, leave them with untenable economic circumstances if the sponsorship should be removed for whatever reason.

Moving into present orientation, therefore, provides the basis for industrialization and independence. Political independence can be maintained when no single country or bloc of countries under the influence of a single country provides aid and assistance as well as market availability. For an emerging country like Bangladesh to achieve present orientation, it must establish the rule of just and equal law to protect its citizens from religious persecution and provide a sound economic infrastructure on which its economy can be built and expanded. International aid and assistance has to be obtained by emerging countries, because these are necessary and important sources of financing. However, the political leaders of the emerging countries must use their skills in obtaining these sources without compromising their countries' independence. In Cuba's case, this compromising was welcomed by the Cuban government, which rejected capitalism, and by the Soviet Union, which obtained a military position of the shore of the United States.

The Middle East is a region in which rulers of many countries have maintained past orientation.[5] Secure in its religious teachings, those countries with great wealth from oil revenues are nevertheless insecure. This is because this wealth is due not to the labors of its people as in the postindustrial countries, but to the exploitation of the main natural resource of oil. Moreover, the exploitation of oil to yield great wealth is a fairly recent phenomenon in this region. Until the Yom Kippur War of 1973, oil was considered a profitable source of revenue, even at its low price per barrel. In the aftermath of the war, output was curtailed and prices were raised, making oil even more profitable with the threat of even greater reductions in output and higher prices for those countries that did not censure Israel for its military victory in the war.[6] Hence, oil was used as a weapon, especially against the postindustrial countries so that they would pressure Israel to retreat from the territories captured in the war. The postindustrial countries, being unprepared for this war, were equally unprepared for the oil shortages and the high prices that resulted. Moreover, the oil-exporting countries used their newly acquired leverage to obtain military and political benefits to increase their influence in world affairs and to protect their precious resource.

The oil profits were used to accumulate great material wealth, but as this resource comes from the ground, its supply is finite. After the initial impact of the use of oil as a weapon and for leverage, other energy sources, such as coal, gas, and atomic energy, have come on line, reducing oil revenues. Use of oil as a weapon against Israel and as political and military leverage in the postindustrial societies has subsided, and OPEC and other oil-exporting countries now exhibit a degree of uncertainty in their destinations. As already noted, their great wealth was not established on the basis of labor and industrialization, which are essential for a society to move from past to present orientation, and eventually into future-oriented postindustrialization. Nor are any real efforts being made to establish sufficient infrastructure necessary for industrialization.

Somewhat ironically, the great wealth accumulated from oil revenues has enhanced the past orientation of the majority of Middle Eastern Countries.[7] In the search for certainty in this uncertain region, plagued by internal conflicts and wars, oil, the one factor that has provided a basis for financial security and political importance, has initiated a state of jealousy among these countries as they seek to perpetuate their wealth. As a consequence, the OPEC cartel was formed to ensure that one country would not undercut the selling price to increase its sales at the expense of the others. Thus, while oil unites these countries in their need to protect their wealth, it also serves as a reason for conflict among them, often leading to military action, as was the case with the Iraq-Iran War in 1980 and Iraq's invasion of Kuwait in 1991.

The combination of religion and authoritarian government, considered necessary for protecting the inheritance of the kingdoms and for maintaining a strong military and internal security, provides the rationale for continuing in past orientation. With their great wealth, these countries can provide the infrastructure needed to move into present orientation and eventually into future orientation as postindustrial societies. The difficulty here is that because the countries are seeking to maintain their security, the socioeconomic changes and the abolishment of their monarchies would be too disruptive.

These countries are extremely conservative, owing to the need to maintain defensive postures in a highly unstable region. The existence of Israel in the region–a country with a different religious orientation and proven military strength–adds to the regions instability. Having previously used oil with great effectiveness to pressure Israel to relinquish the territories gained in war, the effectiveness of this leverage has since diminished, notably because the Soviet Union, which backed these countries, is no longer a force. These countries have thus turned to the postindustrial countries–mainly the United States–for military assistance and defense strategies.

Because of the influence of the postindustrial countries and the prospects of real peace in this region, the changes that are taking place are challenging tradition, especially religion. Religious extremists are therefore coming to the fore, supported by many orthodox leaders, to protect the historical foundations of these countries. In Iran, these extremists have gained political power, and they also pose a threat to Egypt and Algeria. The leaders in other Middle Eastern countries are seeking accommodation with the extremists while seeking to move their countries into present orientation. Hence, the security issue remains important, especially internally, as the secular leaders of these countries try to contain religious extremism and establish sufficient infrastructure to move into present orientation. The uncertainty among these countries over their own historical destinies, their relations with each other, and with the postindustrial countries is nevertheless sufficiently strong to maintain these countries in past orientation.

Throughout their histories, the peoples of the Middle East have demonstrated their ability to make great contributions in the arts, sciences, and commerce. However, because of the uncertainty prevailing in the region, the reliance on past-oriented crisis theories provides the security of the familiar, giving the impression that the changes occurring in the region can be dealt with by traditional political and economic crisis theories. The nontraditionalist leaders, such as those in Egypt, Turkey, and Jordan, have realized that, given the new geopolitical situation, crisis theories that are appropriate for moving their countries into present orientation are necessary. Financial aid from the postindustrial countries is providing the backing for taking the necessary measures for accomplishing this shift. The leaders of these countries are seeking to maintain religion within the spiritual realm of human existence, separating it from politics, while attempting to move their educational systems and their industries into a present-orientation position.

The vision of the new Middle East is that of a common market with mutual industrialization and commerce, and with an exchange of ideas and artistic contributions that can influence the other countries of the world. Once more the countries in this region realize that true peace is the only way that will allow them to structure their education systems and industries toward this visionary goal, the capabilities of the peoples in this region will be brought to fruition, eventually moving them into the dynamics of our contemporary era.

The future-oriented postindustrial countries are firmly within the context of our contemporary era of knowledge. Yet they are not without their difficulties. They are confronted with a paradox of industrialization that is perhaps the most crucial situation they now face. Moreover, the Eastern European countries that were once within the Soviet sphere have industrial bases oriented primarily for production within the old Soviet common market, the Comecon. Since their independence, these countries have not been able to cope with the industrial output of the postindustrial countries. The paradox of industrialization, and its impact on the postindustrial countries and the former Soviet countries, are discussed in the next chapter.

NOTES

1. James Burnham, *The Machiavellians* (Chicago: Gateway Books, 1963), p. 297.

2. *ibid.*, p. 298.

3. Another example is North Korea, another country supported by the Soviet Union. Upon the Soviet Union's demise, the North Koreans sought to establish a similar relationship with China. The Chinese have not been so generous, however, being slow in updating their arms supplies while demanding payment instead of credit for wheat purchases. The North Koreans are now turning to the United States for financial assistance and trade, in return for North Korea's agreement to cease development of its nuclear program. These relationships are just beginning, and the direction they take and the influences on each country will be extremely important, both for Asia and for world peace in general.

4. See Peter T. Bauer's essay, "The Lesson of Hong Kong," in *Equality, the Third World, and Economic Delusion* (Cambridge, Mass.: Harvard University Press, 1981), pp. 185-190.

5. Of course, this is a generalization necessitated by the scope and restrictions of this work. Countries such as Morocco, Turkey, Egypt, and recently Jordan with the signing of the peace treaty with Israel are seeking to move into future orientation, each country undergoing its soul searching with the trend toward modernization and the influences of religion. Iraq, Iran, and Syria are still firmly in past orientation. Israel is a country that seeks to belong to the region, while at the same time establishing its own separate religious and cultural identity. This gives it a status that is ambiguous to other countries in the region and makes this country a highly visible target for animosity in the Middle East.

6. The postindustrial countries of Western Europe readily relented to the Middle East oil-producing countries' demand to censure Israel. Japan, which hesitated at first,

also gave way to the pressure.

    7. For a discussion on this matter and on Saudi Arabia's role as one of the largest oil producers, see Nadav Safran, *Saudi Arabia: A Ceaseless Quest for Certainty* (Cambridge, Mass.: Harvard University Press, 1985). This book and its bibliography provides insightful reading on the dynamics of the Middle East.

CHAPTER 13

Future Orientation and
the Paradox of Industrialization

Thus, the struggle over the riches of the earth has just begun. There are
many imponderables. The faster Europe and Japan develop an industrial
machine to rival that of the United States, the greater the pressure on
the world resource supply and the greater the chances of serious splits
among the nations.

Richard J. Barnett and Ronald E. Müller,
Global Reach[1]

INTRODUCTORY COMMENTS

Whether Europe and Japan can be considered to have developed industrial
economies that can rival the United States, economy depends on two factors.
One factor is statistical in nature, measuring the output and sales of Japan and
Europe, as compared to those of the United States. The European Economic
Community was formed both to compete effectively with the United States and
to realize the historical ambition of European unity. The output and sales of the
member countries can present a decent showing when compared to the U.S.
economy. NAFTA was formed with the same general objective–to unify the
North and South American continents in order to increase economic growth,
abolish poverty, and provide an effective response to the Common Market of
Europe. Because it is too recent to provide a proper historical evaluation,
NAFTA's impact in the region has yet to be determined.

Japan, on the other hand, has provided serious competition to the other
postindustrial countries. Its output has been so tremendous that it has exerted a
strong influence in the world's markets–this, without the benefit of a common
market with price supports and production quotas. Indeed, both the European
Economic Community and Japan have posed serious economic challenges to the
U.S. economy. The success of both has demonstrated that it is not only the fight

for the world's resources that has begun in earnest, but also the competition for the world's markets, expressed in sales and the rise of auxiliary businesses, that is underway.

Barnett and Müller observe that as the emerging countries demand higher prices for both their raw materials and their labor, global corporations will pass these increases onto the consumer unless they are prevented by law from doing so. They comment that

> Whether there is enough statesmanship and true international spirit in the rich countries to recognize that changes in bargaining power and resource pricing (including human labor) are long overdue in the interests of global justice and global stability will determine the character of world politics in the coming generation.[2]

In these countries' movement into present orientation, the reevaluation of pricing policies for their resources and labor provides not only profits but also capital for reinvesting in industrial output. While the multinational corporations are involved in the process of economic development, the establishment of democracies in these countries allows their governments to franchise multinational corporations only if they benefit the domestic economies. For both multinational corporations and domestic industry that is developing as a result of entry into present orientation, pricing for both resources and labor is determined by the crisis theories of business, labor, and the supply and demand conditions of their markets. The fact that the crisis theories of these countries take these factors into consideration indicates the entry of these countries into present orientation, for such considerations are absent to any serious extent in dictatorships and authoritarian regimes. The operation of multinational corporations in these countries indicates their confidence in the local labor forces and the intentions of these governments' and their peoples' willingness to move into present and eventually future orientation.[3]

With resources available and labor costs lower than in the postindustrial countries, the cost advantages for both multinationals and the rising domestic industries allow these countries to move into present orientation. The revenues accured from domestic and international sales will, after taxes, be returned to the economy and increase the social and economic infrastructure to permit further economic growth and expansion. With the labor force gainfully employed, consumption and savings will increase, thereby resulting in increased market development. The arts and sciences will also benefit from these activities because more funds will be available for scientific research and artistic endeavors.

Even in present orientation, however, these countries must face the situation that confronts the future-oriented postindustrial societies. This is the paradox that has arisen due to postwar industrialization and the efforts that resulted in reestablishing in those countries materially damaged during World War II–victors and vanquished alike–industrial infrastructure so that they could enter the new era and compete effectively in the world's markets. For both victors and vanquished, because of the costs and efforts involved, as these countries continued their restructuring, they could no longer maintain their colonies. They had to offer them independence, each at various stages of their economic and political development. The exception was the Soviet Union, which occupied much of Eastern Europe during the latter stages of World War II and developed the infrastructure and industry of these countries to satisfy the Soviet Union's production requirements of goods and services. This is why this region must be discussed in the context of this chapter.

These countries move into present orientation and enter into international competition by producing the goods and services of the postindustrial countries. Specific differences exist among the competing products that provide consumer attraction, and these differences are due to the influences of the countries of their origin. But as these products are similar enough to be close competitors in the international markets, the edge in competition tends to be with the products manufactured by the future-oriented postindustrial countries due to greater technology and marketing experience. The only real advantage in competition betwen the present- and future-oriented countries lies in products for which there is no real competition, such as tourism. The history and scenery of each country, regardless of whether it is past, present, or future oriented, give them some unique and hence noncompetitive advantages.

The problems of competition with the postindustrial countries are not simply related to the present-oriented countries, even though these problems are unique. Postindustrial countries also compete among themselves, as is demonstrated by the issues of quotas and tariffs between the products of Japanese and U.S. industries. Although these issues have been resolved without the threat of a trade war being realized, they illustrate the nature of the paradox that has resulted from industrialization in our contemporary era of knowledge. While the ramifications of this paradox are important in the international arena, they are also significant for domestic production.

FUTURE ORIENTATION AND
PARADOX OF INDUSTRIALIZATION

The postindustrial countries have entered fully into our contemporary era of knowledge and are therefore future-oriented. This orientation is manifested in the formulation of knowledge in these societies within the development of crisis theories. Once accepted, these theories not only enter the country's academic system and its domestic markets, but are also adapted for each country's unique situation and used in the past- and present-oriented countries throughout the world. The knowledge gained from these crisis theories is incorporated into the society's body of knowledge and—apart from patent restrictions which are nullified after time—is available to all concerned. This knowledge can be used for current and new conceptions in the development of crisis theories only if the proper infrastructure and the technological foundation for comprehension and application exist, the lack of which restricts its uses in present- and past-oriented countries.

Two examples will suffice as demonstration. Automobile technology is of such an advanced state that only postindustrial countries and present-oriented countries with strong motivation such as South Korea can compete effectively. Yet not only are automobiles driven throughout the world, but also they have led to the establishment of auxiliary businesses such as garages and service departments in sales offices to handle repairs. Nevertheless, most present-oriented countries do not compete in the field of automobiles, because they lack the infrastructure, knowledge, and technology to compete in this market. Communications is another industry primarily of postindustrial and highly motivated present-oriented countries. The modern cellular phones, computer systems, and facsimile communications are products of the applications of knowledge in the postindustrial countries to the problems of increasing the efficiency of communications systems. The crisis theories that the communications industries posited, once brought into fruition through production and marketing, became highly competitive, resulting in improvements and lower production costs that have been passed on to consumers to increase sales. These systems are used internationally, but only the postindustrial countries and highly motivated present-oriented countries (again, South Korea is an example) can compete in production and sales.

The sales of automobiles and communications systems, as well as all other products of the postindustrial countries, are not only to other postindustrial countries, even though in these countries the sales are the greatest. They are also made to present-oriented and, to a lesser extent, the past-oriented countries. As the present-oriented countries are trying to move into future orientation, and therefore mimic those aspects of the future-oriented countries' living standards that can be advantageous as they develop further, they seek to compete with those products that can be manufactured in their countries, given their state of the arts and technology. With their comparative higher production and sales costs, they, like the postindustrial countries, seek markets, and this is the very paradox of industrialization.

The paradox can be stated as follows: For a country to be postindustrial, its industries must manufacture and sell goods and services that are associated with postindustrial countries, such as high technology, think tank research organizations, computers, automobiles, to some extent airplane manufacture, and advanced communications systems, including space technology and research. Only a few countries can be considered postindustrial in this sense. Such postindustrial countries as Germany and Japan have not yet undertaken serious space research, even though they excel in the other aspects of postindustrialization. Paradoxically if this criterion is relevant for postindustrialization, how are the markets to be developed for these countries' goods and services? Although they compete among themselves, their consumers are offered the opportunities to make the best purchases. But how much can be purchased in countries whose capital taxation policies allow for phasing out equipment over time, while the drive for competitive innovation is intensive? Of course, the past- and present-oriented countries provide markets, but the rates of absorption of these goods and services can only be undertaken at rates appropriate for their countries. This results in a technical market-saturation effect in which the rate of saturation is dependent on each country's technical ability to absorb these products. Industrialization is thus slowed down by the products of industrialization, as industrial output cannot be absorbed at the rate at which it is produced.

Of course, output has to be geared to market expectations, and for lower technological products this has some degree of success. Highly technological products such as top-line computers require that when they are marketed, older computers are sold in the secondary "used" markets, while the new products are consumed. The problems with this are that older equipment is not so readily abandoned but is phased out over time, and that when new products are successful, competitors will come on line fairly rapidly to provide alternative products and reduce the profits of the entrepreneurs.

While this is the situation in all competitive markets, the postindustrial countries that establish innovation, manufacture, and sales in both domestic and international markets maintain production of goods and services that are highly technological and crisis theories and infrastructures for such conceptualizations. The delay in competition from both postindustrial manufacturers and present oriented countries makes significant profits possible. Nevertheless, these profits are short term because when competitors come on line, they must have products at least as good at competitive prices in order to generate sales. This economic innovation maintains the postindustrial countries in their future–oriented positions, as they develop, manufacture, and sell products that the non-future oriented countries are incapable of placing in the markets, but still purchase from the postindustrial countries according to their requirements.

This leads to near-market saturation over each product's cycle, as it is purchased in both the future-oriented countries and those others that need them for their own operations and in their industries. This is more so in the present-oriented countries that aspire to future orientation. They become highly imitative in order to establish the necessary infrastructure and technological base to enter into competition. Hence, South Korea and to a somewhat lesser extent Taiwan are moving into advanced stages of present orientation as they compete by imitation with the postindustrial countries. The paradox of industrialization therefore exists, when the postindustrial countries produce competitive products that result in near-market saturation, both domestically and internationally.

Unlike business cycles during the Industrial Revolution, the paradox of industrialization is a phenomenon of our contemporary era. Where previously markets had reached near saturation bringing the business cycle downward, the governments' policy of abolishing depressions nevertheless intensifies the recessions that occur. This is because contemporary economies are so dependent on cost-intensive highly technological production in all its aspects.[4] Whereas during the Industrial Revolution production costs were relative to the products' sales, this relationship does not hold in postindustrial countries. The costs of product research, of innovation, of testing, marketing, and sales, are far greater now than previously, and while profits are great, competition renders them of short duration comparable to the costs involved. Because these countries are so dependent on highly technological production, the tendency is toward reduced profits after a respectable profit-time as imitators near-saturate the markets. Consequently, the cyclical upswing tends to be of fairly short duration and the downswing to be intense.

The imposition of tariffs to protect domestic industry by reducing imports of competing profits is not a viable solution, as Japan's tariff structure with regard to the U.S. competition demonstrated. This policy led to economic confrontation that almost erupted in a trade war with the United States and has since been resolved amicably for most products. This illustrates the intensity of the competition, and huge investments in education, training and research, as well as in maintaining growing technological bases and infrastructures necessary to ensure the postindustrial and present-oriented levels of innovation and production among the postindustrial countries. It also serves to generate high levels of investment in infrastructure and technology in present-oriented countries that seek to achieve postindustrial future-oriented status.

This is also the reason for the disproportionately high rates of unemployment given these countries' productive capacity. Domestic and international competition reduces profits radically over time, resulting in unemployment, as the downsizing occurring in big corporations demonstrates. The income effect reduces consumption, and while many of these unemployed people will eventually find employment in auxiliary businesses, or may even start their own high-technology businesses, the time factor for this depends on the variables of age, contacts, and experience, and on the markets' receptivity to such new endeavors.

Although innovation is the prescription for easing the intensity of this paradox, it is a temporary "cure," for as innovation becomes successful, it is met with successful imitation. This reduces profits and eventually leads to near-market saturation, intensifying the paradox again. The products of the postindustrial economies extend the duration of cyclical fluctuations, and while depressions have been ruled out by government operations, recessions in our social time are due to near-market saturation for cost-intensive, highly technological products resulting from domestic and international competition.

COMMENTS ON EASTERN EUROPE

Prior to World War II, the Soviet Union exerted a marginal ecnomic and political influence on the countries on its geographical periphery. The world was in the throes of the Great Depression, and the sounds of the impending war were being heard as Germany rearmed and began its plans to invade its neighboring countries, while the League of Nations was ineffective in preventing this situation. Since the leaders of these countries sought to ease the effects of the depression and to rely on the League of Nations and the various treaties they had for their defense, they were caught unprepared when Germany began its invasions. The Soviet Union was considered Germany's natural enemy, but when they signed a nonaggression pact in 1939, Eastern Europe resigned itself to the fact that it could not rely on Stalin's contempt for Nazism for defense. In the aftermath of the war, Stalin had control of Germany's eastern sector as well as most of the East European countries previously occupied by Germany.

This proved to be an advantage for the Soviet Union as it renewed its conflict with its ally-in-arms, the United States. The Eastern European countries had fledgling industries and a fairly skilled labor force to work them. Moreover, they provided markets for Soviet goods and services, as well as products for Soviet consumers. In light of the formation of the European Economic Community, the Soviet bloc was united into Comecon, a customs union in its own right, thereby reinforcing the Soviet Union's mutual relationships with its satellite countries. This was important, because as competition with the United States and its NATO allies in the military and economic spheres intensified, with the Western bloc moving into postindustrial future orientation, the Soviet bloc sought to construct its industrial base to compete effectively. With dictatorship and overburdening bureaucracy prevailing in this bloc, such competition proved impossible, however. When President Reagan upped the ante by seriously considering the Strategic Defense Initiative ("Star Wars"), the Soviet leadership could not meet this challenge. Together with this new defense burden and the comprehension of the competition that would result from both the United States and a strong European Economic Community, the then Soviet leader, Mikhail Gorbachev, initiated the democratization of the entire Soviet society and its satellite countries, in order to establish an effective competitive bloc for the current and upcoming challenges of the postindustrial countries.

Gorbachev understood that for this new approach to be effective, liberalization had to be maintained, not only for the industries within the country and its satellites, but also for these countries themselves. His reasoning was that with grass-roots liberalization, efficient planning and manufacturing could be achieved. Even though the grand economic plans might remain intact, the manner by which they are carried out must be within the economic and industrial echelons, and not the political. The consequences of this policy were a reorientation of Soviet industry and greater freedom in planning, production, and marketing by the satellite countries.

The dynamics of this new approach did not cease with the economic revolution, but instead spread to the political sphere. Economic independence without political independence accomplishes very little, and both the Soviets and the satellite countries demanded the political freedom to conduct their business.

Stalin's tyrannical hold over the Soviet Union and the satellite countries in the aftermath of the war no longer existed. Indeed, the damaging effects of Stalinism were revealed to some extent during Nikita Khruschev's premiership, although Leonid Brezhnev, who followed him, maintained a Stalin-like grip on the region to prevent the kind of anarchy that existed prior to the Communist Revolution. Gorbachev's understanding differed from that of his predecessors in that he realized the limits of power and constraint in light of the new economic challenges. Thus, while providing the basis for economic liberalization, Gorbachev knew that he could not avoid the consequence of the Soviets becoming politically independent. Upon having their independence, they maintained their historical unity in a confederation of the Commonwealth of Independent States.

The satellite countries also achieved their political and economic independence and have sought to go their own way. Economic reliance on–and cooperation with–the postindustrial countries, predominately the United States, once considered a betrayal of principles, became necessary to develop the social infrastructure and the industrial base needed to enter into future orientation. In establishing their independence and economic identities, several of those countries sought to rectify their historical grievances. Czechoslovakia, for example, separated amicably into the Czech and Slovak nations, each establishing its own country. Yugoslavia, while being somewhat independent from Soviet influence under Marshall Tito, but nevertheless a communist regime, had a far different outcome. The Serbs, Croats, and Muslims that formed the country split in anger and fought against each other to resolve the festering historical animosity. Poland and Lithuania became independent and have struggled to maintain their democracies; the Soviet zone of East Germany merged with West Germany to become reunited under a democratic regime. Romania, like Yugoslavia, remained fairly independent for the Soviet Union, and with the fall of Ceausescu's dictatorship, the Romanians are struggling to establish a viable economy and, with Hungary, are trying to resolve their historical differences peacefully. The Bulgarians and Albanians are seeking to establish economic growth. The Bulgarian government, though communist, was fairly lenient, but the Albanian peoples suffered under a severely repressive regime. Bulgaria is now attempting to work within democratic government, while Albania is undergoing social and political unrest.

Hence, while independence has brought opportunities for new political structures and for economic growth and development, it has also given rise to internal conflicts that were previously held in check. There is also the potential danger that some of the independent countries that were formerly under the domination of the Soviet Union may seek to dominate their neighbors. The avoidance of such a situation is the reason why Hungary and Romania have sought to resolve their historical differences without bloodshed. However, given the rise of the new nationalism, the historical tendency for domination as a pursuit of national interests, which is so often the cause of war in this region, may flare up once again and lead to conflict. Given the new situation, a new element has entered the region–an active NATO, which is seeking a viable permanent settlement to the former Yugoslavian territory of Bosnia-Herzegovina. The fear is that the conflict may spread into Macedonia and involve Greece and Turkey in war. The secondary apprehension is that Russia may resume responsibility for the region and become active once again, with the possible consequence of another cold war.

In spite of all their current difficulties, these countries have industrial bases they inherited from the period of Soviet domination. During this period–whether tightly controlled as with Hungary, Czechoslovakia, and Poland, or loosely controlled as with Romania and Yugoslavia–there were established industrial foundations within these countries. During this period of domination, these countries were past-oriented, with allegiances to ideology, despite the attempts at pragmatic policy formulations. In the cases where such policies led to independence, as in Hungary, Poland, and Czechoslovakia, it was met with repression, emphasizing the de facto reliance on the Soviet Union for economic and political support and direction.

Today these countries are neither past- nor present-oriented. Because of their recent common histories under Soviet domination and because of their newly gained independence, both the leaders and ordinary citizens of these countries realize that in order to revitalize their industries and provide effective domestic and international competition, they must become culturally and economically involved in our contemporary era, so that ultimately, they can become future-oriented postindustrial societies.

With their industrial bases primarily unchanged from the period of Soviet domination, these countries are unique in that they must confront the paradox of industrialization without entering the phase of present orientation. Their domestic and international marketing approaches have not deviated significantly from the time when their markets were secured according to decisions of central planning boards. Hence, so far, these countries have managed to exploit one feature–tourism. Low tourist rates, beautiful scenery, rich histories, and the ancestries of many peoples who visit them make these countries very attractive tourist sites, bringing into their coffers much needed foreign currency. These natural and historical attractions, though worthy of tourists, are, however, insufficient for bringing these countries into our contemporary era.

These countries are thus confronted with the paradox of industrialization, perhaps to a greater extent than the present-oriented countries–such as South Korea and Taiwan–that are moving into postindustrial status. For Eastern European countries to enter our era, they must use their existing industrial infrastructures to expand their domestic markets, thereby increasing employment and consumption and generating economic growth. They must also enter into international markets and export goods and services unique to their economies. Although tourism is seasonal and heavily price-oriented, exporting domestic products is more reliable than tourism as a source of foreign currency because tourism is seasonal and highly competitive. The demand for a country's products tends to be inelastic, as the demand for French wines, Russian caviar, and Swiss watches demonstrates.

There is another advantage in production: the experience gained in manufacturing and marketing, which can be developed and adapted for other products that will be marketed. The problem is selecting the products to be exported. Every country has its own unique products for which the country is known. For example, Polish pickles and vodka can be found in international supermarkets, along with French and Swiss cheeses. These products, though foreign currency earners, are insufficient in themselves to establish postindustrial bases and to move the countries into the postindustrial future orientation of our contemporary era.

For the Eastern European countries to enter our era, they must reorganize their industries into high-technology production. They must manufacture automobiles, computers, and advanced electronic and communications equipment, installing in these products whatever unique advantages possible to make them competitive in both the domestic and international markets. Such reorganization involves costs but these costs cannot be passed onto international consumers, for it would place the products at a cost disadvantage. Internal policies, such as taxation, purchasing incentives, and even the call to nationalism, can be an effective means of recouping the investment, research, and marketing costs involved. In addition, monies in the form of loans and grants from the postindustrial countries and various international agencies such as the International Monetary fund and the World Bank can be used to develop infrastructure and to invest in advanced technology. With proper planning and with the understanding of consumer demand and marketing, the political and industrial leaders of these countries can convert their existing industrial bases into viable productive facilities, absorbing workforces that will readily adapt to the new production techniques.

Once industry is geared to modern production, these countries will gain postindustrial status. This is the opening to our contemporary era, because with a strong economic and productive foundation monies can be directed, either by private contributions or government support, into the arts and sciences. Artistic institutions can be endowed, and scientific institutions can obtain research funds from the government and private institutions, such as industrial endowments. In this way, these countries can enter fully into our contemporary era, with its future orientation. However, their postindustrial status will place them within the paradox of industrialization. The goods and services that these countries will provide are the same as those of the other postindustrial countries. Whatever competitive advantage their products may have will be manifested in whatever technological changes are initiated or price incentives offered.

FURTHER COMMENTS

The paradox of industrialization is a fact of our contemporary era and is due to the present-day concept of industrialization. For countries to be advanced industrially, they must produce goods and services that are considered advanced and must do so competitively, so that their products will sell. This results in rapid near-market saturation, and even though there are nuances among the products to increase their competitiveness, these nuances are compensated for by competitive prices and the inclusion of similar nuances in order to move the goods and services.

This paradox, though inherent in our contemporary era, is nevertheless necessary, for it stimulates highly technological production. The initial profits for such products are very high, with technological advantages protected for the duration of their domestic and international patents. Nevertheless, competition allows for nuances on products and for similar competing products to enter the markets. The greater bulk of profits on high technology are earned during the time lapse between the initial products on the markets and the competition entering the field. Depending on the product, this lapse may be of sufficient duration to render the product highly profitable after research, production, and marketing costs are discounted.

The paradox of industrialization has serious implications for our era. The levels of education necessary to work productively in all phases of technological industry are higher in our social time than in any other period. The necessity for technological training places heavy demand on institutes of higher education, and competition for employment in these industries is intense. As compensation, small, specialized, highly technologically oriented businesses are entering the markets, providing employment where big industries are unable to do so because their staff is working on current and planned projects.

With respect to the paradox of industrialization, there are differences in the quality and amount of technological output in the postindustrial countries, as they have an advantage with regard to research, production, and marketing. However, those countries in the latter stages of present orientation have the opportunity to form their own markets as they establish their unique criteria for future orientation based on their histories and understanding of our contemporary era.

The paradox of industrialization encourages neocolonialism, in which the postindustrial countries dominate the past- and present-oriented countries. An example of the present-oriented are the Eastern European countries that, while seeking to establish themselves in our contemporary era, have not yet done so. Since the postindustrial countries have the strongest economies, the most stable political systems, and the highest levels of learning, this neocolonialism manifests itself primarily in industrial domination, and to a lesser but still important degree, in political domination. This domination is prevalent in the past-oriented countries, as they are dependent on the future-oriented countries for

210 Crisis Theory and Its Applications

assistance and aid, as well as for their technology. For the present-oriented countries, this domination is less stringent, as in their processes of moving into future orientation, they develop their own industries and are able to compete in the international markets.

Some aspects of political influences are discernible in this neocolonialism, but in general, it is not political in orientation. Neocolonialism results from the discrepancies in the past- and present-oriented countries' crisis theories. Because the future-oriented countries have stronger industrial bases, their systems allow liquidity to be channeled into research, which results in innovation and initiation and the critical testing that follows. This provides the basis for moving from strict imitation in production and marketing into explorative imitation and initiation in response to deviations in markets due to competition. The explorative imitation that results permits the examination of production and marketing techniques, with initiation allowing for changes to be incorporated after they have been subject to critical testing when differing opinions make such testing necessary.

Although this domination results from the economic strength of the postindustrial countries, quasipolitical dominance in the form of economic assistance and aid is a consequence, with the postindustrial countries exerting their financial–and at times military–influence to achieve their international objectives. With the Cold War over and the present-oriented countries seeking to move into future orientation, with regard to aid and assistance for these and the past-oriented countries, the international objectives of the postindustrial countries tend to be the same.

In regions of past-oriented countries, such as Africa and the Middle East, in which war and strife are common, the political and economic instability of these regions produces conditions such as those that afflict Somalia and the Sudan. There starvation, illness, and military conflict debilitate the people, while the warlords maintain their power through force, living well under the circumstances. The international agencies of the postindustrial countries are removing the scourge of starvation, controlling the spread of epidemic illnesses, establishing democratic forms of government, and bringing these people into our era as soon as possible. Given the depth and intensity of these complicated situations, these objectives are long run.

Whether these objectives can be achieved depends on the acumen of the leaders in these past-oriented countries, on their willingness to relinquish their control for establishing an environment for businesses and competition, a political situation that will move them first into present orientation and eventually into future orientation, and the persuasiveness of the leaders of the postindustrial countries to influence them to do so. As a long-run objective, should this be achieved, these countries will benefit from the future orientation of our contemporary era. Until this objective is achieved, neocolonialism will remain as the postindustrial countries influence the policies of the past-oriented countries that have shown no real ability or willingness to enter our era.

The present-oriented countries have achieved their status because' while in past orientation, they formulated their crisis theories to develop their situations. This has been so in commerce, for example, as the business leaders placed their countries' industries in the production patterns of the postindustrial countries, with labor leaders responding accordingly. Their political leaders have developed their countries' democratic systems according to those of the postindustrial countries, allowing sufficient flexibility for relating to the social problems that arise from industrial urbanization and suburban living. As these crisis theories are subject to entropy, they allow for changes in their languages brought about by innovation and initiation. Because these societies are dynamic, the democratic ambience permits competing crisis theories to be posited and critically tested for their utilities and abilities to function in competition. As these crisis theories become more sophisticated, they will eventually move these dynamic present-oriented countries into future-oriented postindustrial status, thereby competing with the established postindustrial countries. This will also bring them within the paradox of industrialization, as they compete with manufactured goods and services similar to those of the established postindustrial countries.

The way out of this paradox is through the innovation of unique goods and services that are of strong enough demand that a sufficient time lapse is generated for profits to be made before imitative products enter the markets and reduce profit margins. Hence, effective crisis theories of sufficient quantity must be formulated in order to maintain innovative industrial output. Although some countries have present-orientation status, they can rely on imitation, bringing in profits from sales, but at levels that will sustain industrial output without wide profit margins. Once these countries have entered into future orientation, by having achieved postindustrial status, remaining strictly imitative will no longer be sufficient to sustain their industries. Other countries will become present-oriented and will compete rigorously for imitative markets. The new postindustrial countries will therefore have to emphasize innovation in order to maintain their postindustrial status. By emphasizing imitation, they will return to present orientation, remaining without the ability to develop new markets and reap the initial profits that come with highly technological innovation.

Eastern Europe is in an advantageous position for eventually moving into future orientation. This region's industrial base, established to support the Soviet economy in the past social time, can be vitalized sufficiently to move these countries well into present orientation. The formulation of viable crisis theories for planning, marketing, and manufacturing competitive products can improve these countries' situations, so that with sufficient experience in international competition, their industries will move toward innovation, bringing these countries into future orientation.

Hence, for all countries aspiring to future orientation, industrial development must first be undertaken as industrialization requires the establishment of physical infrastructure, such as roads, railways, and airports for moving goods and services to domestic and international markets. Social amenities, such as urban centers, health care services, and educational and recreational facilities, will either follow or will be developed along with industry–depending on the foresight and acumen of the social and political leaders. Industrial development is the primary stimulus for moving into future orientation. Once postindustrial status is achieved, the paradox of industrialization will set in, only to be alleviated temporarily through viable innovation. Innovative and imitative crisis theories will continue to be formulated and refined, generating and maintaining demand from consumers within the future-oriented societies.

CONCLUDING REMARKS

Every historical era has come to an end for reasons internal to the era. In the Dark Ages, the empire that was formed during the previous era of Roman rule had become the Holy Roman Empire under the authority of the Church, while the Eastern Church in Byzantine ruled the Balkans, with its influence spreading into Russia. It was Aristotle's works, translated from the Greek and Arabic into Latin, that influenced St. Thomas Aquinas's thinking, bringing the Dark Ages to an end and initiating the Renaissance. This era was brought to an end by applying the science of the era to the problems of production, culminating in the Industrial Revolution, which in turn ended with the Great Depression. Our era of knowledge began in the aftermath of World War II and will no doubt follow the same pattern, carrying within it the causes of its termination, from which another historical era will begin.

Yet another trend has to be considered, that of the diminishing time duration of an era. The Dark Ages lasted approximately 775 years, the Renaissance endured for approximately 525 years, and the Industrial Revolution that followed lasted some 150 years. Each of these eras had its own unique social times in which changes were brought about within the era and enhanced its unique characteristics. The Dark Ages witnessed the flowering of the Christian religion and the rise of the Moslem faith, the control of education by the Scholastics, and the merging of religious authority with political power. The Renaissance saw the development of the arts and sciences due to the thawing of doctrine on the conceptions and teachings of the sciences and on artistic freedom. During the Industrial Revolution, regions that were separated geographically were brought together through geographical exploration and industrial expansion. The Civil War on the American continent was fought to unite regions of conflicting ideologies; Napoleon in France sought to unite Europe under French domination, and the problems in Europe that led to World War I were unresolved by that conflict, to be fought over again in World War II. The difficulties of the business cycle were brought into sharp perspective when the expected cyclical upswing of the Great Depression of 1929 failed to materialize.

Our era came into its own in the aftermath of World War II, and among is social times, two have been major: the imposition of the Cold War with its subsequent dynamics such as the Korean and Vietnam conflicts and the wars in the Middle East, and the end of the Cold War with the dissolution of the Soviet Union and the great efforts of the postindustrial countries to help the past- and present-oriented countries move eventually into future orientation.

Whether our era will be of shorter duration still and what the factors will be in bringing about its termination cannot be foretold. We can only surmise. For example, when the majority of present-oriented countries enter future orientation, the demand for innovation to get rid of the influence of the paradox of industrialization will be so great and the realization of innovation so costly that innovative crisis theories will decline and an imitative "mature" world economy will prevail. This will be contrary to the very dynamics of knowledge in our era and will result in an excess of knowledge without practical applications. Another plausible scenario can be made for the gap between the future-oriented and past-oriented countries as the inertia involved in moving from past- to present-orientation cannot be overcome. As this gap widens, another major war will be fought, bringing down our era because, with all its knowledge, it had not succeeded in raising up past-oriented countries to present and future orientation. As for our era's duration, it will last as long as its dynamics are able to continue crisis theory innovation, initiation, and imitation, and this is dependent on the abilities of more countries to move into present and future orientation.

Thus, another paradox seems to be inherent in our era. On the one hand, the greater the number of countries that enter our era, the greater the difficulty for crisis theory innovation to be realized in production programs. On the other hand, the resistance to entering our era is resulting in a widening gap in productivity between the types of countries, possibly leading to another global conflict. Our era has great promises, and whether they can be realized for the benefit of all countries in their striving to be unique while at the same time being members of the world's commonwealth will unfold as our era and its social times develop.

NOTES

1. Richard J. Barnett and Ronald E. Müller, *Global Reach* (New York: Simon and Schuster/Touchstone Books, 1974), p. 210.

2. *ibid.*

3. See the argument offered on this point in David Z. Rich, *The Economics of International Trade: An Independent View* (Westport, Conn.: Quorum Books, 1992), Chapter 9, "Circa 1992: Multinational Corporations," pp. 155-163.

4. For a discussion of the four-phased business cycle and the development of the contemporary three-phased business cycle, see David Z. Rich, *The Economics of Welfare: A Contemporary Analysis* (New York: Praeger Publishers, 1989), Part 3, pp. 99-148.

CHAPTER 14

Conclusion—Comments on Philosophy and Physics

> Knowledge would not be possible if there were no sameness. Through them alone are we able to find again the one in the other and to describe the multiform world with the aid of a very few concepts.

Moritz Schlick,
General Theory of Knowledge[1]

FURTHER COMMENTS ON THE CRITICAL TEST

Knowledge would not be possible without a great degree of sameness. In a nonrigorous sense, sameness is necessary for understanding and communicating both within and among societies. In a rigorous sense, the sameness among competing crisis theories allows for their uses in their respective problem areas. Knowledge, however, is discontinuous in its development, and it is not the sameness that is of interest concerning competing crisis theories, but the differences. Indeed, it is on the basis of these differences that crisis theories are competitive.

Schlick's statement is only partially correct. As knowledge is false, it is replaceable; sameness is continuity and is not replaceable. Although knowledge requires sameness for strict imitation relating crisis theories to their problem areas, difference is also required for change and for the general development and expansion of competing crisis theories, and hence for knowledge.

Since the domains of difference provide the basis for competition among crisis theories, when these theories change through expansion or through entropy and their subsequent reconstruction, their knowledge content also changes. Because it is their sameness that provides the common ground for competition, should their problem area change, then if the corresponding changes in the respective crisis theories are inadequate, they are maintained in their usage either until such internal changes of utility are initiated, until they are brought into irreparable entropy, or until an innovative theory enters the area with the sameness in knowledge that characterizes the other theories but with unique domains of difference that bring supporters to the theory and its area.

Since knowledge depends on sameness for its strict imitative activity, explorative imitation of the given knowledge is brought into domains that are not within the crisis theory and its area but as such remains within allowable parameters. If explorative imitation results in entropy, the accepted initiation fitting the theory's probability and utility requirements brings the theory into sharper difference with the other competing theories.

Critique and the critical test have been discussed in this work and have been explained with respect to the processes of evaluating a contribution, be it a statement within a crisis theory, or an innovatively unique contribution in competition with other theories working with the problem area, or on its own. Two other points need explication. These are the rational and empirical aspects of crisis theory. These points are important because they provide the basis for modern scientific inquiry in a domain where innovation and imitation prevail.

First, it must be said that with respect to the argument presented in this work, a more philosophical approach could have been taken, starting with the individual in the process of working with a crisis theory and analyzing the influences of reason, skepticism, and observation on his or her judgment and evaluation processes. There could have been still another recessive step, entering into the dynamics of psychology concerning the processes of innovation, imitation, and initiation. The skepticism first posited by Hume and accepted by Kant could have been explored and pushed into solipsism, with rationalism brought into modern antinomes in the form of logical paradoxes and arithmetic being a case in point with Gödel's argument about its consistency, completeness, but not both.[2]

The need for more fundamental philosophical considerations for establishing crisis theories has been circumvented by the very existence of such theories and the general consensus concerning their utility or entropy by those who use and oppose them. The arguments of the philosophical rationalists and the Humean-Kantian skeptics therefore are of little importance here. Nor is it necessary to discuss in depth the fundamentals of the psychology of epistemology.

The discussion on acceptance and rejection is important, for it describes the dynamics by which these processes occur according to the general subjective and objective criteria of crisis theories. With respect to the critical test, both subjective and objective criteria are brought into question, as was the case with Pasteur's experiment, which, though accepted as correct by the French Academy, was later demonstrated to be incorrect. However, the critical test at the time of Pasteur's experiment determined the acceptance of the results, according to the experiments and the testing conditions agreed upon.

Nevertheless, the critical test takes into account the subjectivity of the people involved, with the possibility that the testing results may be accepted by some and rejected by others. It was necessary to discuss critique for clarification in order to establish support for, or opposition to, the results of the critical test. Crisis theories are not refutable by experience–as with Popper's criterion–but they are viable because of their utility and they decline because of their entropy. Aristotle's physics were not refuted by Galileo, but were shown to be entropic and replaced by a theory of far greater utility. Experiments of balls rolling down inclined planes can be described by both Aristotle's and Galileo's theories, but Galileo's concepts of mathematical calculation and friction provide greater understanding than Aristotle's concepts of wind forces on the balls and their attempt to reach their destination with increasing and decreasing momentum.

The critical test tends to be objectively decisive in terms of the experimental conditions for which it is devised. This decisiveness is, however, tempered by critique, and this depends on the objective and subjective understanding that the innovator, initiator, or critic has for the subject matter. The aspect of critique associated with the critical test, therefore, reduces the possibilities of dogmatic condemnation of a theory. Whether the Freudians maintain that to question Freud's theory is to rebel against it, and hence is a confirmation of the theory, is not relevant for the critical test. The point of Freud's theory contains operational and area statements that can be tested whether or not Freud's supporters agree. If such testing shows that some statements are entropic, they can be corrected within the theory or be left alone. The point is not what the Freudians or the Popperians maintain, but the utility or entropy of the statements within the theoretical context. The Freudians do not want to work with statements that are defective, and no rebellion occurs here.[3]

The logical positivist and the Popperian approaches of proofs and refutations– developed in the previous historical era–have been shown to be lacking. Innovation, imitation, and initiation, as discussed in this work, are appropriate for our era, inasmuch as they account for competing theories. Hence, this work breaks with a long tradition of testing theories to confirm or refute them. The argument is that theories cannot be considered in the tradition that began with Bacon and Descartes, but exist for the duration of their utility. Heisenberg's uncertainty principle is one such theory, and Gödel's proof is another: they will continue to be crisis theories until they become entropic and are replaced by other theories.

Science and philosophy share the pursuit of enduring truth. This present work is a contribution to this endeavor. Since Bacon and Descartes, and from Hume and Kant and the logical positivists and the Popperians, philosophers have presented scientists with issues that they, as practitioners of scientific disciplines, may not have considered, being too close to their fields. In this sense, the division between philosophy and science that began after Newton has been bridged. Because knowledge–*scientia*–is false and changing, philosophers seek to explain the processes by which changes in knowledge occur. The discussion of crisis theory is a contemporary analysis of this process.

COMMENTS ON PHYSICS AND PHILOSOPHY

Although relativity theory and quantum theory cover different fields, nevertheless a philosophical controversy exists between them. According to the Einsteinians, God does not play dice with the universe; the universe is regulated according to the laws of statistical determinism. Opposing this notion is the position of the strict quantum physicists, who, using Heisenberg's uncertainty principle, mainain that the universe is indeterminate. Where statistics operate, these are in limit-case domains in a universe in which uncertainty and indeterminism prevail. However, as the micro sphere of quantum physics is part of the macro universe of relativity, then the universe is either statistically deterministic or statistically and hence physically indeterministic, but not both.

Einstein based his physics on Riemannian geometry because it could handle curvature in space and because its properties allowed the Lorentz transformation of an event that, with Einstein's use, provides the transformations of velocities and tensors in general to either different frames of reference or to other such frames. Since tensor mathematics allows for space curvatures, Einstein applied this mathematics together with an energy-momentum tensor that plots the amount of energy and momentum of mass with the sum of energy within the tensor space. Since Riemannian geometry is both curved and finite, tensor mathematics is appropriate for the transformation of one space-time position to another in Einsteinian theory. Moreover, statistical determinism can function only within finite space-time, allowing Einstein to use this geometry and tensor mathematics for such transformations.

Einstein based his gravitational field on Gauss's differential geometry. This form of geometry represents straight lines, even when the surfaces in question are curved, so that by plotting coordinates on a graphic representation of a shape being considered, and by applying the calculus, the derivations turn out to be straight lines. The set of possible coordinates are intrinsic to the surfaces and are not related to surrounding space. The internal space is the tensor space and is described by a matrix of the space's coordinates and their reflexive relationship, so that coordinates can be transformed onto position q_{21} if symmetric, and onto its reversible equivalent q_{12} in space-time in a nonsymmetric quadratic relation. The important value is thus the coefficient of the coordinate, for this allows the tensor to be transformed onto another space-time matrix area.

With respect to the atom, it is nucleus-centered, with energy flowing within its structure toward the nucleus. Particle shifts from one orbital to another within the atom result in the emission of a photon. Particles shifting orbitals function within the tensor space of the atomic matrix, and when using approaches with Gaussian matrix computation and applying differential calculus, account for the rates of orbital changes and resultant energy shifts. But what of the photon as it travels through macro space? Macro space is composed of micro space, each portion of which is capable of being plotted and analyzed for its atomic content and tensor properties. As the earth is curved over long distances, for example, its micro spaces become subject to analysis of their individual space-time matrices.

Using Riemannian geometry, Einstein unites space and time in the Minkowski continuum.[4] Unlike the classical physics of Galileo and the neoclassical physics of Newton in which space and time are separate aspects of nature, with space having a functional relationship with time, in relativity, space and time cannot be separated, which allows for the matrix transformation in different space-time areas, with all matrices united by the constant velocity of light. This accounts for gravity, as it is related to the presence of physical bodies–no matter how great or small in size–in their specific space-time matrices. The greater the density of bodies, the greater the gravitational field. As for cosmological space, gravity is generated by the presence of stars. When they lose their energies, they collapse into black holes, forming pockets in space of extremely intense gravity due to the densely collapsed material. The gravitational pull of these black holes affects the velocities of passing photons, such as the light from surrounding stars, as it travels through space-time and reaches our planet.

We have, therefore, three operable theories of physics, relating to each other only in limited areas. Quantum theory describes atoms and their subatomic particles, Newtonian theory relates to the world as it is visible to us as observers and applicable in its three-dimensional framework, and Einsteinian relativity, with its supervelocities in space-time continuum operating in Lorentz-Minkowski transformations, employs Ricci-cum Levi-Civita tensors. With respect to quantum theory, relativity shares with it the common ground of mass-energy transformations and photon velocity, all within the atomic structure. Einsteinian relativity shares in common with Newtonian theory the dynamics of bodies in motion computable with the calculus. Newtonian theory shares with quantum theory the heritage of particle theory from the Greek Democritus (c. 460–c. 370 B.C.) and the Roman Lucretius (c. 96–c. 55 B.C.) that formed the basis of Newton's particle theory of light that is included in his overall concept of physical energy.

In spite of their common peripheries, these theories are nevertheless in conflict. Each theory has its different language for its problem area, with Newton's theory being strictly deterministic, Einstein's being statistically deterministic, and quantum theory being strictly indeterminate. Newton's theory is deterministic to the point that, given the present history of the physical world, within the Newtonian domain the entire physical future can be predicted accurately. Einstein's statistical determinism is less extreme by the nature of its statistical foundation. Hence, with respect to quantum physics, Einstein's theory uses probability relations for the energy levels absorbed or displaced by an atom, so that Planck's radiation can be derived from statistical determinism as well as quantum indeterminism.[5]

Heisenberg's uncertainty principle demonstrates the indeterminism of quantum physics by the restriction on the observation of both positions and velocities of quanta. As, we know from Wolfgang Pauli's exclusion principle no two subatomic particles can be in the same orbital. This principle allows us to investigate the weak and strong forces that hold the atom together and allow its subparticles to relate to the nucleus and to one another.[6] On this point, Einstein's special theory of relativity is relevant, for it pertains to different observers and the laws used to describe their observations with respect to inertia and gravitation relative to each other. Its significance for quantum physics is that atoms and their subparticles move in gravitational fields and are either inert or dynamic relative to other atomic systems.

If the space-time continuum is expanded to consider still another dimension, that of matter, this affects Einstein's expansion of the Newtonian three-dimensional view with the inclusion of time. Matter must be included as a dimension in the space-time continuum, for without it, the Newtonian distinction between space and time would still hold, but only in the form of abstract geometry.

By setting space-time relative to matter, be it macro matter as with galaxies or micro matter as with subatomic particles–matter becomes a dynamic component within the space-time continuum. Given the validity of the expanding-universe concept, the presence of matter explains the existence of gravity within the vast reaches of outer space-time. Because galaxies exist at great distances from each other, this separateness accounts for the diminution of intergalactic gravitational pull.

Gravitation can be viewed as an interchange of subatomic particles within and among atoms, owing to their closeness. This interchange explains the existence of gravity among objects, the influence of which is stronger as the objects are closer, as their subatomic particles act and react bringing them together. This also explains the gravitational relationships between objects of different sizes and volumes. The smaller or less voluminous object has fewer atoms and is attracted to the larger or denser object. It also accounts for the lack of gravity among galaxies, even though such subatomic particles as photons and neutrinos travel through macro space.

Setting $\mathbf{h}^*$ for Planck length ($=10^{-35}$), g for gravity and hgt for Planck time, the gravitation equation can be written: $\mathbf{G} = \mathbf{g(h^*+h)}_{gt}/\Sigma \mathbf{mc}^2$, with m for mass and mc2 for Einsteinian energy. Since each atom has its atomic mass, and since this mass approaches high velocities unless bounded by internal and external gravitational influences of other atoms, as each region is composed of atoms, dividing Planck time by Planck length of a region provides the measurement of the region's gravitation. This region is a matrix sector of space-time-matter, and as such is a section of Einsteinian-Riemannian space, curved onto itself in macro space and expanding with the velocity of this continuum.

This velocity imposes a seemingly paradoxical situation on the continuum. With the expansion of space-time-matter, the space within the atomic structures that are either isolated or within larger systems tends to retain its general configuration. This is explained, however, because the region in question is itself expanding owing to the micro expansion of the space-time-matter within it, as the region is itself determined by the same atoms that provide its material density. This expansion toward infinity continues, while specific regions seemingly retain their finiteness, being held together by the very gravitation due to its atomic density. Space is expanding. However, because the atomic density is great rendering this expansion small, it seems imperceptible.

Setting r for the matrix region, $\mathbf{G_r}$ is finite due to the regional gravity, with space-time and its matter content expanding to infinity in the macro realm in the Einsteinian-Riemannian geometrical framework. This accounts for the reduction of matter in the vast dark outer space due to the lack of atomic cohesion. It also accounts for the expansion of space-time as the diminished atomic cohesion reduces the effects of gravitation proportionately.

As this closed but infinite geometry holds, the time relation is each r is fixed. It is relative with respect to other regions, thereby accounting for the Lorentz-Miknowski transformations. This is so because should matter be extremely dense throughout space-time, no space-time expansion could take place, for matter closes in on itself as with atoms and galaxies through atomic and subparticle interactions and the energy exchanges so generated. The velocity of this expansion within the cosmos is so tremendous that even in the darkest space it carries with it pockets of energy in the form of closed regions of gravitation, such as those arising from the decline of stars into black holes with regionally limited space-time motion, but for which macro Einsteinian-Riemannian geometry moves with the velocity of space-time.

For black holes, although the geometrical r region of the star has diminished, Planck length and time remain stable. Internal energy is increased by the entrapment of all matter that passes within the black holes' gravitational ranges, which is then converted into energy. Black holes can therefore be considered not as regions in which space-time has enveloped onto itself, but as regions in which extreme concentrations of energy are converted from mass whose velocity approaches infinity according to our comprehension, due to the intensity of the regions' gravitational fields. This condition is expressed by an energy equation $\mathbf{E_{t+n}=G'_r}$, which is equal to $[l/g(h^*+h_{gt})/\Sigma mc^2]_{t+n}$, with $t+n$ referring to the increase in matter content over time. Thus, as the mass of a region decreases infinitely due to the stars' implosions, the gravitation of these regions increases accordingly as matter is trapped within them.

The greater the density of matter, the greater the gravitational force, owing to the interactions of atoms and their subparticles. The wave effects in gravitational fields are due to these interchanges as orbital shifts within and among the atoms, thereby altering the atomic structures within these fields due to these relations and interactions.

The weak and strong gravitational forces define a symmetry. Thus, such subparticles as positively charged bosons may indeed be responsible for the effects of gravitation, for they exhibit the property of binding with fermions.[7] This binding is regional within matrices and occurs in the continuum of space-time-matter. As the weak and strong forces operate specifically in these regional matrices, they are subforces of the superforce of universal gravitation. This superforce can be considered as the space-time-matter continuum formed during the creation of the universe.

The space-time-matter continuum is symbiotic, for matter cannot exist without space and time, and space and time cannot exist without matter, be it in the form of neutrinos or as black holes or galaxies. The concept of space and time as used by Newton has been replaced by the Einsteinian space-time continuum. Newton's approach allows for strict determinism, whereas Einstein's approach allows for statistical determinism. These philosophical positions not only developed from their understanding of physics, but indeed were strengthened by this understanding. Heisenberg, however, reached the only conclusion consistent with the dynamics of quantum physics–that whether the world is in fact strictly determined or statistically so will never be known to us, because as observers, we influence the events that occur. The world must thus be considered to be indeterministic, with our imposing on it statistics as such with our formulations of crisis theory situations.

What influence does this space-time-matter continuum have on this debate? Given this continuum, all physical systems are in states of quasi-equilibrium, so that although the statistics of change can be narrowed, until the Heisenbergian caveat can be breached to a certain extent, the world will always be unknown to us. This continues to motivate us in our search for knowledge and the ultimate truth, placing our contributions to this search under the scrutiny of those capable of evaluating and working with them within the structures of crisis theories.

NOTES

1. Moritz Schlick, *General Theory of Knowledge*, trans. Albert E. Blumberg (La Salle, Ill.: Open Court, reprint, 1974), p. 399.

2. See Kurt Gödel, On *Formally Undecidable Propositions* (New York: Basic Books, 1962), and Rozsa Peter, *Playing with Infinity*, trans. Z. P. Dienes (New York: Dover, 1976), Chapter 21, "Awaiting Judgment by Metamathematics," and Chapter 22, "What Is Mathematics Not Capable Of?," pp. 243-265.

3. For Popper's comments on Freud, see his essay "Science: Conjectures and Refutations," in *Conjectures and Refutations* (London: Rutledge and Kegan Paul, 1963), p. 35. See also Jürgen Habermas's comments on Freud in *Jürgen Habermas on Society and Politics: A Reader*, ed. Steven Seidman (Boston: Beacon Press, 1989), Chapter 3, "Self-Reflection as Science: Freud's Psychoanalytic Critique of Meaning," pp. 54-76, and the footnotes on pp. 304-305.

4. See Hermann Minkowski's address delivered at the 80th Assembly of German Natural Scientists and Physicians, at Cologne, September 21, 1908, reprinted in A. Einstein, H. A. Lorentz, H. Minkowski, and H. Weyl, *The Principle of Relativity* (London: Methuen, 1923), and for a discussion on Minkowski's theory, see G. J. Whitrow, *The Nature of Time* (Baltimore, Md.: Penguin Books, 1975), pp. 102-107.

5. For example, when radiation in an enclosure has attained statistical equilibrium, the densities of radiation remain unchanged, except for conditions in which inevitable conditions occur owing to the emission and absorption of definite radiation within the enclosure. Setting A_{ij} to represent the energy state E_i, dropping to a lower energy state E_j within one second, the statement A_{ij} pertaining to the various energy drops are known as "Einsteinian probability coefficients of spontaneous emission."

Considering absorption, positive absorption occurs when atoms absorb radiation energy and are therefore excited to a higher level. Negative absorption, which is really emission, occurs when an atom drops to a lower level when influenced by radiation. Einstein introduced probability coefficients B_{ij} and B_{ji}, respectively, to show that the emission and absorption of each individual atom must proceed at the same rate, as is the case with equilibrium. He demonstrated that Planck's radiation law will be obtained if the following relations hold between the two probabilities: $A_{ij}/B_{ij} = 8\pi/c^3 vh$, so that $B_{ij} = B_{ji}$, with c being velocity, v radiation, and h Planck's constant (approximately 6.6×10^{-34} Joule seeonds).

A. d'Abro wrote, "Einstein's deduction of Planck's radiation formula is of historic importance because it marks the first systematic introduction of probability factors in the mathematics of quantum theory." Further in the same paragraph, d'Abro continued stating that the probability coefficients were viewed as "mere expedients which might in theory be deduced from the requisite rigorous laws. . . . In particular, no suggestion was made that these probabilities betrayed any fundamental indeterminacy." He stated that these views were later to be revised. This was so because of the nature of the statistics involved, which are based on statistical determinacy. See A. d'Abro, *The Rise of the New Physics* (New York: Dover, 1952), Vol. 2, p. 599.

6. For a discussion on Wolfgang Pauli's contribution to physics, see his *Theory of Relativity*, tran. G. Field (New York: Pergamon Press, 1985).

7. Bosons are composite particles with spins of 0h, 1h, and so on; fermions are particles with spins of 1/2h, 3/2h, 2/2h, and so on. The weak and strong forces of gravity, operating at a distance and within the atom, can be explained by the space-time-matter continuum, for which distance pertains to the interchange of matter in the continuum. Moreover, the graviton, a hypothetical and as yet undetected quantum particle of gravity, may remain a fiction, with the effects of gravity to be considered within the space-time-matter continuum, as explained in the text.

This also sheds light on black holes, whose intense energy and mass are held in the regional matrix by weak and strong forces, and with the probability of exploding as conflicts in their internal energy result from internal collision, thereby forming new stars. See John Gribbin, *White Holes: Cosmic Gushers in the Universe* (New York: Dell Publishing Co., 1977).

Selected Bibliography

Arendt, Hannah. *The Human Condition*. New York: Doubleday, Anchor Books, 1959.

Bacon, Sir Francis. *New Organon and Related Writings*. Fulton H. Anderson, ed. New York: Macmillan, 1960.

Beasley, W. G. *The History of Modern Japan*. London: Weidenfield Goldbacks, 1967.

Boorstin, Daniel J. *The Discoverers*. New York: Vintage Books, 1985.

Borges, Jorge Luis. *Other Inquisitions 1937-1952*. New York: Washington Square Press, 1968.

Bragg, Sir William. *Concerning the Nature of Things*. New York: Dover, 1948.

Broad, C. D. *Scientific Thought*. Patterson, N.J.: Littlefield, Adams, and Co., 1959.

Burns, James MacGregor. *Leadership*. New York: Harper, 1978.

Cassirer, Ernst. *An Essay on Man*. New Haven, Conn.: Yale University Press, 1962.

——. *The Philosophy of Symbolic Forms vol. 1*, Language. New Haven, Conn.: Yale University Press, 1955.

Cooke, Robert. *Improving on Nature*. New York: Quadrangle Books, 1978.

Crawford, Gregory Philip, and Zumen Zloboban, eds. *Liquid Crystals in Complex Geometries*. London: Taylor and Francis, Ltd., 1996.

Crease, Robert P., and Charles Mann. *The Second Generation*. New York: Collier Books, 1986.

Culler, Jonathan. *On Deconstruction*. Ithaca, N.Y.: Cornell University Press, 1989.

Davies, Paul. *Other Worlds*. New York: Touchstone Books, 1980.

Davis, Philip J., and Reuben Hersh. *The Mathematical Experience*. Boston: Houghton Mifflin Co., 1981.

Demski, Joel. *Information Analysis*. Reading, Mass.: Addison-Wesley, 1972.

Dennet, Daniel C. *Brainstorms*. Cambridge, Mass.: M.I.T. Press, 1981.
——, and Douglas R. Hofstadter. *The Mind's I*. New York: Bantam Books, 1982.
Descartes, René. *Philosophical Essays Discourse on Method: Rules for the Direction of the Mind*. Laurence J. Laffener, trans. New York: Macmillan, 1969.
Diebold, John. *The Innovators*. New York: Trueman Talley Books/Plume, 1991.
Dillen, Daniel C. *Russia and the Independent States*. Washington, D.C.: Congressional Quarterly, 1996.
Dornbusch, Rudiger, and Leslie C. H. Helmers, eds. *The Open Economy*. New York: Oxford University Press, 1990. See especially Part II, Country Studies: "Argentina," by Domingo F. Cavallo; "Brazil," by Mario Henrique Simonsen; "Indonesia," by Malcom Gillis and David Dapice; "Korea," by Yung-Chul Park; "Mexico," by Eliana A. Cardoso and Santiago Levy, pp. 267-369; and the notes and bibliographies for each essay.
Eco, Umberto. *Semiotics and the Philosophy of Language*. Bloomington: University of Indiana Press, 1986.
Fraser, J.T., ed. *The Voices of Time*. 2nd ed. Amherst: University of Massachusetts Press, 1981.
Fuller, R. Buckminster. *Synergetics*. New York: Macmillan, 1975, especially his discussion on Numerology, pp. 727-785.
Georgescu-Rogen, Nicholas. *The Entropy Law and the Economic Process*. Cambridge, Mass.: Harvard University Press, 1981.
Gribbin, John. *In Search of Schrödinger's Kittens*. London: Phoenix, 1996.
Heilbroner, Robert L. *The Human Prospect*. New York: W. W. Norton, 1980.
Heisenberg, Werner. *Physics and Philosophy*. New York: Penguin Books, 1990.
Hillenbrand, Martin, and Daniel Yergin, eds. *Global Insecurity*. New York: Penguin Books, 1983.
Hofstadter, Douglas R. *Gödel, Escher, Bach*. New York: Vintage Books, 1980.
——. *Metamagical Themas*. New York: Bantam Books, 1986, and see the extensive bibliography.
Hume, David. *An Essay Concerning Human Understanding*. New York: Oxford University Press, 1924.
Kahn, Herman. *The Emerging Japanese Superstate*. Englewood Cliffs, N.J.: Prentice-Hall, 1971, and see the bibliography.
——, William Brown, and Leon Martel, with the assitance of the Hudson Institute Staff. *The Next 200 Years*. New York: William Morrow and Co., 1976, and see the selected readings.
——, and the Hudson Institute. *World Economic Development*. New York: Morrow Quill, 1979.
Kasner, Edward, and James R, Newman. *Mathematics and the Imagination*. Redmond, Wash.: Tempus Books, 1989.

Kant, Immanuel. *Critique of Pure Reason*. N. Kemp Smith, trans. London: Macmillan, 1934.

Klitgaard, Robert. *Tropical Gangsters*. New York: Basic Books, 1990, and see the references in the notes on pp. 275-276.

Koestler, Arthur. *The Sleepwalkers*. London: Hutchinson, 1968.

Koyré, Alexandre. *From the Closed World to the Infinite Universe*. Baltimore, Md.: Johns Hopkins University Press, 1968.

Kuhn, Thomas S. *Copernican Revolution*. Cambridge, Mass.: Harvard University Press, 1957.

——. The *Structure of Scientific Revolutions*. Chicago: Chicago University Press, 1970.

Leib, Irwin C. *Past, Present, and Future*. Urbana and Chicago: University of Illinois Press, 1991.

Leibniz, G. W. von. *Three Essays in Human Understanding*. Peter Remnant and Jonathan Bennet, eds. New York: Cambridge University Press, 1981.

Lorenz, Edward. "Deterministic Nonperiodic Flow." *Journal of the Atmospheric Sciences* 20 (1993) pp.130–141.

Lovejoy, Arthur O. *The Great Chain of Being*. Cambridge, Mass.: Harvard University Press, 1938.

Mandelbrot, Benoit. *Fractals: Form, Choice, and Dimension*. San Francisco: W. H. Freeman, 1977.

McKeon, Richard, ed. *Selections from Medieval Philosophers vol 1*. New York: Charles Scribner's Sons, 1957.

Merleau-Ponty, Maurice. *Sense and Non-Sense*. Evanston, Ill.: Northwestern University Press, 1964.

Motz, lloyd, and Jefferson Hane Weaver. *The Story of Mathematics*. New York: Avon Books, 1993.

Myrdal, Gunnar. *Asian Drama*. New York: Twentieth Century Fund, 1968.

Nora, Hamilton, Jeffry A. Frieden, Linda Fuller, and Maunel Pastor Jr., eds. *Crisis in Central America*. Boulder, Colo.: Westview Press, 1988.

Nozick, Robert. *Philosophical Explanations*. Cambridge, Mass.: Harvard University Press, 1981.

Passmore, John. *Recent Philosophers*. New York: Open Court, 1985.

Penrose, Roger. *The Emperor's New Mind*. New York: Vintage, 1990.

——. *Shadows of the Mind*. New York: Vintage, 1995.

Peterson, Ivars. *Islands of Truth: A Mathematical Mystery Cruise*. New York: W. W. Freeman, 1990.

Prigogne, Ilya, and Isabelle Stengers. *Order Out of Chaos*. New York: Bantam Books, 1984.

Quine, W.V.O. *The Philosophy of Logic*. Cambridge, Mass.: Harvard University Press, 1976.

——, and J.S. Ullian. *Web of Belief*. New York: Random House, 1978.

Radetsky, Peter. *The Invisible Invaders*. New York: Little, Brown and Co., 1991.

Reichenbach, Hans. *The Philosophy of Space and Time*. Maria Reichenbach and J. Freund, trans. New York: Dover, 1928.

Ricoeur, Paul. *Freedom and Necessity*. Evanston, Ill.: Northwestern University Press, 1966.

Shackle, C.L.S. *Epistemics and Economics*. New Brunswick, N.J.: Transaction Publishers, 1992.

Supe, Reitmar, Heinz-Otto Pietsen, and Harmut Jurgens. *Chaos and Fractals*. New York: Springer-Verlag, 1992.

"Taiwan." *International Herald Tribune Sponsored Section*, October 10, 1996.

Taylor, Gordon Rattay. *Rethink*. Harmondsworth, England: Pelican Books.

Terkel, Menachem. *Integrative Management, Innovation and New Venturing 2 vols*. New York: Elsevier, 1991; and see the References and Supplementary Reading list.

Torretti, Roberto. *Relativity and Geometry*. New York: Dover, 1993; and see the References.

Tudge, Colin. *The Engineer in the Garden*. London: Pimlico Books, 1993.

"Turkey: Business Update." *International Herald Tribune Sponsored Section*. September 26, 1996.

Weinberg, Steven. *The Frist Three Minutes*. New York: Basic Books, 1977.

Wittgenstein, Ludwig. *Tractatus Logico-Philosophicus*. London: Routledge and Kegan Paul, 1961.

Yates, Francis A. *The Art of Memory*. Chicago: Chicago University Press, 1966.

Index

About the Author

DAVID Z. RICH is an economic consultant, independent researcher, and freelance writer. His most recent books include *The Economic Theory of Growth and Development* (Praeger, 1994) and *The Economics of International Trade* (Quorum, 1992).